THE SHAAR PRESS

THE JUDAICA IMPRINT
FOR THOUGHTFUL PEOPLE

ZALMEN LEIB AND ETTY WEISS EDITION

ZERA

The sefer. The stories. The segulah.

THE
SHAAR
PRESS

זרע שמשון

SHIMSHON
Eishes Chayil

With selections from Sefer Zera Shimshon,
the classic sefer by the 18th-century Rav,
RABBI SHIMSHON CHAIM NACHMANI

RABBI NACHMAN SELTZER
in conjunction with
Rabbi Menachem Binyomin Paskesz and Rabbi Yisroel Zilberberg

Published by **SHAAR PRESS**
Distributed by MESORAH PUBLICATIONS, LTD.
313 Regina Avenue / Rahway, N.J 07065 / (718) 921-9000

Distributed in Israel by SIFRIATI / A. GITLER
POB 2351 / Bnei Brak 51122

Distributed in Europe by LEHMANNS
Unit E, Viking Business Park, Rolling Mill Road / Jarrow, Tyne and Wear, NE32 3DP/
England

Distributed in Australia and New Zealand by GOLDS WORLD OF JUDAICA
3-13 William Street / Balaclava, Melbourne 3183 / Victoria Australia

Distributed in South Africa by KOLLEL BOOKSHOP
Northfield Centre / 17 Northfield Avenue / Glenhazel 2192, Johannesburg, South Africa

ITEM CODE: ZERECH
ISBN 10:1-4226-3176-1 / ISBN 13: 978-1-4226-3176-8

Printed in the United States of America
Custom bound by Sefercraft, Inc. / 313 Regina Avenue / Rahway N.J. 07065

The *Zera Shimshon* — Eishes Chayil is dedicated
in memory of our beloved parents

Chaim Elazar and Rachel Leah Weiss ז"ל
ר' חיים אלעזר בן ר' נתן נטע ז"ל
נפ' ל' תשרי תשע"ג

מרת רחל לאה בת ר' יקותיאל יהודה ע"ה
נפ' כ"ט טבת תשע"ז

Yeshaya Asher and Rivka Basya Frankl ז"ל
ר' ישעיה אשר בן ר' אריה ז"ל
נפ' י' ניסן תשע"ב

מרת רבקה בתיה בת ר' אביגדור ע"ה
נפ' ב' תמוז תשע"ח

◆◆◆

In honor of our children and grandchildren

Avi and Elisheva Weiss
Shragi, Ahuva, Chaim, Heddy

Shauli and Suri Weintraub
Tzvi, Batsheva, Shaya, Estee, Bassi

Eliezer and Chayala Indig
Tzippy, Avrumi, Ashie

Nusi and Chayie Weiss
Eli, Racheli, Sara

Shmulie and Deena Weiss
Shlomo Eliyahu

Tzvi and Shaindy Weiss

Gitty, Tzippy

Zalmen Leib and Etty Weiss

Table of Contents

PART ONE:
Eishes Chayil ❖ אשת חיל

PART TWO:
The Beis Yaakov Treasury

Acknowledgments

To the Ribbono shel Olam for allowing me to hear a story about the *Zera Shimshon* in 2007 — a story that led to the resurgence and reprinting of the *sefer* itself, and on to books of selected pieces in English and eventually to a full-fledged collaboration between the *Zera Shimshon* Foundation and ArtScroll — translating every single word of the sefer into an elucidated multi-volume work.

Once again it is clear to me that Hashem is sending me the things He wants me to write about and I thank Him for giving me a clear mission and the *siyata d'Shmaya* to carry it out.

A big *yasher koach* to **Rabbi Yisroel Zilberberg** and **Rabbi Binyomin Paskesz** for the incredible *mesiras nefesh* they display on each and every day with their involvement in furthering the Torah of the *Zera Shimshon* to Klal Yisrael.

A thank you goes to all the people involved with the actual work that goes into such a *sefer*.

To **Reb Shmuel Blitz** for being an all-around fantastic Yid who sits in an office high above the Jerusalem skyline — while influencing what Klal Yisrael is reading across the globe.

To **Mrs. Miriam Zakon** for editing the Torah part of the book — because she took one look at it and decided that she really wanted to do this one herself...

To **Mrs. Libby Lazewnik** for editing the stories in the book with her usual professionalism and talent.

To **Rabbi Pinchas Waldman** for reviewing the Torah and making sure that everything was translated correctly.

To **Mrs. Esther Ilana Rabi** for her careful proofreading.

To **Mrs. Judi Dick, Mrs. Estie Dicker, Mrs. Esther Feierstein** and the rest of the team at the American office for doing their jobs with passion, excitement, and dedication.

To **Reb Eli Kroen** for applying and adapting the *Zera Shimshon* cover concept to this very unique and special *sefer*.

To **Rabbi Gedaliah Zlotowitz** — If every yeshivah and business was run like ArtScroll, the world would be in good shape.

To my wife **Aliza**

אֵשֶׁת חַיִל מִי יִמְצָא וְרָחֹק מִפְּנִינִים מִכְרָהּ

And as Shlomo HaMelech writes

(*Mishlei* 18:22):

מָצָא אִשָּׁה מָצָא טוֹב

Introduction

It has been quite a while since I wrote my first story about the *Zera Shimshon*, way back in 2007. Since then so much has happened. I wrote several follow-up articles and that led to the first volume of ***Zera Shimshon: The sefer, the stories, the segulah*** in 2017, and then Volume Two in 2018. As the works of *Zera Shimshon* — and the extraordinary *segulah* promised to those who study his Torah commentary — became known throughout the world, a warm relationship developed between ArtScroll and the *Zera Shimshon* Organization. As a result, the entire *sefer* is being translated into English and published in a multi-volume work.

With so many beautiful *sefarim* based on *Zera Shimshon* already published and so many *shiurim* being delivered around the globe, the time had come for Volume Three of the *Zera Shimshon* series, which includes brief Torah thoughts from *Zera Shimshon*, together with true stories that illustrate his teachings and themes.

And here it is — ***The Zera Shimshon Eishes Chayil.***

This *sefer* is devoted to the greatness of the *eishes chayil*, the Jewish wife, the crowning glory of her husband. Rav Shimshon Chaim examines every line of Eishes Chayil with a unique and original *peirush* that leaves the reader fascinated and inspired.

The second part of the *sefer* is called Yalkut Beis Yaakov. It is a collection of the *Zera Shimshon's* Torah thoughts that relate to Jewish women. This is a *sefer* dedicated to the Jewish mother, Jewish wife, and Jewish daughter. More than anything, it is dedicated to the *eishes chayil*, who brings her sons to learn Torah and waits for her husband to return from the *beis midrash*. It hails both the *mesiras nefesh* of the kollel wife and the woman who encourages her working husband to take time from his busy schedule for Torah learning.

As Rabbi Akiva famously said (*Kesubos* 63a) about his wife Rachel: "What is mine and yours — is hers." This applies to every one of us as well.

We'll begin **Zera Shimshon Eishes Chayil**, the beautiful commentary written by Moreinu HaRav Shimshon Chaim ben Reb Nachman Michoel, with a story heard personally by the rabbanim who have dedicated their efforts to disseminate the writings of the *Zera Shimshon*:

> To the members of the *Zera Shimshon* team,
>
> It is now one in the morning, and I am sitting here with tears streaming down my face, unable to believe what has happened to me over the last few days and weeks.
>
> I am forty-one years old and the mother of eight children. My husband was a successful businessman, and our home was a peaceful and happy place. However, nobody knows what to expect from the twists and turns of life, and there came a day when we learned that my husband had become very ill and would not be around for much longer. This would have been a tremendous challenge for anyone. In my case, since everything had been so good in our lives, when my husband passed away at a very young age his loss cannot be described. Suddenly I found myself having to deal with the burden of the family finances in addition to having to raise our children — all on my own.
>
> It wasn't easy for me to consider remarriage, but I knew that this was something I was going to have to do. It was next to impossible for me to handle the *parnassah* for our large family. Besides, I had quite a few young children at home and they needed a father figure in their lives.
>
> At first, I didn't think this was going to be such a difficult

mission. However, the deeper I sank into the world of shidduchim, the more I realized that this was no simple matter — especially since my new husband would have to take on the responsibility of supporting eight children.

It didn't take long for *shadchanim* to stop calling me once they understood that very few men were interested in such a "deal." I soon found myself in a state of abject depression, feeling as if my entire world had come crashing down on my head. Having to figure out ways to make money while dealing with the children was proving too much for me. I felt as if I was collapsing under an incredible burden.

My brother was a great help during this time. To ease my burden, he would often invite us for Shabbos. Being away from home — even for a short amount of time — gave me a much-needed mini-vacation and some sorely needed breathing space. One Shabbos morning, I got up early and went to daven at a nearby shul, something I was unable to do when we were home since I had to be available for the children. That Shabbos morning, I arrived in shul early, giving myself sufficient time to be able to daven slowly and with genuine concentration. I found a seat and as I was settling in, I happened to notice a *sefer* lying nearby. I saw the words "Eishes Chayil" written on the binding.

"I wonder what that *sefer* is about," I thought. "Is this a *sefer* of tips for the *eishes chayil*? Or maybe it's a cookbook?"

I opened the *sefer* and discovered that it was neither of those things, but rather a *peirush* on Eishes Chayil that had been written by the *Zera Shimshon* over 250 years earlier.

I read the author's introduction, where he wrote that a person who learned his *sefer* would merit a home filled with all manner of good things. I felt that this was exactly what was missing from my home right then. I had a house and I had children, but the good that used to characterize my home when my husband was alive had disappeared.

On the spot, I felt very connected to the *sefer*. It was

perfect for a woman who wanted to learn some Torah ideas and absorb Torah messages. I made sure to buy a copy a short while later and began learning the *sefer* every day. Soon I had finished it from cover to cover. A few days after I made my "*siyum*" on the *Zera Shimshon's* Eishes Chayil, a shidduch was suggested to me with a wonderful and special individual, who told me that the fact that I had such a large family was a motivating factor for him and not the opposite. He loves children, is a wonderful father, and considered it a true privilege to have the opportunity of raising a family of *yesomim*.

I cannot accurately describe my feelings of overwhelming gratitude for the turnaround that has happened in my life. So many people have heard about the power of the tzaddik and how his blessings have come true. I know that you, at the *Zera Shimshon* organization, have heard numerous stories of people who have personally benefitted from the tzaddik's promise.

However, I feel the need to tell you my story, because it is clear to me that the *Zera Shimshon* stood by my side in my darkest hours — and that his merit helped clear the pathways of *tefillah* for me, all the way up to the Heavenly Throne.

Brooklyn, New York

The members of Klal Yisrael were long used to having access to the home of the Sar HaTorah, Rav Chaim Kanievsky *ztz"l*, but that access was more or less curtailed during the long months of Covid. Rabbi Yisroel Zilberberg, however, who together with Rabbi Binyomin Paskesz exerts great efforts into spreading the Torah of the *Zera Shimshon*, was given the opportunity to visit Rav Chaim not long ago, and he jumped at the chance to see the *gadol's* glowing visage and to give Rav Chaim all the new *sefarim* that the *Zera Shimshon* team had recently published.

This was also a chance for Reb Yisroel to relay some of the questions that come into the *Zera Shimshon* office on a regular basis and to receive decisive answers, immediately and on the spot. While most meetings with Rav Chaim are generally brief, here Rav Chaim dedicated far more time than was his custom.

Though he appreciated it greatly, Reb Yisroel didn't find that privilege strange or surprising. After all, he had known for quite some time how much Rav Chaim valued the *sefer Zera Shimshon*. In fact, Rav Chaim's acquaintance with the *Zera Shimshon* went back to the days of his father, the holy Steipler Gaon, author of the *Kehillas Yaakov*, who owned a copy of the *sefer* at a time when few others did.

"I will never forget the excitement and emotion that encompassed Rav Chaim when we presented him with the recent additions to the *Zera Shimshon* family that we had just published," Reb Yisroel said. "When I handed him one of the new *sefarim*, Rav Chaim said in a loud and loving voice, "He was an *adam gadol*, a great man," in reference to the *Zera Shimshon*. He then touched the *sefer* with obvious affection and asked that his name be inscribed in the flyleaf of the new *sefarim*.

"Saba," Rav Chaim's grandson Rabbi Yanky Kanievsky said, "these people are the publishers of the *Zera Shimshon*. They brought the newest releases, a compendium of *derushim* on the *parshiyos* and on *Megillas Esther*. They want a *berachah* that they will merit to publish all of the *Zera Shimshon's peirushim* and Torah ideas."

"B'hatzlachah," Rav Chaim said.

Reb Yisroel then presented Rav Chaim with a note containing five specific questions that had been sent in by people who learn the *sefarim* all over the world. Rav Chaim looked at the paper and then answered each of the questions in the order they'd been asked:

Since it is known that the Zera Shimshon wrote that anyone who learns his Torah will be blessed with all manner of blessings, do they need to learn the Torah every day or is it sufficient if they learn it once or twice a week?

"They should learn the *sefer* at least twice a week," Rav Chaim said.

And how many minutes should each session be?
"At least five minutes."

Is this a genuine segulah — that is, a segulah that is effective?

"Yes."

Is it true that the Steipler Gaon owned the sefer Zera Shimshon and even learned from it?

"Yes."

If a person is unable to learn, can they take on part of the cost of the sefarim and still receive the benefits of the berachah?

"*Nachon*," said Rav Chaim. "That is correct. *Berachah v'hatzlachah!*"

Rabbi Nachman Seltzer
Ramat Beit Shemesh

Note: An asterisk (*) next to a name indicates that the name has been changed.

Excerpts From the Introduction to Sefer Zera Shimshon

by the *mechaber*, Rav Shimshon Chaim Nachmani

Full of Biblical and Talmudic allusions, Rav Shimshon Chaim Nach-mani's introduction to Sefer Zera Shimshon gives us a breathtaking display of his Torah genius. Here we bring only a few paragraphs in which he discusses his famous promise: that those who learn his sefer will see great blessings in their homes — a promise that baruch Hashem we are seeing fulfilled more and more.

כַּאֲשֶׁר אֲנִי מְחַלֶּה פְּנֵיהֶם בְּעֶשֶׂר לְשׁוֹנוֹת שֶׁל תְּפִלָּה, לִבְרוֹר הַמָּנָה הַיָּפָה אֲשֶׁר יִיטַב בְּעֵינֵיהֶם בְּחִידוּשִׁים הַלָּלוּ, וּבִפְרָט אַחֲרֵי מוֹתִי כִּי לִימוּדָם יִהְיֶה לִי לְהָשִׁיב נֶפֶשׁ וּלְעִידוּן רוּחַ וְלִזְכוּת נִשְׁמָתִי, וּצְדָקָה תִּהְיֶה לָהֶם וְצִדְקָתָם תַּעֲמוֹד לָעַד, לֶאֱכוֹל בָּעוֹלָם הַזֶּה וְלִשְׂבּוֹעַ בָּעוֹלָם הַבָּא, וּבַעַל הַגְּמוּל יְשַׁלֵּם בִּזְכוּת זֶה שָׂכָר טוֹב לְגוֹמְלֵי חֶסֶד שֶׁל אֱמֶת, בְּמוֹתָב תְּלָתָא בְּנֵי חַיֵּי וּמְזוֹנֵי טָבֵי, דִּבְזְכוּתָא תָּלוּ.
וַאֲנִי בְעָנְיִי וּבִמְרִירוּתִי, לְבָבִי הוֹלֵךְ וּבוֹכֶה עַל כִּי אֵין לִי בָּנִים וְזֶרַע יַעַבְדֶנִי אַחֲרֵי מוֹתִי, וּמוּכְרָח אֲנִי לָצֵאת בְּעִקְבוֹת אַנְשֵׁי שֵׁמוֹת לְהַשְׁאִיר אַחֲרַי - בְּרָכָה.

I implore upon [my friends] in ten languages of prayer to choose [to learn] the beautiful portions of the novel concepts in my work... Even more so, [to learn Sefer Zera Shimshon] after my death, since learning [this sefer] will be a remedy for my essence, soothing to my spirit and meritorious for my soul. [Those who study it,] their righteousness shall remain with them forever,[1] to benefit in this world and have full

---

1. וְצִדְקָתָם עוֹמֶדֶת לָעַד (Mishnah, *Avos* 2:2).

satisfaction in the World to Come. The One Who rewards shall pay them in the merit of doing the ultimate kindness (chesed),[2] with the presence of all three:[3] children, life, and sustenance; which are dependent upon [the person's] merits.

And as for me, in my poverty and bitterness, my heart cries that I do not have children and descendants who would serve me after my passing, which forces me to follow the footsteps of dignitaries, to leave posthumously a blessing.

וָאֶקֹּד וָאֶשְׁתַּחֲוֶה לַה׳, וְאוֹדֶה לוֹ בִּמְאוֹד מְאֹד בְּכָל מִדָּה וּמִדָּה, כִּי בְּחֲסָדָיו הָרַבִּים, אַף בִּשְׁעַת כַּעֲסוֹ שֶׁלָּקַח מִמֶּנִּי בְּנִי יְחִידִי בְּכוֹרִי, יְדִיד נַפְשִׁי, זָכַר לִי אֶת הָרַחֲמִים, כִּי שָׁת לִי זֶרַע אַחֵר, וְהִגִּיעַנִי לִכְלַל זַרְעִי עַל כָּל מָיִם, אֵין מָיִם אֶלָּא תוֹרָה, זֶרַע הַשָּׁלוֹם זֶרַע אֱמֶת. וְלָכֵן קָרָאתִי סֵפֶר זֶה בְּשֵׁם זֶרַע שִׁמְשׁוֹן. וּמֵעַתָּה אַחַי וְרֵעַי אוֹהֲבַי וּמְיֻדָּעַי זֶרַע בְּרוּכֵי ה׳, הֵא לָכֶם זֶרַע, אוֹר זֶרַע לַצַּדִּיקִים כָּמוֹתְכֶם, בְּמַטּוּתָא בָּעֵינָא מִינַּיְיכוּ, זִרְעוּ לָכֶם לִצְדָקָה וְקִצְרוּ לְפִי חֶסֶד שֶׁל אֱמֶת, וְכִי מְרֻבָּה מִדַּת תַּשְׁלוּמֵי חֵן וָחֶסֶד וְשָׁלְמָא רַבָּא מִן שְׁמַיָּא, וְעֵינֵיכֶם תִּרְאֶינָה בָּנִים בְּנֵי בָנִים כִּשְׁתִלֵי זֵיתִים סָבִיב לְשֻׁלְחַנְכֶם חֲכָמִים וּנְבוֹנִים, וּבָתִּים מְלֵאִים כָּל טוּב, גַּם עוֹשֶׁר גַּם כָּבוֹד לֹא יָסוּפוּ מִזַּרְעֲכֶם, עַד יִתְקַיֵּים בָּכֶם הֵמָּה יִרְאוּ כְבוֹד ה׳ הֲדַר אֱלֹהֵינוּ, וְנָשָׂא נֵס לַגּוֹיִם, וְאָסַף נִדְחֵי זֶרַע יִשְׂרָאֵל בִּמְהֵרָה בְיָמֵינוּ אָמֵן.

I shall kneel and bow to Hashem, and I shall be very grateful for all measures[4] [with which He has treated me]. With His enormous loving-kindness, even through His wrath, that He had taken away my only son, who was so close to my soul, He still remembered me mercifully, and He has given me "other descendants."[5] He has brought me to the

---

2. Doing kindness with the deceased is referred to as חֶסֶד שֶׁל אֱמֶת, ultimate or pure kindness, because we cannot expect the deceased to pay back in kind (*Rashi, Bereishis* 47:29, based on *Midrash Rabbah* 96:5).

3. This is derived from what the *beis din* usually writes in the beginning of their official documents: ...בְּמוֹתַב תְּלָתָא הֲוֵינָא — "We [*beis din* judges] were sitting the three of us together..." Here the author uses this term for the three blessings mentioned (cf.) in *Moed Katan* 28b.

4. The author uses beautiful Talmudic language, and it is a reflection of his vast Torah knowledge. However, its deeper meanings are at times lost through translation. The *Mishnah* (*Berachos* 9:5) explains the word מְאֹדֶךָ in the verse (*Devarim* 6:5) [which is the שְׁמַע we recite] that with every measure (בְּכָל מִדָּה וּמִדָּה) that Hashem treats us, whether it is reward or punishment, we should thank Him.

5. The word "*shas*" (He has given) hints at Adam's third child, Shes. When Adam had another child after Hevel was killed, he named his child שֵׁת, to thank Hashem that He has "provided me another child."

level of "planting upon all waters,"[6] "water" meaning Torah. [These are] descendants of peace and descendants of truth.[7] Therefore, I have called this sefer "Zera Shimshon." Now, my brothers, friends, beloved ones, acquaintances, descendants, who are blessed by Hashem — here you have zera, seeds...[8] I beseech you, please plant this... and reap [reward] in accordance with the ultimate kindness. Reward is great for those who do kindness graciously, and you shall have much peace from Heaven. Your eyes shall see children and children's children, like olive shoots around your table.[9] Your homes will be full of all the good.[10] Wealth and honor will not cease from your descendants, until it will come to the fulfillment of: "They will see the glory of Hashem, the majesty of our God."[11] "He will raise a banner for the nations and assemble all the castaway children of Israel,"[12] speedily in our days, Amen.

---

6. The author uses a verse (*Isaiah* 32:20), אַשְׁרֵיכֶם זֹרְעֵי עַל כָּל מָיִם — "You will be so fortunate to sow upon all waters." *Radak* there explains that wherever they will sow, there will be water. is

7. The Torah is referred to as peace and truth (*Midrash Rabbah Esther* 6:2).

8. When Yosef distributed seeds to the people in Egypt, he said, הֵא לָכֶם זֶרַע — "Here is seed for you" (*Bereishis* 47:23).

9. *Tehillim* 128:3. The comparison to an olive tree is: Just as an olive tree does not accept any grafts from other fruits, so will your progeny remain pure (*Rashi* and *Radak* there).

10. *Devarim* 6:11.

11. *Isaiah* 35:2.

12. Cf. *Isaiah* 11:12. There it is written נִדְחֵי יִשְׂרָאֵל — "the castaways of Israel." The author adds the word זֶרַע to fit it in with the *sefer's* title theme.

Part One:
Eishes Chayil

א *An accomplished woman, who can find? —*
  Far beyond pearls is her value.
ב *Her husband's heart relies on her,*
  and he shall lack no fortune.
ג *She bestows goodness upon him and never evil,*
  all the days of her life.
ד *She seeks out wool and linen, and her hands work willingly.*
ה *She is like a merchant's ships,*
  from afar she brings her sustenance.
ו *She arises while it is still nighttime,*
  and gives food to her household and a ration to her maidens.
ז *She plans to buy a field and she buys it,*
  from the fruit of her handiwork she plants a vineyard.
ח *She tightens the belt of her garments,*
  and pays attention to her arms.
ט *She discerns that her business is good —*
  so her lamp is not snuffed out by night.
י *She stretches out her hands to the distaff,*
  and her palms support the spindle.
כ *She spreads out her palm to the poor,*
  and extends her hands to the destitute.
ל *She fears not snow for her household,*
  for her entire household is clothed with scarlet wool.
מ *She made herself luxurious bedspreads,*
  her garments are linen and purple.
נ *Her husband is known in the councils,*
  when he sits with the elders of the land.
ס *She makes a cloak to sell,*
  and delivers a belt to the peddler.
ע *Strength and majesty are her garments,*
  she joyfully awaits the last day.
פ *She opens her mouth with wisdom,*
  and a lesson of kindness is on her tongue.
צ *She anticipates the ways of her household,*
  and does not partake of the bread of laziness.
ק *Her children arise and praise her; her husband, and he lauds her:*
ר *"Many daughters have amassed achievement,*
  but you surpassed them all."
ש *Charm is false and beauty is vain,*
  a woman who fears Hashem — she should be praised.
ת *Give her from the fruits of her hands,*
  and they will praise her actions at the gates.

אֵשֶׁת חַיִל מִי יִמְצָא,
וְרָחֹק מִפְּנִינִים מִכְרָהּ.
בָּטַח בָּהּ לֵב בַּעְלָהּ, וְשָׁלָל לֹא יֶחְסָר.
גְּמָלַתְהוּ טוֹב וְלֹא רָע, כֹּל יְמֵי חַיֶּיהָ.
דָּרְשָׁה צֶמֶר וּפִשְׁתִּים, וַתַּעַשׂ בְּחֵפֶץ כַּפֶּיהָ.
הָיְתָה כָּאֳנִיּוֹת סוֹחֵר, מִמֶּרְחָק תָּבִיא לַחְמָהּ.
וַתָּקָם בְּעוֹד לַיְלָה, וַתִּתֵּן טֶרֶף לְבֵיתָהּ,
וְחֹק לְנַעֲרֹתֶיהָ.
זָמְמָה שָׂדֶה וַתִּקָּחֵהוּ, מִפְּרִי כַפֶּיהָ נָטְעָה כָּרֶם.
חָגְרָה בְעוֹז מָתְנֶיהָ, וַתְּאַמֵּץ זְרוֹעֹתֶיהָ.
טָעֲמָה כִּי טוֹב סַחְרָהּ, לֹא יִכְבֶּה בַלַּיְלָה נֵרָהּ.
יָדֶיהָ שִׁלְּחָה בַכִּישׁוֹר, וְכַפֶּיהָ תָּמְכוּ פָלֶךְ.
כַּפָּהּ פָּרְשָׂה לֶעָנִי, וְיָדֶיהָ שִׁלְּחָה לָאֶבְיוֹן.
לֹא תִירָא לְבֵיתָהּ מִשָּׁלֶג, כִּי כָל בֵּיתָהּ לָבֻשׁ שָׁנִים.
מַרְבַדִּים עָשְׂתָה לָּהּ, שֵׁשׁ וְאַרְגָּמָן לְבוּשָׁהּ.
נוֹדָע בַּשְּׁעָרִים בַּעְלָהּ, בְּשִׁבְתּוֹ עִם זִקְנֵי אָרֶץ.
סָדִין עָשְׂתָה וַתִּמְכֹּר, וַחֲגוֹר נָתְנָה לַכְּנַעֲנִי.
עוֹז וְהָדָר לְבוּשָׁהּ, וַתִּשְׂחַק לְיוֹם אַחֲרוֹן.
פִּיהָ פָּתְחָה בְחָכְמָה, וְתוֹרַת חֶסֶד עַל לְשׁוֹנָהּ.
צוֹפִיָּה הֲלִיכוֹת בֵּיתָהּ, וְלֶחֶם עַצְלוּת לֹא תֹאכֵל.
קָמוּ בָנֶיהָ וַיְאַשְּׁרוּהָ, בַּעְלָהּ וַיְהַלְלָהּ.
רַבּוֹת בָּנוֹת עָשׂוּ חָיִל, וְאַתְּ עָלִית עַל כֻּלָּנָה.
שֶׁקֶר הַחֵן וְהֶבֶל הַיֹּפִי, אִשָּׁה יִרְאַת יְהוָה הִיא תִתְהַלָּל.
תְּנוּ לָהּ מִפְּרִי יָדֶיהָ, וִיהַלְלוּהָ בַשְּׁעָרִים מַעֲשֶׂיהָ.

אֵשֶׁת חַיִל מִי יִמְצָא, וְרָחֹק מִפְּנִינִים מִכְרָהּ
An accomplished woman, who can find?
Far beyond pearls is her value.

A Question for a Chassan

The Contradiction

Zera Shimshon begins with a question.

The opening words of the *pasuk* seem to imply that there is such a thing as an *eishes chayil*, and it is possible to find an accomplished woman in the world. Yet the second half of the verse asks מִי יִמְצָא — "who can find?" — which seems to imply that such a woman is impossible to find.

So we're facing a contradiction. How are we supposed to explain the *pasuk*?

An Unusual Question

Zera Shimshon cites the Gemara (*Yevamos* 63) that relates that in Eretz Yisrael, when a couple married, people would ask the *chassan* the following question:

מָצָא (*matza*) or מוֹצֵא (*motze*)?

What is the meaning of those cryptic words? We are asking the new bridegroom: Have you succeeded in fulfilling the verse (*Mishlei* 18:22), מָצָא אִשָּׁה מָצָא טוֹב — "He who has found (*matza*) a woman has found good"?

In other words: Have you merited to find a good woman — a true find, מְצִיאָה?

Or, מוֹצֵא (*motze*)? Are you a living example of the verse (*Koheles* 7:26), וּמוֹצֶא אֲנִי מַר מִמָּוֶת אֶת הָאִשָּׁה — "I find the woman more bitter than death," referring to someone who fell into the trap of marrying a woman of low character?

That is the question they would ask in Eretz Yisrael.

The Rif's Problem

Here the *Zera Shimshon* quotes the *Rif*, who raises a problem with this.

"The question seems pointless," says the *Rif*.

How is a *chassan* supposed to know on the day of his wedding if he found a "good" woman or not? It is virtually impossible for him to ascertain her personality and character traits in such a short time! This question can be answered only after a person has been married at least for a while.

The *Rif* then brings up another problem with this question. What is the point of asking it at all? If the people in Eretz Yisrael would come to a brand-new *chassan* and tell him how great his wife is — that would be worthwhile, since they are making the husband feel good about his decision. But for them to ask him whether he thinks he made the right choice seems like a pointless and unwise move, since it doesn't benefit anyone!

Even worse, if the *chassan* decided to marry an evil woman — well, he's already married and it's too late for him to do anything about it, so why rub it in?

Is it possible that they are coming to try to make the *chassan* feel better about it? No, because in that case they would approach him with words of comfort, and not the kind of question guaranteed to make him realize that he made a terrible mistake!

The Rif's Answer[1]

This is what you need to know, explains the Rif.

When a *chassan* marries, all his *aveiros*, his sins, are temporarily placed to the side. Not forgiven completely, but placed into a sort of spiritual "holding pen."

If, after he marries, the *chassan* replaces his previous behavior with better behavior, then his sins are turned into merits. וְזֶה מָצָא אִשָּׁה מָצָא טוֹב — and that is an example of "He who has found (*matza*) a woman has found (*matza*) good," because this person's marriage was the catalyst for his *aveiros* to be transformed into mitzvos.

However, if he doesn't change for the better and continues in his previous ways, subsequently he will be asked later why he didn't utilize the opportunity he had been granted to become a better person and to change his sins to merits.

About such a person they will say, מוֹצֵא אֲנִי מַר מִמָּוֶת אֶת הָאִשָּׁה — "I find (*motze*) the woman more bitter than death."

The *Rif* is telling us that asking this question would urge *chassanim* to take advantage of their new situation to become the best people they could be, and to change all their previous sins into merits.

Be Careful What You Daven For

Now *Zera Shimshon* gives us a completely different understanding of the Gemara.

When the Gemara uses the words דְּכִי נָסִיב אִישׁ אִתְּתָא — "when a man marries a woman," in reference to the question they would ask *chassanim* in Eretz Yisrael, מָצָא אוֹ מוֹצֵא, it doesn't mean that they would ask him that question once he was already married.

No, they would ask him the question when he was considering whether or not to marry her in the first place.

Zera Shimshon explains what they were really telling him.

"If you didn't daven to marry this particular woman," they would say to him, "she is your *mazel* and it's clearly meant to be."

---

1. *Zera Shimshon* does not specify the *Rif's* answer. Instead, he simply tells the reader to go and study it. The following segment is a summary of the *Rif's* answer.

"How do you know this?" the *chassan* would reply.

"Because of what the *pasuk* says — מָצָא אִשָּׁה מָצָא טוֹב. The word מָצָא (*matza*) is written in the past tense. It is referring to the idea that you have found the woman you were destined to marry from way back in time, as it says, 'Forty days before a baby is born a Heavenly voice announces who this child is destined to marry' (*Sotah* 2a, *Sanhedrin* 22a).

"And since you have found your destined match, מָצָא טוֹב — 'you have found good' — a perfect shidduch for yourself, since she was sent to you from Above."

And what if the *chassan* had, indeed, davened that he should marry that particular woman? In such a case, they would use the word מוֹצֵא (*motze*), as the Gemara states (*Moed Katan* 18b):

> It is permissible for a person to betroth a woman even on *Chol HaMoed*, since we are concerned that if he does not betroth her now, someone else may come and betroth her with mercy; that is, by praying and asking for mercy because he wants only her.

What does that mean?

We don't postpone a marriage, because someone may come along and daven that Hashem let him marry this specific woman, and his prayers might be accepted.

"We see from here," says the *Zera Shimshon*, "that it's possible for a person to marry someone who isn't their destined match. But such a *shidduch*," he continues, "is called מוֹצֵא (*motze*), in the present tense, because he found her now through his prayers, as opposed to her being his original match as destined from Above.

"While this is a possibility," says the *Zera Shimshon*, "the words מוֹצֵא אֲנִי מַר מִמָּוֶת — 'I find the woman more bitter than death,' were written to describe such a match."

Why?

The reason this is more bitter than death, he explains, is because such a match can cause death or poverty to him or to her, as we see from the following story, cited in *Moed Katan* (18b):

> Rava once heard someone davening. This is what the person said:

"Father in heaven, please allow me to marry this and this woman."

"You are making a mistake by making such a request," Rava told the man.

"Why?" the man wanted to know.

Rava explained, "There is no need to request this. If you are supposed to marry her, she will not marry someone else. If you are not supposed to be together," he continued, "then you shouldn't want to marry her, because when you marry the wrong person, you will end up filled with regret because it won't be a good match."

Warning: Daven!

Zera Shimshon now returns to the original question asked by the people of Eretz Yisrael.

"We can now grasp what they were asking the *chassan*," he says.

"Is this match a case of מָצָא — where you found the shidduch that was destined for you from long ago? Or is it a case of מוֹצֵא — a situation where you found her now, through your prayers, which would not be a good thing?"

That's their question.

And how does this question benefit the *chassan*?

The *chassan* was being given a warning. This is what they were telling him:

"If you received your *kallah* because you davened specifically for her — and not because you were destined for one another — then you need to strengthen your prayers. Hopefully, if you daven really well, you will merit to build a fine Jewish home, even if she was not destined to be your wife."

We find this idea in the *Zohar* (*Parashas Vayeilech*), which states:

> When a person makes a shidduch, since it is possible that this is not the woman destined for him from the time he was created, he should daven not to be pushed away in favor of the original husband.

We see from the *Zohar's* words, says the *Zera Shimshon*, that earnest and meaningful prayer can help smooth things out even when a person marries someone who wasn't his original intended match.

This was the point of the question they used to ask in Eretz Yisrael. They were letting the *chassan* know that even if he wasn't initially intended to marry this woman, he could still have a wonderful marriage — by davening now.

The Eishes Chayil's Protection

Zera Shimshon continues:

"You have to know something," he says. "When a couple are not meant for one another, it can cause problems for both of them, since [if one was destined to] experience a life of poverty, both will suffer. The same is true if either of them is destined to die at an early age — either because she will have the pain of dying young, or because she will now be an *almanah*."

And now *Zera Shimshon* makes a very important point.

These challenging situations — poverty or early death — can be avoided when a woman is an *eishes chayil* even before her marriage. Because if she has a lot of merits, they will protect her from marrying someone not destined for her. The *Zera Shimshon* stresses the point: "A person's *tefillos* will not help him marry an *eishes chayil* who was not destined for him, for one simple reason — she is an *eishes chayil* and her merits will protect her from this."

And that is why the *pasuk* אֵשֶׁת חַיִל מִי יִמְצָא is in the future tense — it is referring to a woman who was not intended to be his wife.

Now everything becomes clear. There are women of valor in this world. Nonetheless when the *pasuk* writes מִי יִמְצָא, "who can find them?," implying they cannot be found, it is referring to the idea that if a man prays to marry a woman who is not destined for him, if she is an *eishes chayil*, those prayers will not be answered.

To sum up:

1. A person's priority should be to marry a good woman — an *eishes chayil*. And when he is lucky enough to find her, he should do his best to improve his deeds so that

he should be worthy of her and turn all his past *aveiros* into mitzvos.

2. There is a concept of davening to marry a particular woman but it is frowned upon, since everyone has someone who was destined for him. That said, if he did daven specifically for someone and they marry, he should continue to daven with great fervor so that their lives should be filled with blessing.

3. If the woman is an *eishes chayil* her merits will help ensure that she only marries the person she is destined for and no one else.

We can learn many lessons from the first line of Eishes Chayil. But it seems obvious that the first lesson is this — the right kind of wife can and will change a person for the better in every way.

I want to tell you about a rosh yeshivah named Rav Daniel Faber who was in an uncomfortable position, and an older man who was afraid of change, and a wife who encouraged her husband to deal with his fears and to grow.

I've been a rosh yeshivah in Eretz Yisrael for many years now, mainly dealing with *bachurim* who are *baalei teshuvah* and are drawn to the world of Chassidus. In fact, I received a personal *tzivui* — or mandate, if you wish — from Rav Mendel Weinbach, rosh yeshivah of Ohr Somayach. The mandate was to establish a yeshivah for these kinds of *bachurim*, where I would "teach them Torah, work with them, and help develop them into balanced *bnei Torah*."

When *Asher Leib came to the yeshivah, he was completely lost. I sat with him for hours, listening as he poured out his heart. He truly wanted to develop into a *talmid chacham* and an *oved Hashem*. At the same time, he told me how much he wanted to make sure that he remained a "normal" person.

"Asher Leib," I said, "you came to the right place. Here at Yeshiva Yeshuas Yisroel, we work with every *bachur* and *yungerman* to help develop their learning and davening capabilities, while keeping them grounded at the same time."

Asher Leib explained that he had a business at which he was good, but he wasn't making enough money. This was making it difficult for him to focus on his learning.

"I am going to help you figure out your business," I promised him. "You will see that once your *parnassah* is steady, you will be able to learn with peace of mind."

So it began. I helped Asher Leib streamline his business and I assigned him a certain number of hours of learning to do. In addition, I spent time guiding him in the area of *shalom bayis* as well. *Baruch Hashem*, things were moving along nicely, and I was happy with his progress.

And then, six months after he joined the kollel, Asher Leib came over to me one morning.

"Rav Faber?"

"Yes, Asher Leib?"

"Rebbi, my wife and I get a *mazel tov.*"

"*Mazel tov!*"

"We just had a baby boy, and we are making a *bris* this coming Shabbos."

"That's beautiful!"

"Yes, we are very happy. I wanted to know if Rebbi would agree to be the *sandek* at the *bris*?"

"Of course! It's a huge *zechus* to serve as the *sandek* at a *bris*!"

Asher Leib smiled, but there was still something else on his mind.

"I'm a little nervous," he said.

"Why are you nervous?"

"My father-in-law is flying in from Mexico for the *bris* and it's possible that he will expect to be *sandek*."

"Is your father-in-law *shomer Shabbos*?"

"No."

"Then you should find some other *kibbud* to give him at the *bris*. He should not be the *sandek*."

"What should I do?"

"You can give him *kvatter* — which is better anyway, in the sense that you will be honoring your mother-in-law at the same time."

We finished the conversation shortly afterward, with the understanding that I would serve as the *sandek* while the *shver* would receive a different honor.

Asher Leib called me that Friday. He wasn't happy.

"What's the good word, Asher Leib?"

"I spoke to my *shver* and told him that I want my rebbi to be the *sandek*."

"And?"

"From the look on his face, I could tell that he was hurt."

"I hear."

"So what should I do? I don't want to hurt his feelings."

"Asher Leib, tell your father-in-law that you want him to be the *sandek*. All he needs to do is commit to becoming a *shomer Shabbos*. If he does, then you will give him the honor without any hesitation whatsoever."

"So I just tell him that he needs to commit to becoming *shomer Shabbos*?"

"Yes."

"Okay," he said dubiously.

The next phone call came in not long before the start of Shabbos.

"What happened?" I asked him.

"My *shver* wouldn't commit. At this point, everything is still open. Interestingly, my mother-in-law is pushing him to agree to the clause."

"So she wants to become *shomer Shabbos*?"

"Exactly."

"Fascinating."

"What do I do?"

"You've done everything you can do. The *bris* will be tomorrow at the yeshivah, and we will see what happens till then. I'll see you later at my house."

Asher Leib and family were all eating at my house that Shabbos. We would also be hosting the *shalom zachar* on Friday night, with the *bris* taking place at the yeshivah the next morning. I knew that his father-in-law was sitting on the fence and that he needed to hear words to help him make the right decision. I therefore devoted much of my talk at the *seudah* on Friday night to a deep discussion about the beauty of Shabbos and how keeping Shabbos changes a person's life for the better.

When the *seudah* was over, the tablecloth was changed and we set up for the *shalom zachar*. More and more people began coming in. Soon the house was filled with a large crowd. Songs were sung, cake was eaten, and a few people spoke. The atmosphere was uplifting.

In the midst of the festivities, Asher Leib's father-in-law came over and took a seat beside me. This meant that, even though the room was full, we were able to speak privately.

"I want to tell you something," I told him.

"Yes, Rabbi?"

"In general, I'm a happy man. I don't need much. Hashem has blessed me with all the important things in life, and I am filled with gratitude. That said, when someone offers me to serve as the *sandek* at their child's *bris*, I always say yes, because it's a tremendous *segulah*." I paused. "But though I know that this is a major *segulah*, I want nothing more than for you to have it. I am just asking you to please consider becoming a *shomer Shabbos*!"

"I hear you, Rabbi," the *shver* replied. "I really do. And part of me wants to take this on. But another part is afraid to make such a huge commitment."

We spoke for a while. In the end, I said to myself, "I guess we will just have to see what happens tomorrow, when this story will be resolved one way or another."

I did very little sleeping that Friday night, tossing and turning for hours as I tried to figure out a way to make it possible for Asher

Leib's father-in-law to make the commitment of becoming *shomer Shabbos.*

Shacharis passed uneventfully, with the *shver* only showing up at the end of *chazaras hashatz,* just before *Krias HaTorah.* Seeing him arrive, I left my place at the front of the room and went outside to speak with him — something I almost never do. The moment of truth had arrived.

"Good Shabbos," I greeted him.

He returned the greeting.

"I want to tell you something. I was up the entire night trying to figure out what to do for you."

He nodded.

"I finally found a piece of important information in the *Seridei Aish* — a famous halachic *sefer* — where the author says that if a person agrees to accept upon himself to keep Shabbos for a significant amount of time, then he has the halachic status of a *shomer Shabbos.* So my suggestion is this. I think it would be a good idea for you to agree to keep Shabbos for a significant amount of time. That way, you will be able to identify yourself as a *shomer Shabbos* and serve as the *sandek* at your grandson's *bris.* What do you say?"

He remained hesitant.

We were still standing there when Asher Leib's mother-in-law approached us.

"Shall we ask the rebbetzin what she thinks?"

"Okay."

I told Asher Leib's mother-in-law everything I had just told her husband. She loved the idea.

"Let's do it," she said enthusiastically.

"I'm afraid to commit," her husband said. "I mean, what if I commit, and I start, and then I mess up? Wouldn't it be better not to start at all, than to start and stop in the middle?"

I smiled at the well-meaning Yid from Mexico. "Did you ever hear the words '*bli neder*'?"

"Actually, I hear those words a lot," he replied. "What does it mean?"

"It means, 'I am going to do my best to keep my word, but this is not a vow.' I think you should commit, *bli neder*, to keep Shabbos from now for a specific amount of time, with the understanding that you will keep on trying after that as well. What do you say?"

He thought for a few seconds.

"You know what, Rabbi? I agree!"

"That's great!"

"On one condition."

"What's that?"

"I'll become *shomer Shabbos*, *bli neder*, until Rosh Hashanah… if *you* will serve as the *sandek* at my grandson's *bris*."

I was shocked. His wife was just as stunned as I was. Neither of us had seen this coming. An explanation was needed.

"Why the change?" I asked him.

"I'll explain. From everything you've been telling me, it seems clear that it's very important that the *sandek* should be a religious Jew, because who he is has a great impact on the baby. This is why we want someone who is truly righteous to serve as the *sandek*."

I waited quietly to see where he was going with this.

"Rav Faber," Asher Leib's father-in-law continued, "I have waited a long time for this grandson, and I want the best for him. So I am asking you to please serve as *sandek* at the *bris*, and I promise to try and become *shomer Shabbos*. That's the deal. I become *shomer Shabbos*, and you serve as *sandek*."

We shook hands on the deal.

I then escorted the *shver* into the beis midrash and banged on the *bimah*. When everyone was quiet, I told the assembled that there was a reason why Hashem chose Klal Yisrael as His nation. Then I related the story of "The *Sandek* Negotiation."

Everyone was moved. Some people even cried.

After davening, we held the *bris* — and I served as the *sandek*.

I had to do it. After all, it was my part of the deal.

The Segulah of the Zera Shimshon

Reb Kalman relates…

A nephew of mine was marrying off his son in London, and because we have a very close connection I decided to fly in and take part in the *simchah*. This nephew had already been learning *Zera Shimshon* for a number of years, and he decided to give out copies of the *sefer* to all the guests at the wedding. He gave the men copies of the *Zera Shimshon's peirush* on *Shir HaShirim* and to the women his commentary on Eishes Chayil. When I asked him why he had specifically chosen to distribute those gifts, he explained that he was sure the *sefarim* would make a positive impression on many of the guests, and that some of them would probably start learning *Zera Shimshon* on a regular basis — which was, after all, what the author had asked people to do.

When I returned to Eretz Yisrael, I found a place for the *sefer* in the *machsan* (storage room) beneath my house, a room which I rent out to a *sofer stam* — and promptly forgot about the whole thing.

Not long ago, I was talking to the *sofer*, and he told me that his wife had just given birth to their first son — after seven years of marriage!

"I just wanted to say thank you! It's all in your *zechus*!"

I stared at him in confusion, wondering what part I had played in his *simchah*. "I see you don't know what I'm talking about. Well, then, let me remind you. When you returned from your trip to London, you put the *sefer* that you were given at the wedding into the *machsan* where I work. I happened to pick up the *sefer*, and there I saw that Rav Shimshon Chaim promises that anyone who learns his *sefer* will merit ...בָּנִים בְּנֵי בָנִים חֲכָמִים וּנְבֹנִים — wise and understanding children and grandchildren."

"I told myself that it would be a good idea to do something small for the tzaddik, hoping that he would keep his promise, with Hashem's help. This is what I did. Every day, while waiting for the ink to dry before rolling up the *klaf* I had worked on, I would learn from the Torah of the *Zera Shimshon*. And *baruch Hashem*, the promise came true! We merited to welcome our *bechor* into the world."

When I heard this story, I realized a number of important things. First, I had merited to serve as the emissary to bring about a Jewish couple's salvation. At the same time, something else struck me: the *hashgachah pratis* that Hakadosh Baruch Hu shows with each of His creations. Think about it. A *baal simchah* in London decided to give the Torah of the *Zera Shimshon*. He ordered the *sefarim* from Eretz Yisrael and gave them in England — where one *sefer* promptly made the return trip back to Eretz Yisrael, taking up residence right in the room of the *sofer* who needed to learn it...

How fortunate I was to have merited to have a part in this exceptional *berachah*!

בָּטַח בָּהּ לֵב בַּעְלָהּ, וְשָׁלָל לֹא יֶחְסָר
*Her husband's heart relies on her,
and he shall lack no fortune.*

Thwarting the Bad Angels

In Her Merit

After finishing his discussion on the first *pasuk* of Eishes Chayil, *Zera Shimshon* tell us:

After the husband has the good fortune to marry an *eishes chayil*, who has earned much merit, he can rely on her — בָּטַח בָּהּ — trusting that he will be blessed with peace and wealth in her merit.

As the Gemara (*Yevamos* 62b) declares: "Rabbi Tanchum says in the name of Rabbi Chanilai: Any person who does not have a wife is living without happiness, without blessing, and without good."

Beating the Mekatrigim

Zera Shimshon continues:

The *mekatrigim* (heavenly angels that speak badly of humankind) do not want a person to live in peace and goodness. Even when it was decreed that a person will live a good life, they never stop trying to ruin it for him.

We find this idea brought down by *Chazal* on the *pasuk,* וְאָכַלְתָּ אֶת שְׁלַל אֹיְבֶיךָ — "You shall eat the *shlal* (booty) of your enemy" (*Devarim* 20:14). This can be understood to mean that the heavenly enemies (*mekatrigim*) want to take away everything good that a man has, but in the merit of his *eishes chayil* he can be sure that וְשָׁלָל לֹא יֶחְסָר — he will not lack fortune (*shalal*, similar to the word *shlal*). He will have whatever he needs — and the *mekatrigim's* efforts will be thwarted.

When that happens, it will be as if he merited not only to have his own blessings, but even managed to take the bounty of his heavenly foes!

Five Types of Chesed

Zera Shimshon gives us another explanation of the words וְשָׁלָל לֹא יֶחְסָר.

He explains that the word שָׁלָל has the *gematria* (numerical value) of 360, which is the same value as the word *chesed*, kindness, multiplied by five. (The numerical value of the word *chesed* is 72, and 5x72 = 360.)

This hints to us that a person who merits to marry an *eishes chayil* will be *zocheh* to benefit from the five types of *chesed* that were known to the *Chachmei HaKabbalah*, the wise men of the Kabbalah (*Zohar Idra Rabbah* III 142a).

This is the opposite of what the *mekatrigim* are trying to achieve. With the right wife, they will have no power to harm him.

The heroine of the following story is an *eishes chayil* in her own right (and she was even before she married...). In this case, she went out of her way for her brother, doing her best to help him get engaged and find his own *eishes chayil*.

In a fascinating turn of events, the Sefer *Zera Shimshon* played a major part in the proceedings...

Tziporah speaks:

My brother had been in *shidduchim* for quite a while. I know that my parents had been listening to prospective ideas for a good two years, but for some reason he was having a difficult time finding the right one. This story occurred during the first Shabbos after my grandmother finished *shivah* for my grandfather, and a group of cousins, her grandchildren, were at her house. I was in the kitchen, enjoying a chat with my brother. My brother is an interesting person and talking to him is always a pleasure, but I was a little surprised when he turned to me in the middle of the conversation and started speaking about his business.

"Recently, I closed a great deal," he said.

"I'm very happy for you."

He went on, discussing the financial elements of the deal. I was beginning to be pulled into the discussion, when I recalled that one is not supposed to discuss business on Shabbos. I decided that it would be better if we held off until Shabbos was over.

It was at that moment that I had a great idea. I don't know why it came to me at that exact second, but when an idea comes your way, it pays to grab hold of it immediately. When Hashem sends an idea, it's like a gift just entered your world...

"You know what I think?" I said to my brother.

"What do you think?"

"I think that you should start learning a *sefer*. I think you need more learning in your life."

I could see that the idea intrigued him.

"To make it easier for you," I continued, "I am offering to serve as your *chavrusa*."

I know this sounds strange, but I hadn't been thinking that way until the offer emerged from my mouth. I don't know how or why; I just decided to offer to learn with my brother, hoping that my offer would make it easier for him to decide to start a new learning regimen. Oddly enough, he took my offer seriously. I guess he was really ready to do some learning.

"The only question," I said, "is what we should start learning together."

He considered for a moment, and then replied, "Why don't we

start learning *Zera Shimshon*? One of my friends recently started learning *Zera Shimshon* and saw major *yeshuos*!"

"Sounds good," I said. "Where can we pick up a copy of the *sefer*?"

"I don't know if you know this," my brother said, "but Zeide (the grandfather who had just passed away) was very into *Zera Shimshon* and he also wanted all his children to have the opportunity to study the *sefer*. So he purchased a copy for each of them. I think we should take a look in his study. There's a good chance that we will find a copy of the *sefer*."

No sooner said than done. We went upstairs into his study, and there, sitting right in the middle of his desk, was a copy of the English version of *Zera Shimshon*. It was the one written by Rabbi Nachman Seltzer and published by ArtScroll, with pieces of *Zera Shimshon* on every *parashah* and stories that connect to the Torah thought. My zeide's copy of the *sefer* was on his desk, as if he were still in the middle of learning from it.

It was a really nice feeling, almost as if my grandfather was still talking to us and helping us understand what he wanted us to do.

My brother brought the copy of my zeide's *Zera Shimshon* downstairs, and on the spot my mother began reading out loud from that week's *parashah*, *Yisro*. The piece she chose to read was about none other than Moshe Rabbeinu and Tziporah. You probably won't be very surprised when I tell you that my name is Tziporah and my brother's name is Moshe. Just a nice coincidence, right?

My mother went on to read the story that was connected to the Torah idea. All the cousins in the kitchen listened as she read. Basically, it was the story of the wife of a *talmid* who called their rebbi, Rav Nissan Kaplan from Yerushalayim, and told him that their child was in the hospital. They were waiting to hear the doctor's diagnosis as to how serious the illness was. Rav Nissan offered to go to the Kosel to daven for them.

"That's not the only problem," the *talmid's* wife said.

"What else is going on?"

"My husband's business is losing a lot of money right now and the situation is looking problematic."

"I'll daven about that as well," he promised.

Rav Nissan went to the Kosel on Friday morning, as he had said he would. After he davened for them, he tried to catch a taxi to Har Nof, but there were none available. In the end, he was forced to take a bus. By that time, he had a pounding headache and mistakenly boarded the wrong bus. He put his head down on the seat in front of him. Suddenly, he felt someone tapping him on the shoulder. He looked over at the person sitting next to him on the bus. It was a chassid.

"Yes?" Rav Nissan said. "What can I do for you?"

The chassid introduced himself. Then he said, "I want to tell you a story."

Rav Nissan really didn't feel well at that moment, but he told the chassid to go ahead. The chassid told him how someone once came to his Rebbe saying that his child was very sick and needed a major *yeshuah*. The Rebbe looked at his chassid and said, "Next Friday night, when you are making *Kiddush*, keep in mind that you are a partner with Hashem in the creation of the world — and that, as a partner, you are asking that your child should be given a complete *refuah sheleimah*."

Rav Nissan didn't understand why the chassid had decided to share that particular anecdote with him at that exact moment, but he thanked his seatmate for the story and put his head back down on the seat in front of him. A minute later, the chassid again started tapping him on the shoulder.

"I want to tell you another story."

Rav Nissan understood that Heaven had sent this man to him. He listened.

"A chassid came to his Rebbe and told him that his business was losing a tremendous amount of money every day. The Rebbe heard him out. He then asked him a question.

"Tell me, do you ever discuss business matters with your wife at the Shabbos table?"

"I'll tell you the truth," the chassid replied. "I am so busy with my business during the week that my wife and I barely have time to talk to one another. Sometimes we slip and we speak about the business on Shabbos."

"I want you to undertake never to discuss business matters on Shabbos anymore," the Rebbe told him.

Rav Nissan thanked the chassid for the two stories. When he arrived home and his wife asked him how his visit to the Kosel had been, he started telling her all about the chassid who had tapped him on the shoulder, and how he had told him two stories. Suddenly, he realized that both stories were exactly tailored to the reasons he had gone to the Kosel in the first place!

Rav Nissan called his *talmid's* wife in America and told her what had happened. He explained what intentions her husband should have when he made *Kiddush* that Friday night. He then asked her a question.

"By any chance, do you ever end up discussing business matters with your husband on Shabbos?"

She thought about the question for a few seconds.

"It's funny you should ask," she replied. "Usually, we don't talk business at the Shabbos table. But because we barely get a chance to talk to one another during the week, sometimes we slip and talk about the business on Shabbos."

"I want you to make a *kabbalah*," Rav Nissan told her, "that from now on, there will be no more talking business at the Shabbos table."

She called Rav Nissan back on Motzaei Shabbos.

"I just wanted to let you know that the doctors have given us a very positive diagnosis. *Baruch Hashem*, we are out of the woods."

"And what about the business?"

"We are looking at a turnaround."

That was the story that my mother read to all of us that night. The message seemed clear to one and all.

In a fascinating development, three weeks after my brother began learning *Zera Shimshon*, we had the great joy and privilege of celebrating his engagement. In my mind, the connection seemed pretty obvious.

It was also beautiful that we were able to feel that my grandfather was still with us, still doing his utmost for the family he loved so much.

גְּמָלַתְהוּ טוֹב וְלֹא רָע, כֹּל יְמֵי חַיֶּיהָ

She bestows goodness upon him,
and never evil, all the days of her life.

You Can't Put a Price on Loyalty

Good, Not Bad

The *eishes chayil* gives her husband only good, and nothing bad.

If she gives him only good things, isn't it obvious that she isn't going to give him things that are bad? Why the double *lashon*? Wouldn't it be enough to celebrate her giving him only good things?

Zera Shimshon answers this question by discussing a Gemara (*Bava Metzia* 59a) that states, "The blessing of wealth enters a person's house only in the merit of his wife."

It is through the wife's hands that the money is drawn down to the home, as the *navi Yechezkel* states (44:30), "to bring the blessing into your home." This means that blessing comes to the home in the merit of the wife, who is called the בָּיִת (the home) by *Chazal*.

Why is it that the blessing of wealth in the home is a result of the *eishes chayil's* merit?

The reason, says *Zera Shimshon*, is her loyalty.

A good wife is supremely loyal to her husband — and in reward for that loyalty, Hashem sends her husband blessings through her hands.

Why?

In *Mishlei* (28:20) it says, "A man of loyalty will increase blessings." The Midrash in *Parashas Pekudei* (*Shemos Rabbah* 51:1) explains this *pasuk* in the following way. Hashem sends blessings through everyone who is loyal — not only someone who is loyal to Hashem, the Master of the World, but even someone who is loyal to his friends.

Or a wife who is loyal to her husband.

In all those cases, Hashem sends blessing through the loyal person.

Since this is so, when a woman is loyal to her husband, she brings blessing to their home.

Let us now return to our initial question.

The *pasuk* already told us that she brings only goodness. Why does it have to stress that she also doesn't bring bad?

Says the *Zera Shimshon*, this is what it means. גְּמָלַתְהוּ טוֹב — goodness and blessing come to the husband through his wife.

And why specifically through her?

וְלֹא רָע — Because she (the *eishes chayil*) doesn't do any evil, and is completely loyal to him.

Whose Merits?

Yet now we have another question. How will the husband know that blessing is coming to the home in his wife's merit? Perhaps the blessing comes because of his own merit, and not hers?

To answer this, the *pasuk* in Eishes Chayil adds the words כֹּל יְמֵי חַיֶּיהָ — "all the days of her life," which implies that the blessing will last as long as she lives, and will cease when she passes away. This is, of course, a very obvious and true proof that the blessing is coming because of her.

As *Rashi* writes on the *pasuk,* וַיִּנָּחֵם יִצְחָק אַחֲרֵי אִמּוֹ — "Yitzchak was comforted [for the loss of] his mother" (*Bereishis* 24:67): "When Sarah Imeinu passed on to the next world, the blessing ceased in the dough in Avraham Avinu's tent."

From here we clearly see that the blessing was coming to Avraham Avinu's home because of Sarah, his wife.

From the *Zera Shimshon's* beautiful explanation we see how much a good wife — an *eishes chayil* — benefits her husband. She benefits him with her loyalty and love, and she benefits him because it is precisely that loyalty and love that draw down endless blessing from heaven into their home.

I want to tell you about a couple that I know.

A couple that exhibited true loyalty to one another and to Hashem. And at the end of their quest — and it took a while — they were rewarded with the most beautiful blessing in their home.

This is the story of Efrat and Itzik Churi. A story of loyalty, love, and complete faith in Hashem — and the reward that came in its wake.

My name is Itzik Churi. I was raised in the Ramot section of Yerushalayim. My wife's family lived there as well when she was a young girl — we were actually neighbors. My sister made our *shidduch*. We were married on the 3rd of Teves 5760 (2000), and like all our friends and every other young couple we knew, we waited for our children to arrive. But nothing happened. One year passed, then another, and still our apartment was as quiet as it had been when we first married.

This story began more than twenty years ago, when the resources that exist today for a couple in our situation were virtually nonexistent. Bonei Olam had yet to establish itself in Israel. Zir Chemed had already begun helping people, but it was a far cry from the professional organization it is today. Which meant that we were stumbling in the dark as we tried to make our way through the maze in which we found ourselves.

Eager to end our wait, and understanding that our situation was of a serious nature, we submitted ourselves for a battery of tests. We eventually were sent to Shaarei Tzedek Hospital, where we underwent our first treatment. It took a lot out of us, especially since

nobody knew what we were going through, and we were a.
own. Unfortunately, we were informed by the doctor that it had no
been successful.

"I have to be honest with you," the doctor told us. "This hospital
doesn't have the equipment that you need."

"So where should we go?"

"I recommend that you go for more thorough testing at Tel
HaShomer Hospital near Tel Aviv."

After conferring with Rav Schlesinger (who today heads an organization called Pri Chaim) we followed the doctor's advice.

Efrat and I were never one of those couples who, unable to
have children of their own, shy away from having anything to do
with kids. In fact, Efrat actually worked with children as a *ganenet*
in her very popular *gan*. Yet as much as being around children was
a balm for us, it also brought home our childless state each and
every day, making us more determined than ever to try every form
of *hishtadlus* possible.

The consciousness of what we were lacking, coupled with our
intense desire to hold our child in our arms, led us to Tel HaShomer,
where we underwent another five treatments — at a rate of two per
year — all of which were unsuccessful. It was at this point that we
had a meeting with our doctor, the head of the fertility department.

"I am sorry to say that we have tried everything, to no avail.
Something is just not working. There is no earthly reason why the
treatments shouldn't have been effective, but facts are facts."

And we understood that, for the time being, there was nothing
left to do.

It was around this time that Bonei Olam opened a branch in
Eretz Yisrael. After conferring with them, they recommended that
we meet with a fertility expert at Ichilov Hospital. There we met with
the head of the department and went through another treatment.
This was also where my wife made an outstanding *kiddush Hashem*.
Often, hormone supplements can cause very adverse reactions. The

the medications can be extreme and can cause normally ...headed people to act in ways that are completely foreign to their normal mode of behavior. We saw this many times.

Efrat made an impression for the exact opposite reason. Here she was, a patient just like the other women, yet instead of allowing the medication to control her, she was helping the nurses with the other patients, calming them and making sure they were doing as well as possible under the circumstances.

"I have to tell you something," the head nurse said. "The religious women who come here — and specifically your wife — are shining examples of humanity, both in terms of their own behavior and in how they help us with the other patients."

She was speaking the truth. And she was right. Efrat constantly served as a prime example of the nobility of the Jewish woman. I remember how overcome and incredulous the other patients were when they discovered that Efrat actually ran her own *gan* for little children.

"How can that be?" they would marvel.

"I am an atheist," one woman told Efrat. "But if your G-d is real, I am sure He will give you a child..."

So saying, the self-proclaimed "atheist" raised her hands in the direction of heaven, as if begging Hashem to reward my wife with a child of her own.

Unfortunately, that treatment was also unsuccessful.

By the time we had been married fifteen years, you can imagine how burned out we were from our many years of trying to have a child. The hopes and the disappointments. The shattered dreams, and the need to carry on as if everything was okay, even when you just heard, yet again, that everything you were hoping for was not meant to be.

Yet we never gave up on our goal. Raising the money we needed was no simple matter. While the kupat cholim does contribute toward some of the medications, if you want to use private doctors you have to raise the funds yourself. Which meant that every single treatment cost in the region of thirty to forty thousand shekel.

I had two good friends who helped me all the time. One was Reb Yigal Bresman, a contractor in Ramat Beit Shemesh who passed away not long ago. The other friend — I am pretty sure he wants to remain anonymous — insisted that my wife and I go away on vacation after we finished yet another treatment. I offer this to every couple in a similar situation as priceless advice:

"When the treatment is done, go away to a hotel."

A rosh kollel of mine helped me from time to time, discreetly handing me money without asking if I needed it. As for us, we didn't save a shekel. We used all our money, whatever funds came in, toward our goal.

At one point, we began another round of treatments at Assuta Hospital with yet another doctor. There we did yet another five treatments, with the doctor continually trying different ideas and methods to help make our dream come true. Still nothing worked.

It had been years of different ideas and hopes that had been dashed time and again. Years of davening, *segulos,* tears and going to the Kosel for forty consecutive days. At that point, my wife and I looked at one another and said, "Okay, we tried everything there is to try. From a medical perspective there is no point in trying again. Now the question is: What comes next? Where do we go from here?"

Medically, it hadn't happened. But there was another whole world out there that had nothing to do with the universe of hospitals, doctors, and medicine. Clearly the time had come to put more effort in other directions. The only question was which direction to take.

One of my relatives runs the kollel at Kever Rochel. He said to me, "Listen Itzik, Kever Rochel is a special place. I myself have seen countless miracles since I have become involved with running everything for Mama Rochel.

"Itzik," he went on, "Kever Rochel is the only place that the Torah tells us was actually established so that Klal Yisrael has somewhere to daven. And another thing — Rochel Imeinu knew how to cry. She knew how to use her tears to plead for what she needed from Hashem. When you come here, you'll feel emotions you have never felt in your life."

I listened to him and began traveling to Kever Rochel.

I went one day. I went the next. Suddenly, I felt as if my heart was opening up. I had been to so many places and never experienced the reaction I felt at Kever Rochel. It was completely unique. I would recite the entire *Sefer Tehillim* every day, joining the kollel that learns in the building and divides the entire *sefer* among themselves. After saying the entire *Sefer Tehillim*, I'd learn *daf yomi* with a *chavrusa* and then focus on learning *hilchos Havdalah*.

The reason I started learning those halachos was due to a visit to Rav Chaim Kanievsky *zt"l*. I asked the *gadol hador* for a *berachah*, and he told me that I should begin reciting *Havdalah* every Motzaei Shabbos on wine instead of grape juice. After a year, I returned to Rav Chaim, and he told me that I should now start learning the halachos of *Havdalah*.

That Rosh Hashanah I went to daven at Ohel Yaakov, my local shul. While I was waiting for the *chazzan* to begin *chazaras hashatz*, I pulled a *sefer* from a nearby shelf and began leafing through the pages. The *sefer* was called *Ahavas Chesed*, one of the many *sefarim* written by the Chofetz Chaim.

There I read the words of Rav Yisrael Meir HaKohen.

"Why do people spend so much money on different *segulos* for having children," he wrote, "when the greatest *segulah* of all for having children is to support poor *talmidei chachamim*?"

Suddenly, I had an awakening.

I was part of a *daf yomi shiur* in Ramat Beit Shemesh that had begun with four participants and was given by a *talmid chacham* named Reb Meir Chein. Before we knew it, the *shiur* had grown to fifty people. While I had been proud to watch as the *shiur* grew in size, a part of me had always felt that it would be a great thing if people could be part of a kollel where they could learn the daily *daf* in a way that was more in-depth than just participating in a morning *shiur*.

On the spot, I decided that I would establish a kollel for *avreichim* to do just that.

One of the beautiful *minhagim* of our *shiur* was that it would be held on special occasions in the homes of different members. My day to host the *shiur* had always been on Erev Yom Kippur. That Erev Yom Kippur, I made a special announcement, informing everyone that I planned to establish a kollel for people who wanted to spend more time focusing on the daily *daf*.

The *maggid shiur* asked me what I planned on calling the kollel.

"The kollel is going to be called Zera Yitzchak." On the spot, a few of the *shiur* members pledged specific amounts toward the upkeep of the kollel.

The kollel opened its doors that Rosh Chodesh Cheshvan, with eight *yungeleit*.

As time passed, more and more *yungeleit* heard about the kollel and asked if they could join. And the Ribbono shel Olam made sure that the *avreichim* who came our way were of the finest caliber. For my part, I always told them, "This is not my kollel. I am not the rosh kollel. My name is Itzik (Yitzchak) and we are doing this as a *zechus* for me and for my brother (who also was waiting for children of his own). I thank you all for learning Torah in our merit! It is your kollel!"

Baruch Hashem, the kollel has been very successful, and I have been able to pay the *yungeleit* on time every single month.

With the passing of time, the kollel grew ever stronger. And then we heard the tragic news that my dear friend and long-time supporter Reb Yigal Bresman had been diagnosed with a horrendous illness. He became sicker and sicker, until he passed away.

Yigal!

Yigal was no longer alive!

The neighborhood joined together to try to raise money for his wife and children. One of the things they did was to put together a video where people spoke about Yigal and what an amazing and caring person he had been.

I was one of those asked to speak about my dear friend, a person to whom I owed so very much.

Needless to say, I agreed. How could I not? Yigal had been there for me and my wife in our darkest times. He had given us so much. If there was anything I could do in return, there was no question that I would give it my all. And so, I sat down in front of the video camera and began to speak.

From the heart.

In a way I had never spoken in public before.

They filmed the video in a house not far from where I live.

"My wife and I have been married for twenty years without children," I began. I found that I could barely get the words out. I tried. I tried again. And suddenly, for the first time in my life, I found myself losing control, breaking down live and on camera! The walls with which I had always surrounded myself had crumbled.

I cried as I understood that Reb Yigal was gone. While his family would miss their father and husband, I would also miss the man who had been a rock in my life.

The video was released, and it went viral. Large amounts of money were raised, with many people telling me that watching me melt down on screen had moved them to donate more than they'd ever planned on giving. I was overjoyed that I had been able to repay my dear friend just a little bit for everything he had done for me over the years. People had been able to feel my emotion over the loss of this *tzaddik*, and they responded.

It is about authenticity. It's always about authenticity. Everyone who watched knew that I was speaking from the core of my soul, and they reacted accordingly. Yet even I had no idea where that video was going to take my wife and me.

Reb Meir Kenig showed the video to Reb Akiva Veiner, the CEO of an organization called Mercaz Taharas Hamishpachah — an organization that builds and refurbishes *mikvaos* around Eretz Yisrael — and asked him for a donation toward the fund they were putting together for Yigal's family.

After watching the clip, Reb Akiva said, "I want to show you something."

He then showed Reb Meir Kenig a video featuring a couple that hadn't had children for many years.

"This couple donated a mikveh," he told Reb Meir.

He then showed him the rest of the video. At the end, the same couple was shown holding twin babies in their arms.

Reb Meir came to see me at the kollel the next day. On a normal day, Meir's enthusiasm level is at ninety-nine percent. That morning, he was operating at three hundred and twenty.

"I need to show you something," he said. "Watch this."

I watched the video.

"Listen to me," he said when it was over, "I am taking you to Rav Chaim. We are going to tell him about this. If he says that you and your wife have to build a *mikveh*, we will build a *mikveh*! I am ready to travel abroad with my brother-in-law Benzy, and we will raise the funds needed to turn this dream into a reality."

Meir Kenig and his brother-in-law were ready to drop everything and put their respective businesses on hold, travel to America and raise the money we would need to build a *mikveh* to stand in our merit. Do you understand what a *tzaddik* this man is?!

The next thing I knew, we were getting out of the car and going in to see Rav Chaim. It was the 8th of Cheshvan, 2020.

Rav Chaim's grandson told his zeide, "This man has been married for twenty years without children. They want to build a *mikveh* in order to earn the *zechus* of having children. What does the Rav say about this?"

Rav Chaim thought about it for a few seconds.

"That's the *eitzah* (idea)," he said.

Meir Kenig interjected in Yiddish to Rav Chaim.

"They've been married for twenty years without children. He opened a kollel. And today is his birthday. What does the Rav say — will he have children?"

Rav Chaim lifted his eyes and replied, "I am not a *navi*. But, *b'ezras Hashem*, I can give him a *berachah*."

Meir asked, "*B'karov*? Soon?"

Rav Chaim replied, "*B'karov*. Soon."

I left Rav Chaim's home on Rashbam Street with a feeling that this was it. It was finally going to happen. The next thing I knew, my wife and I were making our own video, in which both Efrat and I spoke about my visit to Rav Chaim. The *mikveh* we chose to refurbish was located in Moshav Zohar. It was in major disrepair and Reb Akiva told us that it was going to cost 640,000 shekel to redo it to the highest standard.

We accepted the challenge, jumping into the ocean without a clear idea of how we were going to get to the other side. Reb Meir Kenig and his brother-in-law flew to the States and returned with 30,000 dollars. While the video we had filmed was not supposed to have been shown locally, somehow it got out. Suddenly, the entire neighborhood knew what was going on and what we were trying to do.

While I had not planned on showing the clip to my friends and neighbors, once everyone knew what was going on they responded in a way we had never anticipated! Money came in from many different directions.

Meir Kenig's son lives in a community in Raanana, where he learns with a boy. One day, the boy's mother told him, "My husband and I are the owners of a successful business, with branches around the country. We have put aside some money that we want to contribute to *tzedakah*, but we don't know which organization to give it to. Do you have any suggestions for us?"

"I have a very good idea," he told her, and showed her the video that we had made for the *mikveh*.

The next day she handed him a check for 75,000 shekel — the exact amount that we were still lacking!

And so it all came together, with donations from generous people around the world and a surge of effort from all our friends, neighbors, and the people of Ramat Beit Shemesh.

Having been so successful when it came to our *mikveh* campaign, my brother went to see Rav Chaim as well. The *gadol* was asked whether he, too, should undertake a similar campaign.

"No," Rav Chaim said. "They have to start being even more *makpid* on taking *maaser* from fruits and vegetables."

While all of this was taking place, things were moving on the medical front as well. This was due to my sister-in-law, who said, "We find ourselves in a situation right now where we don't know what to do. We are going to rely on Hashem and follow every clue He sends our way."

She was true to her word. She asked everyone she knew for advice and followed up on the answers. We had a long meeting with an elderly expert who recommended that we meet with a doctor with whom she worked. Thus began a year of cleansing treatments under the auspices of that doctor.

At the start, we would have never considered going the homeopathy, alternative, and non-conventional route. By then, however, we had tried everything else and had come up empty-handed. No government office or organization was willing to help us fund these treatments. You can imagine how much everything was costing us. Yet we didn't hesitate. For the next two years we continued raising the money we needed to carry on, consistently helped by my sister-in-law.

We tried to be strong. We didn't discuss our situation with our parents, since we knew how much they were hurting from our pain. We knew that talking about what we were going through wouldn't make us feel better and would only hurt them more. For my parents it was especially difficult, since I had a brother who also had been married for a long time without children.

Which meant that all the pain remained bottled up inside us for years and years.

It was at that time, after we'd been on a special diet and doing the cleansing treatments for two years, that the old woman told us about a new doctor who had recently arrived in Israel from Australia. She strongly recommended that we meet him.

Dr. Shlomo Barak possessed a truly noble spirit, and was extremely accepting of our opinions and thoughts. He understood that as religious Yidden we followed *daas Torah,* and he respected us for it.

Dr. Barak studied our file and sent us for some more tests. When he received the results, he sent us for a procedure at Laniado Hospital in Netanya.

"I did everything possible," he told us. "Now it's in His hands."

After hearing him speak, we knew that we would forever recommend Dr. Barak to anyone in need.

It was true. We really had done everything possible. We had followed a special diet, done cleansing treatments, and undergone a minor operation at Laniado. We had also been in touch with the experts at the Puah organization, who offered guidance and advice.

From a physical perspective, my wife had never been more prepared for a treatment. I had spent years davening at Kever Rochel and had established a kollel. My wife and I had undertaken to raise the funds for a *mikveh*. Everything was now ready — both physically and spiritually — for Dr. Barak, Hashem's emissary, to take the final step and perform the treatment.

Everything was in place and we were about to take the next step, when Covid hit the world. Everything came to a sudden halt.

"I am very sorry," the doctor said to us, "but the government has ordered us to close our doors. We are going to have to push everything off until we get permission to open up again. You waited for so many years," he said, "it seems like you will have to wait just a little longer."

In the early months of the summer, the clinic reopened its doors and we went inside for the long-awaited treatment. It was very expensive, costing us in the region of 80,000 shekel. A friend gave me a significant amount, and I took out some loans to cover the rest.

The Chanukas Hamikveh ceremony took place on the 14th of Tammuz, right around the time of the treatment. I'll never forget traveling to Moshav Zohar for the big moment: the opening of the *mikveh* that Efrat and I had raised the money to refurbish. It was a small ceremony. Not many people were there. Our parents. Siblings and their spouses were present, and Meir Kenig was there. A small ceremony, but truly emotional.

And when it was over, Efrat and I went home.

A week later, I went to the local kupat cholim and asked the woman there for the results of the treatment we had undergone.

"It's positive," she said.

The woman didn't know me and had no idea of the import of her words. There was no way in the world she could have guessed that I had been waiting for more than twenty years to hear those words. I looked at the papers she handed me. Read the results myself. It was really true.

It was positive.

I drove home. Went downstairs to the *gan*. The room was filled with children milling about.

Efrat looked at me. I looked back at her. Then I gave her a thumbs-up sign.

We were overcome.

We immediately called the doctor and Efrat was given a host of shots to strengthen the pregnancy. Forty days into the pregnancy, we drove to Assuta Hospital in Tel Aviv for an ultrasound. Dr. Barak examined the results.

"Wow," he said, "there's a heartbeat! Everything is wonderful! *Mazel tov*!"

From the hospital we drove to my parents' home in Ramot. We arrived at the house around 11:45 at night.

"What are you doing here?" they asked in alarm. "What happened?"

"We have good news."

They understood immediately. My mother burst into tears. My father immediately took out a bottle of wine and made a *l'chaim* with me. We raised our glasses, made a *berachah* and drank.

My father looked at me.

"Go to Efrat's parents right now," he said.

"But it's very late."

"Doesn't matter. Go this second."

We embraced my parents. It was a true moment of joy after more than two decades of ongoing sadness. Then we drove to Efrat's parents' home. We punched in the code. The house was quiet. Everyone was asleep. Efrat knocked on the door of her parents' bedroom. Her father opened the door and was shocked to see his daughter standing there.

"What happened?" he asked.

Efrat told him.

Once again, the news was followed by tears of joy and another *l'chaim*. What a night that was!

We hired another *ganenet* for the afternoons. Efrat told everyone that, while she was still working in the morning, she needed a little break in the afternoons. Barely anyone saw Efrat during all those months, and so very few people knew that she was finally expecting a baby.

Our daughter was born at 5:55 on the afternoon of *Shabbos Vayikra*. Labor lasted from 10:30 Friday night until 5:30 Shabbos afternoon, at which time the doctor said they were going to have to perform a C-section.

And then the midwife finally held our baby daughter in her arms, and we heard the sound of her cries.

Efrat looked at me. "Did you hear that?"

"Yes," I replied. I could barely get the words out.

"Give her to me," Efrat said to the midwife.

"Let me clean her first."

"No, give her to me right now."

The midwife quickly wrapped the baby in a towel and handed her to her mother. Holding our daughter in her hands, Efrat said to her, "I waited for you for twenty-one years!"

Then she kissed our daughter over and over and over...

The entire medical team stood around us. There were tears streaming down every face. As for me, I couldn't help but remember that our baby had been born exactly nine months and one week after we had celebrated the Chanukas Hamikveh in Moshav Zohar.

Wonder of wonders, my brother also learned that he and his wife were expecting their first child, shortly after we did. How's that for a miracle?

On the following Monday, I went to daven at the 6:30 *minyan* at the Mercaz Daf Yomi across the street from my home. The *beis midrash* was decorated in pink. There were balloons and streamers, bottles of baby lotion and shampoo. The table was covered with a pink tablecloth and bottles of drinks and cakes and cookies and refreshments...

I was given an *aliyah*, and the *gabbai* recited the words one says before naming a child. He looked at me and waited for the name.

"Rivka," I said.

The room broke out in song, as everyone threw candies at the brand-new father. My friends hugged me, tears in their eyes, and then we started to dance. There was a smile on my face that felt as if it were glued on. We danced and danced. It was a great moment in my life.

And when davening was over, I, Itzik Churi, father of Rivka Churi, went home.

We named her Rivka for a number of reasons.

On the Thursday before *Parashas Toldos*, we had an ultrasound where we learned that we were expecting a baby girl. Years before — I was still learning at Kever Rochel — a friend had told me that it was a *segulah* to learn the *sefer Zera Shimshon*. After that, we started learning the *sefer* at the Shabbos table during every *seudah*. That Shabbos, we read in the *Zera Shimshon* about how Yitzchak and Rivka had davened for a child, who was finally born more than twenty years after they first married.

I looked at Efrat.

"Rivka had a child after twenty-two years," I said.

At that moment, there was no question in our minds what the baby's name would be.

There were two more good reasons to name our daughter Rivka: that had been the name of both my father's mother and Efrat's grandmother. My father, never an overly emotional type, breaks down whenever he thinks of his new granddaughter.

I find that I am also crying a lot these days. People have commented on my newfound effusions of emotion.

I just smile and explain that twenty years of pent-up emotion are finally being allowed release. My friends and siblings are marrying off their children now, while we are just starting the process. It's hard to wrap our minds around the tremendous blessing we have been granted.

(Author's note: At this point in the story, both of us are sobbing together. I was there when Itzik named his daughter, I hugged him hard, and we danced together. How could one not cry with happiness after witnessing such a wondrous *simchah*?)

My phone hasn't stopped ringing since my baby was born. I have been interviewed by many radio stations, and I tell the story gladly. I know what a *kiddush Hashem* this is, and I want to glorify Hashem's Name as much as I possibly can.

I want to leave you with a few thoughts.

When a couple is faced with this kind of challenge, there is no need to ask them if they need money. Rest assured that they do. It is very difficult to request financial assistance from other people. *Baruch Hashem*, I had friends who possessed the wisdom to know how to give without asking questions.

You need to understand how important it is for a couple who has gone through treatment to go on vacation, someplace where they can rest and relax. Not with others who are in the same situation, but rather as if they are regular guests at the hotel. After what they have just been through, they deserve it.

If I had the funding, I would be so happy to establish an organization dedicated to one thing: making the process that so many couples are going through as easy and painless as possible. I would want the couples to have all the tests administered in the easiest and quickest way, one after the next, so that they will be granted the answers they need as rapidly as is humanly possible.

Everything takes so much time. You cannot begin to comprehend the complexities of the bureaucratic process that every infertile couple faces. It is like a mountain that needs to be climbed, over and over. And when you finally reach the summit, you find another mountain that you need to climb — and this one is even higher than the one before! I wish I could streamline the process for the couples that are waiting and waiting and waiting…

There are so many things I would do if I could, because I've been down that road and I know the parts of the highway that need improvement.

When my wife was interviewed for the clip we did for the *mikveh*, she said something that touched many people's hearts.

"I love being with the children in the *gan*," she said. "But at the end of the day they go home, and I am there putting away the toys."

And she will still be putting away the toys.

But now the toys will be upstairs, in our home, and they are going to be used by our daughter Rivka.

My name is Itzik Churi and I am the proudest father in the world. Our quest has finally come to an end.

I can say only one more thing.

"Thank you, Hashem! Thank You. Thank You. Thank You! From the bottom of my heart, thank You a million times for the gift You have given us!"

דָּרְשָׁה צֶמֶר וּפִשְׁתִּים, וַתַּעַשׂ בְּחֵפֶץ כַּפֶּיהָ
*She seeks out wool and linen,
and her hands work willingly.*

Doing Nothing – Not a Good Idea

The Dangers of "Batalah"

There is a rabbinic decree that states that a husband is obligated to provide food and clothing for his wife. In return, the money she earns belongs to her husband. However, the wife may declare at any time that she forgoes the food and clothing and she wants to keep her earnings (*Kesubos* 58b; *Shulchan Aruch Even HaEzer* 69:4).

If the woman does not forgo the food and clothing, there are specific halachos dealing with what her husband may and may not ask of her (*Even HaEzer* 80:1). In a society where it is accepted for women to weave for a living, the husband may ask that she do so. If they live in a society where women embroider or sew pictures and designs onto clothing, then the husband can ask that his wife do that kind of work. And if they live in a town or city where the women spin both wool and flax, then her husband can ask that she spin both wool and flax.

However, if they live in a society where the women are not occupied with these forms of work, the husband cannot ask his wife to do them. The one thing he can ask that she do is spin wool. He cannot even ask her to spin flax, which is more difficult than spinning wool.

Zera Shimshon now quotes the *Beis Shmuel* (*Even HaEzer* 80:1) who says the following:

> Even if the women of the city where they live don't usually work, and even if the girls in her family have never been active members of the workforce, a husband can still ask that his wife work.

Why?

When people have nothing to do, they are in a state of *"batalah,"* idleness. Being idle is dangerous. It leads to sin. When people are bored, with nothing to do, they will end up using their spare time in ways they shouldn't. For that reason, a husband may ask that his wife at least occupy herself by spinning wool.

However, writes the *Zera Shimshon*, the *eishes chayil* looks at life from a very different perspective. In her mind it doesn't matter what the women around her are doing. Why? Even if the other women in her community don't work, and even if the women in her own family don't work, she doesn't want to be "free" like them. She knows that idleness leads many people to places they should have stayed far away from.

Which is why the *eishes chayil* not only doesn't wait for her husband to tell her to go to work — she "seeks" wool. That is, she goes and finds wool to spin.

Zera Shimshon continues:

> Not only does the *eishes chayil* search for wool to spin, she even looks for flax, which is much more difficult to work with. Even if she lives in a place where her husband cannot ask that she work with flax, she chooses to do so.

Why?

Because the *eishes chayil* has a desire to work. She has pleasure from her work. More than that — she reaps the praise and the honor that come along with hard work. And she is a prime example of וַתַּעַשׂ בְּחֵפֶץ כַּפֶּיהָ — someone who "does her work willingly and happily" — even before her husband asks or demands it of her. She doesn't need that. She wants to do it for him, and for herself.

Shaatnez and Sheep

Zera Shimshon now offers another explanation of this *pasuk*, this one involving the prohibition of wearing *shaatnez*, a mixture of wool and linen. (Linen is made out of *pishtim*, flax.)

The Torah forbids a person from wearing clothing that was made from *kilayim*, a mixture created by weaving together wool — which comes from the fleece of a lamb or sheep — and linen, which grows from the ground. It is forbidden to spin, weave, or sew them together. It is even forbidden to take two pieces of material — one of wool and the other of linen — and produce an article of clothing from them.

There is, however, one case in which the Torah allows a person to join wool and linen, and that is when the wool comes from a sheep whose mother was not a sheep. That is to say, the wool is from a crossbred sheep, whose father was a sheep but whose mother was a goat. The Gemara (*Bechoros* 17a) tells us that if the wool of a crossbred sheep was used together with linen to create a garment, the person who made the garment would not be guilty of the prohibition of *kilayim* and would not be given *malkos* (lashes), the punishment for not observing the prohibition of *kilayim*.

Why is that?

To explain, the *Zera Shimshon* quotes the source of the mitzvah: לֹא תִלְבַּשׁ שַׁעַטְנֵז צֶמֶר וּפִשְׁתִּים יַחְדָּו — "You shall not wear combined fibers, wool and flax together" (*Devarim* 22:11).

Here we are taught by the Gemara that just as flax has not been altered over the generations — it is the same species today as it was when it was created — the prohibition of *shaatnez* applies only to wool that is the same as it was when it was created. It does not apply to the wool of a crossbred animal.

If a sheep is crossbred — if it is the offspring produced by the union of a goat and a sheep — it is not purebred, and the Torah does not forbid using its wool together with linen.

Now *Zera Shimshon* quotes the *Rambam* (*Hilchos Kilayim* 10:2) and adds his explanation for the rabbinic decree that prohibits mixing these materials, even though the Torah does not:

Although such wool (from a sheep that is the hybrid off-spring of a female goat and a ram) is not forbidden from the Torah, *Chazal* forbade it due to *maris ayin* (the appearance of wrongdoing).

Since it looks like regular wool, people might erroneously come to think that using wool with linen is permitted, since they saw a person do it. Since they will not know that he is actually using wool from a permissible source, they might come to err in this matter.

The Eishes Chayil and the Sages

Finally, the *Zera Shimshon* puts all this information together.

This woman, this *eishes chayil*, "אַף עַל פִּי שֶׁ"דָּרְשָׁה — even though she knows the "*derush*," the deeper explanation of the Torah's words לֹא תִלְבַּשׁ שַׁעַטְנֵז צֶמֶר וּפִשְׁתִּים יַחְדָּיו [that the wool has to be the same kind of wool as that from a species created on the sixth day of creation, just as the flax is identical to the flax of creation], and she knows that certain types of wool may be used together with linen, on the Biblical level; even so, וַתַּעַשׂ בְּחֵפֶץ כַּפֶּיהָ — "her hands work willingly": she only wants to do work that is in accord with both Torah and rabbinic precepts. She refuses to do anything that is forbidden by the Sages, even if it is permissible from a Biblical standpoint.

This, writes the *Zera Shimshon*, is what makes the *eishes chayil* so unique. There are women who are not as stringent when it comes to rabbinic prohibitions, which were not written clearly in the Torah. As the *Shulchan Aruch* writes:

> There are women who eat and drink on Erev Yom Kippur until it grows dark... and they do not begin the fast from earlier in the day even though we are obligated to add time to the holy day of Yom Kippur and start fasting from before Yom Kippur begins, which is from before sunset.... We do not protest to them about their eating and drinking, since we do not want them to do it *b'meizid* (on purpose), since we are afraid that they will continue doing this even once they know it is not allowed (*Orach Chaim* 608:2).

Of course, once we are discussing the mitzvah of *shaatnez*, I cannot help but share the following story with you, a story that I heard from the protagonist himself, and which brings home the severity of the prohibition of *shaatnez*.

While still a *bachur*, I landed a job teaching at a day school in the Bronx. This was a few decades ago, when all of the Bronx still had a prominent Jewish presence, not only in Pelham Parkway and Riverdale. In honor of this auspicious occasion, I decided to purchase a new jacket for the upcoming school year. Until that point, clothing had been of little importance to me, but, as the ancient adage goes, "clothes make the man." This was my first teaching job, and I wanted to stack the odds in my favor.

A few days before the semester began, I boarded a bus to the nearest men's clothing store. Feeling very mature and grown-up, I made my way through the door (a tinkling bell heralding my arrival), into a world of shiny shoes, garish ties, cubbies full of white, blue and pinstriped, button-down Christian Dior or Pierre Cardin shirts, and rows and rows of coats and suits. As I meandered down the aisles taking it all in with keen-eyed interest, I was accosted by a salesman who doubtless saw me for the easy mark that I was.

"My name is Ernest, young man. Can I help you today?"

"I hope so."

"What's on the agenda for today? A pair of cufflinks, a tie clip, a nice sweater?"

"No, I need a new jacket."

"Very well," he replied, taking in the jacket I was wearing and nodding his head up and down as if concurring with my judgment that I did, in fact, need a new jacket. Then he got busy, pulling garments off the racks, handing them to me and watching as I tried them on. I have a slight build and we needed to find the perfect fit — a jacket that would complement me instead of enveloping me. In the end, Ernest found me something that looked really sharp. It sat on my shoulders looking for all the world as if it had just rolled out of some Italian fashion house.

"It looks great on ya, kid," Ernest grunted between puffs from the drooping cigar clenched in his mouth.

I nodded my head in agreement.

"Okay, kid." He took the jacket to the counter, removed the tags, pressed it for me and slipped it onto a hanger and into a large suit-carrier bag.

"That'll be forty-five dollars."

I removed the money from my wallet and handed it over.

"Come again!" he sang out.

I slung the suit bag over my shoulder, nodded to Ernest, pushed open the door and exited stage left.

On the first day of school I dressed fastidiously, making sure that my shirt was ironed, my pants pressed, and my tie knotted well. I folded the jacket carefully over my arm, planning to put it on, crisp and fresh, right before I started this new adventure, and walked jauntily out the door. The crisp scent of autumn filled the air, and I enjoyed the sight of the russet and orange leaves lying in crackling piles at my feet. Ten minutes later I carefully put on the jacket, walked up to the school's front door, and let myself in.

Part of me was nervous about my newfound responsibilities, while the other part was thrilled to be in a position of authority, with the opportunity and the privilege of imparting the Torah I had learned through the years. A secretary gave me directions to the principal's office, where I was welcomed with a handshake and a few kind words and then escorted down the hall, up a flight of stairs, and into my classroom.

Twenty-five pairs of eyes looked me over curiously as we walked into the classroom. Twenty-five pairs of eyes made snap judgments, either positive or negative.

"Class," the principal introduced me, "this is *Rabbi Zecharia Leiner. He will be your rebbi this year."

With that, he turned and left the room, leaving me to begin my first teaching job.

I said hello to the kids, wrote my name on the board, explained what I expected from them, and outlined our classroom rules. Then

I began the first lesson of the year. The kids were moderately well-behaved and I got the feeling that this would be a manageable experience.

Suddenly, everything changed.

Without warning, I began to feel faint. One moment, everything was fine, and the next I was sweating, my breath coming in shallow gasps. I touched my forehead in disbelief. What was happening to me? I felt terrible, as if I were going to collapse within the next few minutes!

Ninety percent of my brain power was being directed at preventing myself from fainting in the classroom in front of the kids, while the remaining ten percent was trying to figure out what on earth was going on. I hadn't eaten anything out of the ordinary. There was no reason for beads of sweat to be popping out all over my face! And yet, they were.

Somehow, I managed to soldier through to the end of my time with the boys. I said my goodbyes and raced from the classroom, my head spinning and my mind whirling. I was a mess. As soon as I exited the premises, I removed my jacket, and holding it over my arm, began gulping huge breaths of fresh air. To my utter shock and immense relief, the blurred vision and nauseous, sickly feeling disappeared as instantaneously as they had first appeared. I was healed.

It was a miracle. I felt hale and hardy and ready to tackle the universe. But it was also most unnerving. I had gone from being ready to teach my class with humor, patience and charm, to someone who could barely wield a pencil. What had happened to me back there in the classroom?

As I strode home, I mentally reviewed every move I had made since arising that morning, but I could not put my finger on what had made me feel like I needed a trip to the emergency room.

Never mind, I told myself. The day was done. I had survived, and even found that I was a satisfactory rebbi. It was time to put this bizarre first day behind me and hope that tomorrow would be better.

The morning found me feeling just fine. Not a trace of the

dizzying illness of the day before. Nothing but good, healthy educational feelings coursing through my bloodstream. I had a nice bowl of Cheerios, did the dishes, and then donned my jacket and headed for the door. The street was crowded with people heading for work and school and I sauntered among them, at ease with myself and the world. The painful claustrophobia of yesterday was a nightmare of the past. I stepped into a pile of leaves with a satisfying crunch and hurried on until I reached the double doors leading into the elementary school building.

I left my hat in the teachers' room and made my way through the crowded hallways and into my classroom, where I took a seat beside my desk. I opened my briefcase, withdrew some teaching materials that I had prepared the day before, and proceeded to write a list of *Chumash* words on the blackboard. The boys filed into the room. They took their seats. A jumble of laughing, teasing, noise-making kids, mine for the year to educate. Pliable, impressionable minds that were mine to teach. I could turn these children into *talmidei chachamim* if I just discovered the keys to their hearts and made them excited about Torah learning. The possibilities were endless!

I turned to the boys. Put a finger to my lips. The noise in the room gradually quieted down. I began to teach… and, a minute later, my mind fogged up. My brain began to dance with fatigue and a painful buzz permeated my mind with gray noise. I couldn't think, I couldn't talk. I was a mess. And to think that I had been fine just a few minutes before! What was happening to me?

I don't know how I got through that day.

Or the next.

Four days after I'd begun teaching at the elementary school, I entered my classroom fully expecting my head to begin pounding and my eyes to start closing of their own accord, as if I were lacking days of sleep. I felt so sick. I assigned the boys some reading and sat down in my chair, yearning for the nice, simple, uncomplicated life I had enjoyed before entering the world of education. The boys were engaged in their work, and I had a few minutes to myself. Sighing with relief, I rested my head on the desk and tried to relax.

I couldn't do it. I was too hot. My new jacket was smothering me. I eased it off and laid it carefully on the desk. Then I put my head back down with a sigh of relief. But there was no need to do that because my mind was suddenly sharp as a tack. I was healed. I felt incredible! I was back to myself, as good as new.

I stood up, trying to comprehend what was going on. One second, so sick; the next, completely healed. It didn't make any sense!

I glanced at my jacket, lying so innocently on the desk, and suddenly a far-out possibility hit me with all the subtlety of a sledgehammer as I recalled a story of the Arizal and his *talmid*, Rav Chaim Vital, that I had heard years earlier.

Once, Rav Chaim Vital, *talmid muvhak* of the Arizal, began to suffer from a pain in his shoulder. When he realized that it wasn't going away, he paid a visit to his rebbi to ask for his advice. Upon describing the pain and its location, his rebbi had this bit of practical advice to offer:

"*Teikef l'netilas yadayim berachah*," the Arizal said, quoting Rav Chiya bar Ashi (*Berachos* 42a).

Rav Chiya bar Ashi lists three things that must be done in tandem, with no interval between them. One of the three is that there should be no significant time lapse between washing *mayim acharonim* and beginning to *bentch*.

"The word *teikef* (immediately)," continued the Arizal, "contains the same letters as the word *kateif*, shoulder. This hint seems to imply that the pain you are currently experiencing in your shoulder is due to your not making sure to *bentch* immediately after washing *mayim acharonim*."

That story made a real impression on me. It taught me that the things we do or don't do can have a physical, tangible, actual impact on our bodies! Most importantly, it led me to understand how real the mitzvos are, and how they correspond to our actions in this world.

And now, I thought of that story. And I thought of how sick I felt — every time I put on that new jacket...

Teikef, kateif... the same letters. A person has to understand that sometimes physical pain reflects a spiritual malaise or illness that needs to be addressed. I summarized the situation in my mind. I'd purchased the jacket in honor of my class. To make a good impression. But every day, at school, wearing my new jacket, I was being afflicted with major headaches, dizziness, and a foggy mind. On the other hand, when I took the jacket off I was sharp as a tack. No ailments. Fit as a fiddle....

Finally, after a wonderful day of jacket-less teaching (my first) and another few minutes of deep thought, I elected to bring my jacket to the local *shaatnez* checker for a little "under the microscope probe." I was not surprised, and neither will you be, to learn that my innocent-looking jacket was not so innocent at all. It was chock-full of *shaatnez.*

It's been many years since I lived through this episode, but the lesson never faded. The world of the physical and the world of the spiritual are not as far apart as we sometimes imagine. Sometimes they collide... And then it's up to us to recognize that Hashem is sending us a message that we ignore at our own peril.

The Segulah of the *Zera Shimshon*

Rabbi Menachem Binyomin Paskesz ran into a friend who had a story to tell.

"My youngest son was almost thirty," the friend told Rabbi Paskesz, "and nothing was moving on the *shidduch* front. You can understand how upset I was by this! It was hard for me to believe that my son, whom I loved so much, was about to turn thirty and was still unmarried! It was especially difficult for me since he is a truly outstanding young man.

"At some point, I was introduced to the wonders and *segulos* of the *Zera Shimshon* and felt as if I had been given the most incredible strengthening for my broken soul. I began learning from the *sefarim* on a regular basis, and I accepted upon myself to learn from the *Zera Shimshon's* commentary on Eishes Chayil (which is brought down in *Parashas Chayei Sarah*), focusing on a different *pasuk* every week. In the *zechus* of that learning, I hoped that my son would find a *shidduch*.

"I did this for more than five months. Every Shabbos, I learned the *peirush* on one *pasuk*, finishing the entire commentary in twenty-two weeks."

Reb Binyomin listened, and waited.

"A few days after I finished learning the *Zera Shimshon* on Eishes Chayil," his friend concluded, "a *shidduch* was suggested for my son. Two weeks later, he was a *chassan*...

"*Nu*, Rabbi Paskesz? What do you say to that?"

הָיְתָה כָּאֳנִיּוֹת סוֹחֵר, מִמֶּרְחָק תָּבִיא לַחְמָהּ
*She is like a merchant's ships,
from afar she brings her sustenance.*

The Eishes Chayil's Business Model

The Gemara (*Pesachim* 50b) says: אֵינוֹ רוֹאֶה . . . הַמְצַפֶּה לִשְׂכַר אִשְׁתּוֹ סִימָן בְּרָכָה —"Someone who relies on his wife's earnings will not see a sign of blessing."

What does this mean? What kind of financial support are we discussing?

Answers the Gemara: This is referring to "*maskulta*" (מַתְקוּלְתָא), a kind of scale that people used to weigh goods in stores. A woman invests in such a scale. She then makes the rounds of the businesses in the marketplace, offering the use of her scale for payment.

Such a job will not bring her family financial success.

However, if instead of running around with a scale, the *eishes chayil* has a business selling different products, and people come to her to buy her goods, then she is praised for her initiative. We see this in the words of Eishes Chayil, which praise her because she "makes a cloak to sell" (*Mishlei* 31:24). It is clear that a woman is praised for manufacturing and selling her own goods.

The Maharsha's Guide to Financial Success

When is there a *siman berachah* in a woman's work and when is there not?

Zera Shimshon cites the *Maharsha*, who explains that a *siman berachah* comes from the goods the *eishes chayil* produces and sells. But there is no *siman berachah* when she is unable to produce her goods herself, and she acts as a middleman, purchasing goods from others and selling them.

The *Maharsha* continues: "Why is it so much better when she runs her own business, without relying on other people's merchandise?"

The answer? When she runs her own business, she is able to exemplify the verse, כָּל כְּבוּדָה בַת מֶלֶךְ פְּנִימָה — "The glory of a princess is within" (*Tehillim* 45:14).

When a woman manages her own business, she is able, for the most part, to remain at home, while clients and customers come to her. On the other hand, when she works as a salesperson, taking products and merchandise from other people and selling the goods herself, her business takes her to the marketplace, where she makes the rounds of all the stores trying to make a sale: the opposite of "the glory of a princess is within."

From Far Away

Zera Shimshon continues: Since the *eishes chayil* is the producer of clothing that she manufactures herself, בְּחֵפֶץ כַּפֶּיהָ — "willingly, with her hands," she becomes "like a merchant's ships" and she will see blessing in her work.

What kind of blessing?

The blessing of מִמֶּרְחָק תָּבִיא לַחְמָהּ — "she brings her sustenance from afar."

What does that mean?

She will become very successful. The clothing that she sews or manufactures will be in such demand that orders will come from far away, and she will have to hire ships to transport her goods to those distant lands.

This is telling us that the *eishes chayil*, the woman who found a way to do business while remaining as modest, as *tzniusdik*, as possible, will achieve mega-success in her line of work.

Danger?

Zera Shimshon now raises a question. The Gemara (*Pesachim* 50b) relates that there are four methods of doing business that do not bring blessing to the businessman. One of these is sending goods overseas.

The problem with shipping goods across the ocean is that the businessman is putting his merchandise in danger, since there is always the risk that his ship might be lost in a storm.

Since the businessperson is taking this risk, he is, in essence, relying on a miracle — which is why there is no *siman berachah* in such a venture.

Then why are we being told that the *eishes chayil* will be so successful that she will become an international businesswoman who sends her goods across the ocean? Why would she want to be part of a business that relies on miracles and doesn't see blessings?

Zera Shimshon explains: There are two ways of sending merchandise across the sea.

In any business, there are the people who take the safe routes and the people who take risks. It is the same thing with shipping. There are businessmen who use the fastest ships and send their merchandise to the farthest places. They do this because if they are successful they will make a lot of money. They choose to play the risk game because the payoff is much greater.

Such business, relying on miracles, does not have a *siman berachah*.

Our *eishes chayil* takes a different route. She plays it safe. She uses the best and sturdiest boats, and ships her merchandise during the months when the sea is usually calm. She takes precautions and she is careful. She follows the approach of the businesspeople who take fewer risks and make less profit, but are able to sleep at night, knowing that their investments are reasonably safe. This type of business is not called relying on a miracle, and she will see a *siman berachah*.

The *Zera Shimshon* says about the *eishes chayil*:

Because וַתַּעַשׂ בְּחֵפֶץ כַּפֶּיהָ — "her hands work willingly," and סָדִין עָשְׂתָה וַתִּמְכֹּר — "she produces her own merchandise and sells it [in a modest way]," her business will grow and she will become a businesswoman who הָיְתָה כָּאֳנִיּוֹת סוֹחֵר — "is like a merchant's ships," sending her goods across the sea. And because she is careful in how she does business and doesn't take unnecessary risks, מִמֶּרְחָק תָּבִיא לַחְמָהּ — she is able to cultivate international business interests and will see blessing in her endeavors.

Untouchable Goodness From on High

Zera Shimshon gives us still another way to look at the concept that a person who relies on his wife's earnings will not see a *siman berachah* from the money.

He writes:

The *pasuk* tells us that the *eishes chayil* draws down *parnassah* from a distance. This refers to the goodness of *Olam Haba*, the World to Come.

This idea is found in the *Zohar* in *Parashas Beshalach*. The *Zohar* quotes the *pasuk*, מִמֶּרְחָק תָּבִיא לַחְמָהּ — "she brings her sustenance from afar," and explains that we learn from a *gezeirah shavah* the idea that the term "afar" is referring to *Olam Haba*. [A *gezeirah shavah* is one of the ways we derive halachos, from the use of similar words in different places in the Torah.] There is a *pasuk* (*Yeshayah* 30:27) that states: הִנֵּה שֵׁם ה' בָּא מִמֶּרְחָק — "Behold, the Name of Hashem is coming from afar." The word מִמֶּרְחָק (*mimerchak*, from afar) seems to refer to things that come from the goodness of *Olam Haba* through Hashem's holy Name. Here too, we find the same word, "*mimerchak*," used in reference to *parnassah*, telling us that the *eishes chayil's* financial support is coming from a distance — from the highest places — through the Name of Hashem.

Zera Shimshon brings proof from a *pasuk* (*Devarim* 28:8) that states, יְצַו ה' אִתְּךָ אֶת הַבְּרָכָה בַּאֲסָמֶיךָ — "Hashem will order the *berachah* to be with you in your storehouses." The word "storehouses" can also refer to the rewards that are "stored" for us in *Olam Haba*.

Since the source of the blessing in these "storehouses" is emanating from the highest places possible, no one can derail the blessing, not through *ayin hara* (evil eye) and not through *mazikin* (spiritual forces that seek to harm a person). We know that because the word used is יְצַו, which refers to a command of Hashem. Such a command is enduring; it will never vanish and no one will be able to harm it.

We find a similar idea in *Targum Onkelos* (*Devarim* 28:8), where he translates the word יְצַו as יְפַקֵּד, which means that by the command of Hashem, the blessing is given as a *pikadon* — something given to Him to watch over, and something that no one will be able to harm.

Mazikin are unable to approach this kind of holiness because it comes from the upper worlds.

This, then, is the ability of the *eishes chayil*, who is able to draw forth bounty and blessing from *Olam Haba* — blessing that cannot be touched by any negative force.

No Benefit From Miracles

Zera Shimshon now returns to the concept of benefiting from miracles.

Rashi (*Taanis* 24a s.v. "*ele ke'echad*") says, "It is forbidden for a person to benefit from miracles." For example, if wheat rained down from heaven onto a person's field, it would be forbidden for a person to enjoy more of the wheat than he needs to sustain himself.

A proof of this idea can be found in the phrase הָיְתָה כָּאֳנִיּוֹת סוֹחֵר — "She is like a merchant's ships."

How?

The *pasuk* could have written הָיְתָה כָּאֳנִיּוֹת — "She is like ships," without using the additional word *socher* (merchant).

The fact that the word *socher* is added teaches us that we should strive to bring down the abundance from the upper worlds, but not through miracles. Ideally, a person should act in a natural way — like a *socher*, the way a person generally conducts his business.

This means that the *eishes chayil* should occupy herself with a limited amount of business — and her efforts will provide the basis for Hashem's miracles. At the same time, whatever happens to her will look completely natural and not like a miracle. She should also strive to do business like those people who do not rely on miracles, who ship their merchandise in the most secure and risk-free way, earning fewer profits, but not putting their inventory at risk. Seeing her actions, Hashem will do His part as well, and will send her bounty and blessing מִמֶּרְחָק — from distant *Olam Haba*.

The *pasuk* specifically uses the words מִמֶּרְחָק תָּבִיא לַחְמָה — "she brings *her* bread," rather than simply saying "she brings bread." The word *lachmah* (her bread) refers to her needs; in other words, it is limited to what she needs. Had it simply said "bread," that would imply unlimited quantities, but the *eishes chayil* takes only what she needs. The Torah wants us to understand that the *eishes chayil* should not hesitate when it comes to enjoying the fruits of her labor. But not in an unlimited way.

Elazar Ish Birta's Miracle

The Gemara (*Taanis* 24a) tells of Elazar Ish Birta, who went to the marketplace with money he planned to use for his daughter's dowry. When the neighborhood *askanim* (community activists) caught sight of him, they ran in the opposite direction. Since they were well acquainted with Elazar, they knew that the moment he realized they were collecting for a worthy cause, he was going to give them all the money he had.

When Elazar saw the *askanim* running away from him, he ran after them.

"What are you collecting for?" he wanted to know.

They tried brushing him off, but he wouldn't let them. When they realized that there was no getting away from him, they admitted that they were raising money to marry off a young couple who were both orphans.

Upon hearing the story, Elazar Ish Birta gave them everything he had, leaving one lone *zuz* for himself.

With his one remaining *zuz* he purchased some wheat and left it in his storehouse. A miracle occurred and the entire storehouse filled with wheat.

Seeing what happened, his daughter came to the *beis midrash* to tell her father of the miracle.

"The wheat is like *hekdesh* to you," he said, "and you can only have access to the wheat like any poor person. You cannot use it to pay for your entire dowry, because that would be having extra enjoyment from a miracle."

From this story we can learn that an *eishes chayil* is allowed to benefit from what she brings down from the upper worlds, as it says (*Tehillim* 136:25), נוֹתֵן לֶחֶם לְכָל בָּשָׂר — "[Hashem] gives sustenance to everyone." Since that is the case, the *eishes chayil* is allowed to benefit even from a miraculous event. But only as much as she needs, and not without limit.

That is why the *pasuk* uses the word לַחְמָה — "her bread." Since the *pasuk* is referring to miracles that come her way from Heaven, she can only benefit as much as she needs to, and no more.

Speaking of the *eishes chayil's* unique ability to draw forth spiritual goodness from the upper worlds, I am reminded of three anecdotes that were told to me by Reb Yisrael Ury. All three have two factors in common. They have a connection with the famed Reb Shaya'le Kerestirer, and they deal with the kind of goodness and *shefa* (abundance) that special people are able to draw down from heaven.

First Story

While reading a book about the renowned Reb Shaya'le, I came across the following story, which took place when the legendary *gadol* was only seventeen years old and studying with the Lisker Rebbe in Lisk.

The Rebbe used to give out *bilkelach* (challah rolls) to everyone who came to him in Lisk. He once commented to a visitor, "When a Yid eats a *bilkelah* by me, I am in his service for all eternity."

Clearly, the Rebbe's *bilkelach* weren't just rolls. There was something much greater taking place.

For some reason, the Rebbe decided that he wanted the young Shaya'le to begin distributing the *bilkelach* in his stead. One of the more prominent chassidim — perhaps wanting to understand why the Lisker Rebbe decided to give the task to Shaya'le — began to observe the *bachur* closely as he made his rounds in the *beis midrash*, dispensing *bilkelach* to one and all. It didn't take the chassid long to confidently remark that the young *bachur* would grow up to become a Rebbe himself. This had become obvious to him just from watching the way R' Shaya'le handed out the special rolls.

The Lisker Rebbe, too, was very happy with his choice of roll dispenser. "When my Shaya'le gives out rolls," the Rebbe said, "the *berachos* rest within them."

One Shabbos, many chassidim arrived to spend Shabbos with the Rebbe in Lisk. Just prior to Shalosh Seudos, Reb Shaya'le circulated throughout the *beis midrash*, handing *bilkelach* to all the chassidim. The Lisker Rebbe stood by his chair and didn't make a move to go wash his hands. Instead, he stood and watched young Shaya'le make his rounds.

Nobody knew what the Rebbe was looking at, or what he was watching so intently. For all practical purposes, it was just a young chassid giving out rolls. And yet the Rebbe stood and watched the scene, unmoving, as if caught up in some fascinating drama. Eventually, one of the *gabbaim* approached the Lisker Rebbe and reminded him that the hour was growing late and it was time to wash.

Still the Lisker remained motionless in his place, staring at the *bachur* circulating among the chassidim, his hand entering the sack of *bilkelach* and emerging seconds later with another roll to hand to a guest.

"I am looking at how Shaya'le is doing such a good job handing out the rolls," he said at last, as if to explain his intense fascination with what seemed to be a mundane scene.

The *gabbai* didn't understand. "But Shaya'le gives out the *bilkelach* every Shabbos," he said, as though asking "*Ma nishtanah haShabbos hazeh?* How is this Shabbos different from all the others?"

"That is true," the Rebbe replied. "But today he is dispensing *bilkelach* from an empty sack!"

Some of the chassidim, seated in the Rebbe's vicinity, overheard the Lisker's words. They hurried over to Shaya'le, wanting to confirm the miracle for themselves. They reached his side and looked into the burlap sack in his hand. Just as the Rebbe had said, it was empty.

Caught in the act, as it were, Shaya'le ceased distributing *bilkelach* for the day.

Second Story

In the 1920s, a Yid by the name of Chaim Boruch Kleinbart was experiencing challenges in the area of *parnassah*. While he had a job, Reb Chaim Boruch was not earning enough to pay off all his debts. Not sure about how to proceed, he did what Yidden have been doing for generations and went to seek advice from the Rebbe. In this case, the man he sought out was none other than Reb Shaya'le of Kerestir.

Sitting with the holy Reb Shaya'le, he poured out his heart and asked Reb Shaya'le what he should do to make the situation improve.

"You should open a bakery," Reb Shaya'le said.

Reb Chaim Boruch was surprised. In those days, a bakery was not considered a money-making operation for the simple reason that every housewife baked her own bread. He did not see how establishing a bakery would help rid him of his debts.

"Who is going to buy their bread from me, when everyone bakes their own bread?" he asked Reb Shaya'le.

"Your bread will have a special *'chein'* — a unique appeal to the customers. They will want to purchase it for their needs."

With Reb Shaya'le's blessing in hand, Reb Chaim Boruch opened a bakery. It wasn't long before it had become an outstanding success, affording the family with a plentiful livelihood, just as the Rebbe had promised.

Third Story

Years later, Reb Chaim Boruch's daughter, Yitty, would find herself a prisoner in several horrendous camps during the war. She suffered through the horrors of Auschwitz and was sent to Ravensbruck as well, along with so many other Jewish women who were by then mere skeletons and barely alive. Yitty was also forced to participate in the death march at the very end of the war, where so many other innocent Yidden collapsed and perished despite having almost made it to the end.

Later, she would tell her family the following:

"I do not remember suffering from hunger (this despite the fact that everyone was starving). On the other hand, I do recall the terrible thirst. At that time, I used to have a recurring dream where I'd find myself standing in the bakery back home. There I would see my father, Reb Chaim Boruch, who would hand me a roll.

"When I woke up, I no longer felt hungry.

"It was almost as if I was somehow being sustained in my dreams by the rolls that we baked in our family bakery! The fact that the rolls filled me up, even though they weren't 'real,' didn't bother me at all. In fact, to me it made perfect sense. After all, the reason my father had opened the bakery in the first place was because he had been instructed by Reb Shaya'le to do so — the advice coming along with a *berachah* for the bread to possess a unique '*chein.*' It also went back to the *beis midrash* of the Lisker Rebbe, who had famously said, 'When a Yid eats a *bilkelah* by me, I am in his service for all eternity.'"

Once again, Reb Shaya'le was handing out rolls that weren't quite there. He had done so as a *bachur* in the *beis midrash* of the holy Lisker Rebbe, and he continued to do so many years later in the bakery he had blessed with '*chein,*' when his chassid's daughter so desperately needed sustenance to survive.

וַתָּקָם בְּעוֹד לַיְלָה, וַתִּתֵּן טֶרֶף לְבֵיתָהּ וְחֹק לְנַעֲרֹתֶיהָ
She arises while it is still nighttime, and gives food
to her household and a ration to her maidens.

What to Do
With the Extra Money?

Pushing Herself to the Max

When it comes to supporting her family, the *eishes chayil* pushes herself to the maximum, even awakening in the middle of the night if that is what's needed. She does more than is expected from one person, and can be found working at times that most people are asleep.

(Even today there are plenty of *neshei chayil* living in Eretz Yisrael who work late at night [American hours] to support their families.)

The *Shulchan Aruch* (*Even HaEzer* 80:1) writes: "If [a wife] pushes herself and makes more money than her family needs, the remainder belongs to the husband." For example, if she works extra hours during the night, or takes on two or three jobs, that money will belong to her husband.

There are other opinions that disagree with the *Shulchan Aruch* and state that any extra money belongs to the wife. The *Bach* (ibid.) writes that the accepted *minhag* is that any extra money above and beyond what the family needs for their living expenses is retained by the wife. She made the money by working very hard and has earned the right to keep it for herself.

Zera Shimshon writes: This is what the *pasuk* means when it uses the words וַתָּקָם בְּעוֹד לַיְלָה — "She arises while it is still nighttime." The *eishes chayil* wakes in the middle of the night and works extra jobs. But even though the *minhag* is that she can take the money for herself, nevertheless, the *eishes chayil* acts differently, as it says וַתִּתֵּן טֶרֶף לְבֵיתָהּ — "she gives food to her household." That is, she gives the extra money she earned to her husband and asks him to use it to purchase food with a generous hand. She does not want him holding back on the family's needs; she wants an abundance of blessing in her home.

Because the money really belongs to her, and not to her husband, and she gives it to him only because she wants to be a good wife to him — an *eishes chayil* — in a sense, the husband is being טוֹרֵף (grabbing it) from her. That is another reason the word "*toref*" was used in this *pasuk*.

Zera Shimshon now discusses the words וְחֹק לְנַעֲרֹתֶיהָ — "and a ration to her maidens." He explains that the word חֹק (*chok*) means a ration; the word is used that way in *Mishlei* (30:8), הַטְרִיפֵנִי לֶחֶם חֻקִּי — "allot me my daily bread."

The Question of the Maids

The Mishnah and Gemara (*Kesubos* 59b, 61a) discuss the topic of a woman having maids to do her work. If the family employs a number of maids, the wife does not have to occupy herself with the work that a woman normally does, but she is required to at least weave wool.

The *poskim* debate the question of who has to pay for the maids — husband or wife. The *Ritva* writes that since the husband benefits from the fact that his wife doesn't have to work that hard, he is the one who has to pay for the maids. *Tosafos* disagrees and explains that the husband would rather not have to pay for additional help, since this is yet another financial burden on him. *Tosafos* therefore states that the wife has to pay for her maids herself.

We have two arguments in this *pasuk*:

The first is about who gets the extra money earned by the wife — husband or wife. We said that the *minhag* is that the wife gets it.

The second argument was regarding who pays for maids — husband or wife.

Here, the law sides with the husband.

Since the *eishes chayil* is someone who pushes herself and works extra hours, she can use the extra money that she makes to pay for her maids.

To sum up:

וַתָּקָם בְּעוֹד לַיְלָה — "She arises while it is still nighttime": She pushes herself and works more than she needs to.

וַתִּתֵּן טֶרֶף לְבֵיתָהּ — "and gives food to her household": She uses the extra money to make sure there is an abundance of whatever the family needs.

וְחֹק לְנַעֲרֹתֶיהָ — "and a ration to her maidens": She also uses the extra money to pay for the maids that help in the house.

The sixth *pasuk* of Eishes Chayil is devoted to the idea of someone pushing themselves above and beyond what is expected of them. The following story is a genuine example of how a *mechanech* can and should learn from the *eishes chayil* to do the same thing.

I remember reading something that Rav Yaakov Weinberg, rosh yeshivah of Ner Yisroel of Baltimore, once said in a speech. He was addressing a gathering for Torah Umesorah, an organization that was close to his heart. Rav Yaakov was a brilliant man, and here, too, he transmitted a brilliant principle — something which I internalized and came to adopt into my own life.

"You have to try harder," he told the assembled.

He then explained to what he was referring. He told them about a boy in the yeshivah who needed a *chavrusa*, and how he tried to find him one but was unsuccessful.

"I tried a few times, with no success. For some reason, it was just not happening. I felt bad for the *bachur*, but I didn't see what more I could do. Then I heard that his father was coming to visit the yeshivah. Upon hearing that piece of news, I decided to try yet again. Interestingly, this time I found him the perfect *chavrusa*.

"From here we see it's not enough to try once or twice and then give up. You have to keep on trying — and, after you've tried a few times, try again. You'll see that just when you think there's no way to solve the problem before you, the solution will be right there in your face."

Those words made a deep impression on me. You see, I too am involved in finding *chavrusos* for boys in a yeshivah. No, I'm not the rosh yeshivah, but part of my job is making sure that every boy in the *beis midrash* has someone suitable with whom to learn.

It's not that simple. There are any number of boys who don't make it easy for others to study with them. There are boys who aren't "holding in learning." Boys who have a difficult time comprehending the Gemara. Boys who have a hard time getting up in the morning. Boys who like to chat instead of learn.

And yet, every one of them needs the right *chavrusa*, and it's my responsibility to see that he gets one. I carry around a little paper on which I write the names of the boys who need *chavrusos* at any given time, and am constantly on the lookout to make a match. Over the years, I have found myself in Rav Yaakov Weinberg's situation many, many times. Times when I've searched everywhere for a *chavrusa* for someone, with no luck. But I've never forgotten Rav Yaakov's message. When I am unsuccessful, I pick myself up and try again. And in the end, somehow, I always find someone for them to learn with.

It's a fact of life. Like the old saying goes: If at first you don't succeed, try, try again.

Recently, it happened again. The *bachur* in question was a young man by the name of *Michoel. Michoel was a very fine boy, with good *middos* and a ready smile. Maybe he was having trouble finding and keeping a *chavrusa* because he was so quiet, or perhaps there was another reason I didn't know about. Whatever it was, nothing worked out for him.

He approached me in the *beis midrash* one day.

"Rebbi, I need another *chavrusa*," he said. "I'm having a hard time preparing for *shiur* all by myself. Some guys don't have a problem learning on their own, but I need a *chavrusa*."

"I hear you. I'm going to try again to find someone."

I tried again that afternoon, but despite circling the *beis midrash* a number of times, I didn't come up with any ideas.

The story repeated itself a few days later. Again, Michoel approached me in the *beis midrash* and explained how challenging it was for him to learn on his own. I told him that I understood, and promised to try and look for a *chavrusa*. I tried — and again, I came up empty-handed.

I felt terrible. I can still remember what it was like as a *bachur*. My heart went out to Michoel and I resolved to do whatever it took to find him someone.

But you know how it goes. Life is so busy, and even with the best of intentions it's very easy to forget to do the things you promised to do. Also, Michoel kind of stopped coming to the *beis midrash*. I guess he decided that since he had nobody to learn with, there was no real point in exerting himself.

A week later, I saw him in the hallway.

"Michoel, how's it going?"

"Not great."

"What's the matter?"

"I guess you noticed that I haven't been around, right?"

I nodded.

"Well, the reason I haven't been around is because I can't sit by myself any longer. It's not working for me. I'm going out of my mind trying to figure out the Gemara all by myself."

"I hear you, *tzaddik*," I said. "I want you to come to the *beis midrash* every day, even if it's just for a few minutes. That way, I will see your beautiful face and remember to try again for you. Can you do that?"

He nodded. "I guess so."

"Good."

I shook his hand, and he gave me a smile.

In this case, that was probably progress.

He was standing in the back of the *beis midrash* the next morning. From his stance, I grasped that he wasn't planning to stick around for long. He was merely keeping his word to me. In another few minutes, he'd be gone.

"Yisroel," I said to myself, "it's time to try harder. Time to do what Rav Yaakov Weinberg said. This guy needs a *chavrusa*. Sure, you tried a bunch of times. But the need didn't disappear. It's time to try again."

Standing up, I began walking around the packed room, taking a good look at every *bachur*, trying to ascertain if he was learning with someone or on his own. Most of them were busy learning. Some were by themselves. When I asked them why, they explained that their *chavrusa* had gone out for a minute to make himself a coffee or to freshen up. Whatever the reason, none of them were available.

I didn't give up.

Leaving the room, I went downstairs. There was another *beis midrash* there, used by the members of a kollel. I figured maybe I could find a *chavrusa* for Michoel among the kollel members. I walked around, asked a number of people. None of them were looking for a *chavrusa*.

I kept on looking. Nobody had said it was going to be easy. I walked down the next flight of stairs. Here was an Israeli kollel. I entered that room. Spoke to some people I knew there. Asked around. Made inquiries of anyone who looked like they were sitting by themselves.

No luck.

Now what?

By this point, I had already asked a good twenty people if they were interested in trying a new *chavrusa*. If this had been a baseball game, I would have been benched long ago for all my strikeouts. But it wasn't a baseball game. It was the life of a sensitive yeshivah *bachur* who needed help.

I found myself exiting the building. There were a couple of guys milling around in front of the yeshivah.

"Why not?" I asked myself. "Can't hurt to try."

I approached them. Asked my standard question.

"I have a *chavrusa*," said one.

"I need to return to my *chavrusa*," answered the third.

"I don't learn in this yeshivah," replied the fourth.

Game over?

No. I was down, but not out yet.

I crossed the street in front of the yeshivah. There was a mini-market on the other side. Maybe I'd find someone there. So far, I had struck out more often than usual, but maybe Michoel's luck was about to change. Wasn't this exactly what Rav Yaakov was talking about? Going the distance, making the move, not giving up...

I entered the store. Strolled around. Found a few *bachurim* buying snacks. We chatted for a few minutes. I asked them about their *chavrusa* status. They told me they were all set. I wished them well and told them I looked forward to seeing them back in the *beis midrash* soon.

They smiled.

I turned and left the store. That was it. I had done everything possible. I could not think of another place to look or of anyone else to ask. The game was over — except that I knew it wasn't. I had seen the same story many times. Rav Yaakov's concept was solid. Just when a person thinks it's over, try again.

I was willing to try again. I just didn't know where.

I retraced my steps and crossed the street, into the building and up the stairs to my *beis midrash*. I had honestly done my best and still didn't have an answer. I wasn't looking forward to having to tell Michoel that I had nothing for him.

Then, just as I was about to enter the *beis midrash*, I saw Yanky Presser standing and talking to someone. Yanky was a star. He was always busy doing something important. Sometimes he was learning. Other times he was filming one of the rebbeim and sending it out to the alumni. A real mover and shaker.

"Stranger things have happened," I said to myself.

"Reb Yanky."

"Yes, Reb Yisroel."

"Question."

"Go on."

"Are you by any chance learning with a *chavrusa* at this time in your life?"

He thought for a second, as if pondering my question for deeper meanings.

Then he shook his head.

"No. The last *chavrusa* you set me up with didn't last. I'm on my own."

This was the absolute last thing I had been expecting to hear.

"Are you ready to start with someone new?"

"Sure."

"When?"

"Now is fine."

"Great. I'll send him over to you very soon."

I introduced the two of them fifteen minutes later. *Baruch Hashem*, they hit it off. Michoel is happy. So is Reb Yanky. They like each other. They're learning well together. And to think that I found Reb Yanky after I tried everything else with no success!

But it's like I told you before. Rav Yaakov was right. Don't worry so much when something doesn't work out. Just get up and try again. All the puzzle pieces will fall into place in the end.

So that's my story, friends. Rav Yaakov's principle can be applied across the board. Use it, and may it help you with your *chesed* and your *avodas Hashem*.

The Segulah of the Zera Shimshon

I needed to consult with one of the important rabbanim in Yerushalayim, but I discovered that this would be no easy task. When I finally received an appointment with him at a very late hour in the evening, I told the *gabbai* that I would be there on time. It would be difficult for me to come to him so late at night, but I was prepared to go above and beyond because I looked at it as doing *hishtadlus* to improve my situation. Sometimes you have to push yourself, and I felt that this was one of those times.

During the course of our conversation, the *rav* suggested that I start learning from the *sefer Zera Shimshon*. He told me about a number of cases where people made the *Zera Shimshon* a part of their lives and saw the most beautiful and incredible *yeshuos*. These weren't things that he'd heard about, but rather stories that he'd seen himself, because he had been the one to advise the people to learn the *sefer* and afterward they had come to tell him what had occurred. Not only did he advise me to start learning *Zera Shimshon*, but he even gave me a copy of the *sefer* so that I would be able to begin immediately.

Our conversation continued for quite a long time, and I left his house at two in the morning, an hour when all public transportation had long ceased to be an option. Not having extra money, I was not able to afford a taxi to take me to my home, which was in a different city. I stood in the street, unsure of my next move. I didn't have any relatives in Yerushalayim where I could spend the night, and it was getting colder and colder in the frigid outdoors.

I made my way to a nearby bus stop, not far from the exit of the city, in the hope that someone would happen to pass by and give me a ride at least to the entrance of my city.

I stood there for a few minutes, and then I suddenly had an idea.

The *rav* had just given me a copy of the *Zera Shimshon*. I had it right there with me in my bag. The *rav* had warmly recommended the *sefer* and told me most assuredly that it was the harbinger of *berachos* and *yeshuos*.

"I'm not even going to wait until tomorrow," I decided. "I'm going to start learning it right now! Maybe, in the merit of my learning, someone will come along and give me a ride."

You are not going to believe what happened, my friends. I myself am still overcome when I think about it. The moment I started reading from the *Zera Shimshon* — literally, as I read the opening words — a car pulled up beside me and the driver inquired if perhaps I needed a ride to Elad, where I live.

"That is exactly what I need," I replied.

He took me right to my front door.

זָמְמָה שָׂדֶה וַתִּקָּחֵהוּ, מִפְּרִי כַפֶּיהָ נָטְעָה כָּרֶם
She plans to buy a field and she buys it,
from the fruit of her handiwork she plants a vineyard.

Zera Shimshon's
Real Estate Advice

"Nichsei Milug"

A brief introduction:
And so our *eishes chayil* is busy night and day taking care of her home, working incredibly hard for the success of her husband and children. She works at her jobs and she is paid, giving the money to her husband to support the household in a generous fashion. Our *eishes chayil* is not stingy. She wants everyone in the house to feel comfortable and looked after, and it is very important to her that there should always be enough food — and even more than enough.

That's how she likes it.

And as we explained, if the *eishes chayil* is so good at her job that there is extra money, halachah says that this money remains with her and she doesn't have to give it to her husband.

That said, this money has the halachic status of "*nichsei milug*."

Nichsei milug is an interesting concept. It usually refers to property that a woman brings into a marriage. Property that falls under the category of *nichsei milug* has a particular status. The actual property remains hers. However, while they are married, the husband is the one who retains ownership of the profits that come in from the property.

So, for example, if the wife owns a cabin in the Catskills that is rented out during the summer, the cabin belongs to her, but the husband receives the rent money — the *peiros* (fruits) from the property.

Now, when our *eishes chayil* makes extra money, it falls under the category of *nichsei milug*. If the couple uses it to purchase a piece of property — a house or a field — while the property itself will be owned by the wife, the *peiros* (fruits; that is, the profits) go to the husband.

In the case of a divorce or if the husband passes away, the property is hers and his heirs have no claims. Similarly, if she passes away before he does, and she has children of her own from a previous marriage, the property belongs to them.

Field or House?

Now the question is this: What happens if the husband and wife have a disagreement over what type of property to buy?

This brings us to this *pasuk* in Eishes Chayil, which addresses this very point.

As I stated earlier, writes the *Zera Shimshon*, the *eishes chayil* takes the money that she acquired with so much effort and gives it to her husband to purchase the things a home needs. But not only the necessities; she wants him to buy extras, too, so that everyone (including her maid) feels looked after and well taken care of. In this way, she is acting *lifnim mishuras hadin* (above and beyond what is expected of her).

This particular *eishes chayil* is so good at her job that even after using lots of money for their home, she is still left with funds that the couple now wants to invest.

Suppose the wife has a natural knack for and understanding of agriculture. Maybe she grew up on a farm. In such a case, when she wants to purchase a piece of land to cultivate, growing her own wheat or fruit and vegetables, there is no question that she may do this, even if her husband prefers to use the money to buy a house to rent out to others.

This is the meaning of the words זָמְמָה שָׂדֶה וַתִּקָּחֵהוּ:

זָמְמָה שָׂדֶה — She plans to buy a field, unlike her husband.

וַתִּקָּחֵהוּ — The halachah is with her, and they do as she wants.

We find this halachah in the eighth *perek* of *Kesubos* (79a), where the Gemara writes: פְּשִׁיטָא, אַרְעָא וּבָתֵּי, אַרְעָא — "It is obvious that if there is a question as to whether to buy a field or a house, a field should be bought." This is referring to when a husband and wife disagree as to whether to purchase a house for rent or a field for produce and fruit. The law favors whichever side wants to buy the field since, as the Gemara states, a field is a better investment than a house.

Why?

The Gemara explains: Houses eventually fall into disrepair and are demolished. Land, however, lasts forever. And that is why the law is with the spouse who wants to use the extra money for the purchase of land, as opposed to a house.

[Author's note: It is possible that the outcome of such a question will depend in which country this question comes up. In the times of the Gemara, when homes often just collapsed (see *Bava Metzia* 117a-b) and people sometimes squatted in other people's houses, it would have been wiser to invest in fields. Nowadays, it is often preferable to invest in homes that are built well and that command high rents, such as in Manhattan, Paris, London and, certainly, Yerushalayim.]

The Vineyard of Love

Now *Zera Shimshon* introduces a new scenario.

Let's say, he writes, that the husband enters the marriage with a vineyard. Of course, vineyards are expensive and need a lot of work to maintain. Yet the husband wants to hold onto his vineyard, since he makes a lot of money from the sale of his grapes.

Tosafos addresses this in *Kesubos*, writing regarding the *pasuk*, מִפְּרִי כַפֶּיהָ נָטְעָה כָּרֶם — "From the fruit of her handiwork she plants a vineyard": The wife pushes herself and works in the vineyard, doing whatever labor is needed and guarding it from predators. She does this, *Tosafos* explains, to save them the expense of having to hire workers to do these jobs. And she does this on top of all her other obligations, because she wants to bring her husband wealth.

Fruits or Grapes?

Here the *Zera Shimshon* introduces another question facing our intrepid couple.

What if the *eishes chayil* and her husband have another question as to what to do with the money?

What if one of them wants to use the money to purchase fruit trees and the other wants to buy a vineyard?

Well, what are the different sides of the dispute?

Let's begin with fruit trees. Fruit trees don't generate as much profit as grapevines do, but they also do not require a lot of work. Vineyards require a huge amount of work, but they have the potential to bring in a lot of money!

In this scenario, the *Zera Shimshon* explains, we follow the spouse who wants to purchase fruit trees, even though the profits are less than those of a vineyard. And there is an additional reason for not investing in vineyards: because grapevines are delicate and not as sturdy as regular fruit trees, it is easy to lose money on them.

But What If the Eishes Chayil Wants a Vineyard?

Even though the Gemara told us that the halachah is with the spouse who wants to buy fruit trees, and even if she wants to use her own money to purchase a vineyard, her husband can prevent her from doing this.

Here the *Zera Shimshon* introduces another fascinating idea.

When can she be prevented from buying a vineyard? Only in a situation where the vineyard is already old, and has been in existence for a long time. Since the vineyard is already past its prime, it may not be the most lucrative investment — especially since it costs a lot of money to buy and who knows how many more seasons you will get out of it?

However, our *eishes chayil* wants to do something else. She has it all worked out. She has already purchased a field with the extra money that she earned.

Since she already owns the property, the only cost she has in planting a vineyard is buying new grapevines, which are not expensive.

And even in the worst-case scenario — if she plants a vineyard and it doesn't do well — she knows that she can always uproot the vines and use the field to plant other things, like wheat or different kinds of fruit trees.

A Savvy Businesswoman

To sum up:

זָמְמָה שָׂדֶה וַתִּקָּחֵהוּ — She will buy a field and not a house. Why? Because it's a better investment and she's a savvy businessperson.

מִפְּרִי כַפֶּיהָ נָטְעָה כָּרֶם — Once she owns the land, she works it herself, planting a brand-new vineyard, since she knows the financial potential. And she even keeps the costs down by doing much of the work herself, thereby making it even more profitable.

Of course, if things don't work out as planned, she knows that the vineyard can always be turned into a regular field.

What an *eishes chayil* we have here! She will do whatever it takes to make sure her family is provided for. But she doesn't stop there. She puts lots of thought into what to do with their extra money and is an active partner when it comes to investing for the future.

And in many cases she hinges her family's financial future on the mighty grape.

Which reminds me of a story.

It's the story of a team of *mashgichim*, and the story of doing outreach, and the story of the power of the right words — and all of this occurred right in the middle of the grape capital of America.

In the words of the *mashgiach*:

The scent was the first thing that hit me. The closer we came to the place, the stronger the scent became, until it was almost overpowering in its intensity. We were surrounded as far as the eye could see by rows and rows of grapevines stretching to eternity. Just one giant vineyard, producing some of the best grape juice in the United States. Smuckers Jelly harvests their grapes in the area, as well as other giants in the industry.

We had flown in as part of a team of *mashgichim* to oversee what is known in the business as "The Grape Crush," the gigantic harvest of tons and tons of grapes. The "Crush" lasted a few months, and during that time we would be on call to ensure that everything was carried out according to halachah. This was Washington State, and we were separated from the rest of civilization by fifty miles of grapevines and apple orchards. It was heady but boring work, and it paid very well.

On our arrival, I saw that we had enough guys for a *minyan*, so I walked over to the *mashgiach* in command of our detail and asked him what we could do about obtaining a Sefer Torah, so we could hear *leining* when we davened together.

"That's a problem," he admitted. "I didn't think we were going to have a *minyan*. Yep it's *mamesh* a problem." Obviously, he was at a loss.

I, for one, didn't think the problem was that complicated. I got hold of a phonebook for the closest three cities and leafed through it, looking for listings of temples. I struck pay dirt when I found a number for Temple Beth Shalom in the city of Yokama. I dialed the number, and it was picked up after a few rings by a man with a pleasant voice who introduced himself as Rabbi Dale.

"Good morning, Rabbi Dale," I said. "My name is Rabbi Greenstein, and I am here in Washington State as part of a team from the OU to oversee the Grape Crush."

"What's that?" he asked. I explained.

"Oh, that's so interesting," he said. "But what can be unkosher about a grape?"

And this was the rabbi!

I wasn't going to give this "rabbi" a halachah *shiur*. Instead, I simply asked if he could help out. "We desperately need a Sefer Torah for the days of the week that call for Torah reading," I explained.

The "rabbi" was intrigued. Apparently, he had never heard about reading the Torah three times a week. It seemed a bit much for him.

"Well," I said, "as Orthodox Jews, we follow halachah, Jewish law, in the way we practice, doing things the way the Rabbis prescribed thousands of years ago."

"I see," he said. "I would love to help you, but I am only a rabbi in training here and I don't have the authority to let you remove a Torah from the sanctuary. You'll have to speak with Dr. Leimann, the president of the Temple."

"What is Dr. Leimann's medical specialty?" I wanted to know.

"He's an anesthesiologist," he said, "and he's in charge of the three biggest hospitals in Yokama, Washington."

"This is just great," I thought. "I have to call up this bigshot doctor, who heads the Reform temple in town as well as the three biggest hospitals, and beg him to lend me a Sefer Torah. There is no way this guy is going to do that!"

Baruch Hashem, I was wrong.

The man who answered the number that Rabbi Dale gave me spoke in a cultured voice that sounded as if it belonged to a person who had been around the world once or twice.

"Hi," I said. "I'm one of the rabbis here for the Grape Crush and I was wondering if we would be able to borrow one of the Torahs from the Temple?"

"No problem!" he said. "Why don't you come down here

tomorrow so that I can meet with you? If everything looks okay, I'll lend you the Torah and you can be back in an hour."

"Sounds good," I said.

The following morning found me and one of the other rabbis comfortably ensconced in Dr. Leimann's office. He was most cordial and offered us coffee and tea, which we declined. The Temple was located in a restored colonial structure with a grace reminiscent of grander days. As it was, there was something forlorn about the place. On the doctor's desk were piled two stacks of notebooks.

"I hope you don't mind," he began, "but I cannot recall having had the pleasure of hosting Orthodox rabbis in the past. I would like to take the opportunity to ask you a couple of questions that have been bothering me for the last few years."

"Fire away," we said.

"Well," he began, pointing to the smaller stack of notebooks, "these books contain all of my Jewish knowledge. And these," he said, pointing to the other much larger stack, "contain all the questions that I have on that information."

And so began a conversation that lasted way past the time we had allotted for meeting with him, but it was time well spent. The doctor was intelligent and articulate, and above all genuinely interested in pursuing the truth. We spoke for about three and a half hours. As we were beginning to get ready to leave, he asked us if we knew what *tefillin* were.

"Sure," we told him.

"Well, do you put them on every day?"

"We do."

"Can I put them on as well?"

It seemed as if he was holding his breath as he waited for our answer.

"Of course. Of course you can put them on. But are you really ready to drive ninety miles, all the way from Yokama to the Grape Crush and another ninety miles back, just to put on *tefillin*?"

"Wouldn't you?"

I have to admit, I didn't see that one coming.

He escorted us from his office into the sanctuary, a large though rather functional room, and over to the *aron*. He opened the *aron* and removed the Sefer Torah that he had agreed to lend us. On the way, he related the history of this particular scroll. How it originated in Prague, had somehow survived the Holocaust, and how many years after the war there had been an offer to come see if there was anything that his Temple might need from the large assortment of religious artifacts, all that remained of the once-thriving Jewish community of Prague.

He had seen the scroll and fallen in love with it on the spot. It was very, very large — about a third larger than the largest Sefer Torah I had ever seen. The letters were huge. The wooden handles were much bigger than on the usual Torah Scroll and there were carvings in the wood and careful etchings of *pesukim* all around the handles. It was very heavy, and we handled it with care.

Before we left, we arranged to meet the doctor the next morning at our *minyan* ninety miles away, and bade him farewell. The entire episode became more and more dreamlike the farther we drove. Somehow, I doubted that he would come.

But there he was bright and early the next morning, waiting outside our motel and eagerly awaiting his chance to don our *tefillin*. I have never seen anyone waiting to do a mitzvah with as much anticipation. I helped him put them on, and as he was sitting down at the table wrapped in my *tallis* and *tefillin*, he suddenly burst into tears! It was as if we had unleashed a storm of emotion within him and he didn't even know why. He had never put on *tefillin* in his entire life until that day, but the moment he put them on they became part of him and something cracked inside.

Again, we spent many hours in conversation with this man, and again he impressed us more than we had ever imagined possible. Then he invited us to come down to Yokama over Succos, telling us that he was going to build a succah and that it was going to be kosher according to halachah. I explained all the rules, and he told me where he was planning to build it. Carefully we drew up a diagram of what he needed to avoid while building, and then we planned the Simchas Beis Hashoevah to which the Temple would be invited. He asked me what he could serve. I told him that soft drinks and fruits would be fine, and that we were all looking forward to the party. He left us feeling that we had been in the presence of greatness. We checked the Sefer Torah as brought down in halachah, and when we found that it was fine, we figured that we were in great shape.

The next day I received a phone call from a rabbi I knew in Portland, Oregon. He had a situation, he said, and needed my help. His wife was due to give birth smack bang on Yom Kippur, and she was usually right on target. It was very probable that he would be called away in the middle of the services. Could I come down to Portland for Yom Kippur and lead the davening if he was called away? I agreed to come, and the other *mashgichim* asked to join as well, but we weren't sure what to do with Dr. Leimann's Sefer Torah. I called the doctor and told him the situation.

"Would you mind if we bring the Sefer Torah along with us to Portland?" I asked.

"I don't have a problem with that," he said, "but why don't you just leave it in your motel room until you get back?"

I explained that you didn't just leave Sifrei Torah lying around in motel rooms. You guarded them and watched them and made sure that they were well taken care of.

"No problem," he said. "Take it along with you and have a meaningful Yom Kippur."

The drive to Portland was long, tedious, and mostly filled with monotonous scenery. It certainly lacked the charm of, say, the Grand Canyon or Yellowstone National Park. We arrived on Erev Yom Kippur at the home of a very relieved rabbi.

"You are a life saver," he told me.

"Good," I said. "I need all the *zechusim* I can get before Yom Kippur."

He took us to his shul, which was like something out of Europe.

I guess the Yidden who settled in Portland before and after the war wanted a shul that would remind them of home. It was a huge, beautiful structure with shining wood, graceful candlesticks holding electric candles and lights, and polished floors. There was a very large balcony for the women. The whole place made a grand impression. It was a shame that it was barely used. Even on Yom Kippur, the rabbi told us, the shul was mostly filled with Holocaust survivors and their grandchildren who came to spend the day with them. Somehow, the second generation had been skipped over.

I stood in the empty shul on Erev Yom Kippur looking around at the rows and rows of wooden seats crying out to be filled by Yidden who never came, and shivered at the thought of what lay in store for the Jews of Greater America. We moved the Sefer Torah into its temporary home and the rabbi brought out a couple of white mantles to cover it. The Sefer Torah was so big and tall, however, that none of them fit well and the mantle ended up covering only about two thirds of the Scroll. In the end, we just left the original blue mantle on the Sefer Torah and we went to get ready for the big day. Me, to polish up my davening, and the rabbi to work on his *derashah*.

Yom Kippur dawned grey and cloudy. There was a slight mist in the air, which accentuated the somber mood, and the walk to shul was one of silent contemplation. The rabbi's wife had, in fact, gone to the hospital in the middle of the night, and so I was the one leading the services that Yom Kippur morning. The shul was fairly full of older people and a handful of younger ones, and I davened Shacharis in the opulent sanctuary where my voice was the only one that was really raised. The congregation sang along just a little bit. The acoustics were delightful, however, and after a few songs the old men started to get more into it.

I had to *lein* for them as well, since the rabbi hadn't returned. The rabbi did arrive in time for Mussaf, with the grand news that he had just had a boy. The day felt lighter and seemed more favorable as the rabbi davened Mussaf in the joyful tone of a man with much to thank Hashem for. Then he left to go back to the hospital, and I took the congregation through Minchah and Maftir Yonah. It was almost time for Neilah. It was then that I was informed that the congregation expected a speech prior to Neilah. I wasn't prepared to deliver a speech, nor was I in the mood to deliver one. But there they were, all the old men, Holocaust survivors waiting with expectant looks. I couldn't let them down. So I stood up to speak.

I stood there at the front of this crowded room and I wondered what I should talk about. I hadn't prepared anything on Maftir Yonah, or on the meaning of Yom Kippur. And then I suddenly realized that there was something very special to talk about. I could speak about the Sefer Torah that I had brought with me. This had been a long journey for one Sefer Torah. From Prague to Yokama, from Yokama to the Grape Crush, and from the Crush to Portland — all because the rabbi's wife had given birth to a boy Yom Kippur night. Through a chain of circumstances, that Torah had ended up here for the day, in a place it had never been before.

I explained that the Torah is the *neshamah*, the soul of Klal Yisrael, and that it will never die. As much as they attempt to destroy our nation, I said, they will never be able to destroy our soul.

"Many of you are survivors of the worst Gehinnom the world has ever known. Many of you lost parents and families to the Nazi murderers. But there is one thing you must never forget! As much as it seems like they are gone, that is not really the case. Their bodies may be gone, but their *neshamos*, their souls, are here — just like this Torah is here from Prague!"

I really got into it, using my hands and shaking my fists, and the crowd was loving it, following my gestures with their heads as here and there someone wiped away a tear. And then, from among the crowd, an elderly, frail man stood up and interrupted me right in the middle of my speech. He was openly weeping, tears streaming down his face.

"Do you know where I am from?" he asked me in a trembling voice.

"Where are you from?"

"I am one of a small group of survivors from the city of Prague."

The shul was quiet. Everyone waited to hear what was coming next.

"Do you know something? I was honored last night to stand by the *bimah* with one of the Sifrei Torah in my hands. And do you know which one? It was that tall one, the giant Sefer Torah that I was holding."

He paused for a moment. You could have heard a pin drop in the shul.

"All the time that I was holding the Sefer Torah I felt something, a connection that I have never felt before with any Sefer Torah that I have ever held since my bar mitzvah so many years ago. Last night while holding the Sefer Torah, I felt the same exact connection that I felt so many years ago. And now I know why! This is my Sefer Torah! This is the Torah from my hometown! I recognized the wooden handles, the inscriptions along the edges. But I wasn't sure. And now I know!"

He was crying, tears of joy rolling out of his eyes, and we cried along with him.

"The Torah and I, we are both survivors. As you say, they can try and try, but they'll never be able to take our *neshamos* away from us!"

I, for one, never experienced a Neilah like that one, neither before or after.

That was the old man's final Neilah. He was *niftar* on Chanukah that year. May his memory be blessed.

I returned to Yokama many times after that first unforgettable trip, and witnessed a profound change in a community that all had given up for dead. Quite a few of those Reform couples are completely *frum* today, and Dr. Leimann is going strong. And all this because of something as far removed from the spiritual as one can imagine. All because of something known as "The Grape Crush."

ח

חָגְרָה בְעוֹז מָתְנֶיהָ, וַתְּאַמֵּץ זְרעוֹתֶיהָ
She tightens the belt of her garments,
and she pays attention to her arms.

The Tznius Challenge

Careful — Even in the Fields

*T*he *eishes chayil* is a modest woman. She makes certain that her clothing is *tzanuah*, especially since she works in the fields. When she is doing manual labor it would be easy to stop focusing on how modest her clothing is, or whether her body is properly covered.

But not our *eishes chayil*.

She never loses track of who she is.

After she plants her vineyard, she carries on with the rest of the many different tasks needed to ensure the grapes grow well, like pruning the branches and tending to the land surrounding the vines.

When a person is so busy with physical labor — which some women are unaccustomed to — her clothing might fall into disarray. Or she might lift her hands up to pick the grapes off the vine, exposing her arms.

To ensure that this does not happen to her, the *eishes chayil* חָגְרָה בְּעוֹז מָתְנֶיהָ — "she tightens the belt of her garments" at all times;

וַתְּאַמֵּץ זְרֹעוֹתֶיהָ — "and she pays attention to her arms," ensuring that her sleeves cover her elbows. When the time comes for her to pick the grapes off the vine, she makes sure to do the harvesting in the most modest way possible, lifting her arms in a way that is totally *tzniusdik*.

Our *eishes chayil* is a person who knows the truth about life. She knows the enjoyment of dressing up and looking good, and she knows the temptation that people have to sometimes purchase the wrong type of clothing.

And because she is a person who works on herself, she gets it right. Because she knows what real enjoyment and happiness are, and what life is really about.

Liora didn't know what to do with her sixteen-year-old daughter. Tami was a serious girl, smart, personable, sweet and caring — everything that a parent would want to see in a daughter. There was just one thing that Liora wished would be different: the matter of Tami's dress.

Tami didn't fight the system. She wasn't the kind of girl who showed up at school and had to be sent home because she was wearing something that was just plain wrong. No, Tami wasn't like that. She had too much *derech eretz* for her teachers and principal to behave that way. But vacation time was a different matter entirely.

Days with no school uniform brought out a different side in her daughter. It was a side that Liora didn't know or recognize, a side that scared her with its casual approach toward *tznius*. Why was it that so many girls today weren't connecting with the whole concept of modest dress in a real way? Why was it that they were listening and not really hearing? She didn't want to preach. That had never been her method of parenting. And yet, every time Tami walked down the stairs and into the kitchen, she had to force herself to keep quiet, at the risk of alienating her daughter further.

She tried to console herself with the thought that there were many girls who dressed far worse than her daughter did, but that was small comfort and it did not ease the pain. She just didn't know what to do. Any time she brought up the subject, Tami stiffened up and became angry. Things would deteriorate quickly after that, which Liora hated. If only Tami would meet the perfect person who knew the magic words to help her realize that the pleasure she derived from dressing a certain way wasn't the real thing. But who knew those magic words?

And then, one Shabbos afternoon, Tami went to a *shiur* at the local shul. When she came back, her eyes were shining. She was practically glowing with happiness.

"What happened to you?" Liora asked her daughter.

"I just heard the most amazing idea," she replied.

"Will you tell me what it was?"

"At Shalosh Seudos."

Finally, they were sitting together at the kitchen table. Abba was in shul with the boys and Chavi was away at a friend's. The world seemed to recede, until it was only the two of them illuminated by the soft yellow light coming from the fixture above.

"So, tell me," Liora urged.

"Well, it was this rebbetzin that I never heard before. She didn't preach at us. It wasn't like that at all. You know our crowd. One word of preaching, and half of them would have stood up and left the room. But she said something that made us think. That *really* made us think."

"What did she say?"

"Okay, here goes. She gave a *mashal* about peaches and diamonds. I'm going to try to remember exactly how she said it."

Tami closed her eyes, concentrated for a minute, and then began repeating what she had heard.

"Peaches are a really delicious fruit. Who doesn't love a peach? Let's say you're in the mood to buy a peach, what do you do? It's easy enough. Just leave your home, walk down the street, and find the nearest fruit store. There you'll find a giant pile of peaches — enough peaches for everyone in the neighborhood. The peaches just sit there on the stand, available for every person to touch and squeeze, to see if they are firm enough and if the consistency is the way they like it. So you feel a few of them, select three or four and pay for what you purchased. Not too complicated.

"That's the way it works when you're in the market for a peach.

"Now, let's say you need to buy a diamond ring. Shopping for a diamond is an entirely different experience. Instead of an open-air display, the jewelry shop is surrounded by closed-circuit cameras for maximum security. You can't enter the establishment unless someone buzzes you in. Once inside, you find yourself in a wondrous world of mirrors and soft recessed lighting showcasing the beautiful gems. After browsing for more than an hour, you finally decide on the type of diamond ring you want. You'd like nothing more than to try it on. But you can't. Because every piece of expensive jewelry is under lock, key, and alarm. The only way you'll be able to see, examine or try on the ring that interests you so, and whose lovely gleam has attracted you from beneath the glass, is if you ask the woman behind the counter to unlock the case. Otherwise, no dice.

"The big question every single person should be asking themselves is: "What do I want to be in life — a peach or a diamond? A peach, which anyone off the street can touch and throw from hand to hand, or a diamond, an object of class and beauty, cherished by its owner and accessible to only a select and worthy few.

"I don't think there's a person alive who'd rather be a peach than a diamond. And none of us can afford to leave it at the philosophical level, where they know this is what they should be doing, but don't because it's just too hard. The choice they make will impact how much Torah enters a person's home and the lives of their children, their husband, and ultimately themselves as well.

"It's a truly challenging battle, but one truly worth fighting for."

There was a magic spell in the kitchen by the time Tami finished talking.

"Wow. That was something," Liora said.

"It's *emes*," her daughter replied. "It's truth. For the first time ever, I actually feel like I understand the concept of *tznius* and the real pleasure that comes from holding yourself back when it comes to how you dress."

Liora wanted to dance with joy.

טָעֲמָה כִּי טוֹב סַחְרָהּ, לֹא יִכְבֶּה בַלַּיְלָה נֵרָהּ

She discerns that her business is good,
so her lamp is not snuffed out by night.

The Right Balance

Slowing Down

Zera Shimshon tells us that this *pasuk,* טָעֲמָה כִּי טוֹב סַחְרָהּ, is a continuation of one of the previous *pesukim,* הָיְתָה כָּאֳנִיּוֹת סוֹחֵר, and that the connection lies in the word סוֹחֵר, *socher,* which literally means "merchant," but which refers to business practices as well.

He explains:

There will come a time, says the *Zera Shimshon,* when the *eishes chayil* will decide to rethink and then slow down working on her business interests and financial pursuits.

In the second explanation of the *pasuk* הָיְתָה כָּאֳנִיּוֹת סוֹחֵר, *Zera Shimshon* wrote that the merit of the *eishes chayil* brings blessing and abundance for her family from *Olam Haba.*

Yet he stresses that though she does her best to help her husband by taking care of her business, she is content to put in the effort that she feels is the minimum expected of her.

She is also very careful to stay away from money that she feels is coming to them in a miraculous fashion.

Hishtadlus (effort) — yes.

A certain amount of work — yes.

Miracles — no.

The Problem With Miracles

A person is not allowed to benefit from miracles, and if the *eishes chayil* feels that the money she is making is coming to her in an abnormal fashion, she will shy away from it.

Why?

What's wrong with enjoying a miracle?

Miracle money comes off a person's portion in the World to Come — as the Gemara (*Taanis* 25a) shows in the famous story of Rabbi Chaninah ben Dosa and his wife:

One day, Rabbi Chaninah ben Dosa's wife asked her husband how long they were going to suffer from poverty.

Her husband replied, "What do you want me to do?"

"Pray to Hashem to give you financial help."

So Rabbi Chaninah ben Dosa prayed and a hand came down from the heavens and delivered a golden table leg into their home.

That night Rabbi Chaninah's wife had a dream. She saw *tzaddikim* sitting in *Olam Haba* at golden tables. Everyone else's table had three legs. Their table had only two golden legs.

When she woke up, she asked him to pray that the golden leg should be taken back.

What's the upshot of all this?

"If a person benefits from miracles, the enjoyment will be deducted from his portion in the World to Come" (*Taanis* 20b).

This is an explanation of the phrase טָעֲמָה כִּי טוֹב סַחְרָהּ — "She discerns (*taamah*) that her business is good."

When the *eishes chayil* comes to the realization that the money she is making is way in excess of the norm, and is therefore being deducted from her portion in *Olam Haba*, she doesn't want it. A *pasuk* (*Tehillim* 34:9) states: טַעֲמוּ וּרְאוּ כִּי טוֹב ה' — "Taste (*taamu* — from the same root as the word *taamah*) and see that Hashem is good" — and that the great abundance in this world comes from Above.

When she realizes that this is the case, and that the abundance is coming to her from Above, she doesn't want it.

Because having such abundance in this world — a world that is compared to night (*Bava Metzia* 83b) — isn't a good thing, in the sense that it will have a hand in extinguishing the light of her portion in *Olam Haba*, as it says, לָאוֹר בְּאוֹר הַחַיִּים (*Iyov* 33:30), referring to the World to Come.

Because she understands that her business is causing her to lose what is really important, she doesn't want it; לֹא יִכְבֶּה בַלַּיְלָה נֵרָהּ — she wants to avoid extinguishing her spiritual light. She doesn't want to extinguish her candle, the light of heaven that comes down to this world.

To sum it up: The *eishes chayil* does her best to find the happy balance between work and *hishtadlus* and not benefiting from the reward that awaits her in the World to Come.

A Time to Rest From Work

Zera Shimshon provides another explanation of the *pasuk*.

When she is טָעֲמָה כִּי טוֹב סַחְרָהּ, when she enjoys success in her business — clients are coming to her and she is making money — then she begins cutting down on some of her extra work. Since she is doing well, she no longer sees the need to get up in the middle of the night and do even more work by candlelight, just to increase her wealth.

In other words:

When she has reached a situation of כִּי טוֹב סַחְרָהּ — she's already comfortable and doing well, and לֹא יִכְבֶּה בַלַּיְלָה נֵרָהּ — she has ceased rising in the middle of the night to work because she doesn't need to do so anymore, then יָדֶיהָ שִׁלְּחָה בַכִּישׁוֹר — the only additional job she will do is work with wool, as we will see in the next *pasuk*.

Stay tuned…

Smart Yidden like our *eishes chayil* understand that making money is not the point of life and should not be the focus. Of course a person needs to do *hishtadlus* and make a *parnassah*, but at the end of the day we need to remember that we are on a journey — and when that journey comes to an end we want to be sitting at a table with three golden legs.

The following story is the tale of just such a person — a man who had no problem spending his hard-earned money for the right reasons. It seems pretty obvious what type of table he's sitting at right now…

This story began over half a century ago, but its ramifications continue to this day. In the middle of the city of Jaffa — a city which is populated by both Jewish people and Arabs — there is a famous bakery. It is called "Abulafia." Above the name of the bakery, written in both Ivrit and English, the date 1879 appears — the year the bakery was first established.

During the rest of the year, Jaffa was filled with numerous bakeries that provided its citizens with fresh-baked goods. On Pesach, however, virtually every one of those bakeries closed its doors and shuttered its windows. Production ceased, since the majority of Jews made sure to stay away from all *chametz*.

This created a problem for the minority of Jewish people who did not appreciate being told what to do. They wanted to continue eating bread and pita during the eight days of Pesach, and since most of the bakeries were closed, the search was on to find an alternative source for their bread supplies. For this group, not being able to partake of a fresh pita for eight days felt impossible, and they were unwilling to commit to such a thing. "Luckily" for them, there was a bakery that stayed open. A bakery that had been around and in full operational mode since 1879.

The Abulafia Bakery.

This could explain the traffic jams that resulted near the bakery during the entire week of Pesach, as people drove in from the nearby moshavim and kibbutzim around Jaffa, intent on purchasing the *chametz* they were unwilling to forgo.

Reb Shlomo Zalman Stauber lived in Jaffa and owned a shoe factory located across the street from the Abulafia Bakery. As everyone knows, for a *frum* Yid even seeing a piece of bread on Pesach is difficult. This was so much worse. Abulafia was a big bakery, a large operation. A huge amount of bread products were being carried out of its capacious ovens every day of Pesach. Traditional Arab breads and flatbreads, pita, laffah, cake, and all sorts of Arab pastries were being produced on premises. Reb Shlomo Zalman was able to see many Yidden streaming toward the bakery — only to emerge with bags laden with *chametz* that they planned to feed their families!

Observing the traffic jams near the bakery caused Reb Shlomo Zalman infinite sorrow. It wasn't right. Pesach was a Yom Tov for which Klal Yisrael has sacrificed and which they have honored for thousands of years. And now, right here in Eretz Yisrael, an Arab bakery was operating at full capacity, selling poison to so many unsuspecting and ignorant Jews who didn't understand the severity of what they were doing.

It bothered him to no end.

Finally, in the year 1969, he resolved to do something about it. So many people were eating *chametz*, for which the punishment for eating even a *k'zayis* is nothing less than *kareis*.

After giving the matter a lot of thought, Reb Shlomo Zalman walked out of his shoe factory and approached the bakery of his neighbor, Saeed Abulafia. Having been neighbors for many years, they knew one another. It was a few weeks before Pesach. Reb Shlomo Zalman walked into the bakery and asked one of the Abulafia boys to ask his father if he had time to speak with him for a few minutes.

Saeed Abulafia emerged from the back of the store moments later and greeted his neighbor with a big smile.

"*Adon* Shlomo!" he said. "What can I do for you? My son told me that you wish to talk to me. Is something the matter? Is there a problem that I can help you with?"

The two of them sat down together in a quiet spot and Reb Shlomo Zalman began to explain.

"Saeed," he began, "you know that the festival of Pesach is fast approaching."

"Of course," the Arab replied.

"And you know that on Pesach, the majority of bakeries are closed all over the country."

The Arab nodded again.

"There is a reason for this. We Jews are not allowed to eat *chametz* on Pesach."

Reb Shlomo Zalman explained to Mr. Abulafia what *chametz* is, why Jewish people bake matzos, and that the Torah is very, very unhappy with any Jew who dared consume even the tiniest morsel of leavened bread on Pesach. The smile on Saeed Abulafia's face gradually decreased in size as he grasped what Reb Shlomo Zalman was telling him.

"Saeed," Reb Shlomo Zalman said, "I don't expect you to close your store over the week of Pesach just because I ask you to. You are not Jewish and have no obligation to cease baking bread. However, this is so important to me that I am asking you to sit down and make a calculation of how much money you will make over the week of Pesach. I will pay you the entire amount, on condition that you close your business during that time. Take your family and go on a vacation. You deserve it! What do you say?"

Saeed Abulafia was silent for a few seconds. Finally he spoke.

"Mr. Shlomo," Saeed replied, "do you have any idea how much money I make during that one week? While it is true that most Jewish people are careful not to eat bread products during Pesach, the minority all seem to hop to my store! I want to tell you a secret. So many people buy bread in my store during Pesach that I make more money in that week than I make the entire rest of the year!"

"I understand, Saeed. But knowing that my fellow Jews are buying and eating *chametz* on Pesach hurts me so much that I feel obligated to pay for your week so that the Abulafia Bakery will close up shop just for Pesach. Tell me the amount and I will give it to you."

"If that's how you feel, Mr. Shlomo, I am willing to make a deal with you."

Saeed Abulafia placed a piece of paper down on the table and wrote down the details of the agreement.

> *"That the store will be closed from April 20th–9:30 in the morning until the evening of April 27th."*
>
> Signed — *Saeed Abulafia*
>
> Signed — *Shlomo Zalman Stauber*

The amount of money that Reb Shlomo Zalman agreed to pay Saeed Abulafia was also written in the contract, as was the time by which he would transfer the funds to the Abulafia family.

When the contract was finalized, they shook hands. Both were satisfied with the deal they had made. Saeed Abulafia was happy that he had been able to help his neighbor without incurring a financial loss. He was also happy that he was not causing Jewish people to go against their religion.

As for Reb Shlomo Zalman — he was filled with incredible *simchah* at the knowledge that this year, the bakery would be closed and the *chillul Hashem* of the Pesach traffic jams would be averted. Each felt like they had made a good deal.

That year, for the first time ever, the Abulafia Bakery was closed for the entire Pesach. Car after car drove up to the bakery, expecting to see long lines of people waiting outside the open exterior. But that year there were no lines. There were no tables filled with fragrant cakes, fresh rolls, pita and bread. Instead, the passengers of those cars were treated to the sight of a shuttered Abulafia Bakery. Turning around, they left Jaffa and went home. But before they left, they couldn't help but notice the huge sign hanging from the front of the bakery:

> *"The Abulafia Bakery blesses the entire Jewish people with a Chag Kasher V'sameach!"*

For the next six years, the same scene repeated itself. A few weeks prior to Pesach, Reb Shlomo Zalman would leave his factory and make his way over to the Abulafia Bakery, where he asked one of the boys to please call his father. The two of them would sit down. First a little friendly conversation, then down to business. Every year Saeed Abulafia would make his monetary calculation and tell Reb Shlomo Zalman the price. They would write it down and sign the contract.

That's the way it went for six years.

(After Reb Shlomo Zalman passed away, the Stauber family examined all their father's documents and made a calculation of how much their father had spent to close the bakery for six years running. It emerged that their father had paid Mr. Abulafia an amount that would have enabled the baker to purchase a four-bedroom apartment in Tel Aviv!)

In the seventh year, things changed. When Reb Shlomo Zalman came over to talk business with his neighbor, Saeed Abulafia said to him, "*Adon* Shlomo, this year we are not going to make the same deal as we have done for the last six years!"

Reb Shlomo Zalman was taken aback. What had happened to change Saeed Abulafia's mind? Did he no longer enjoy an all-expenses-paid vacation? Why the change?

"Don't worry, my friend," Saeed Abulafia reassured Reb Shlomo Zalman. "The bakery will still be closed. But from now on, my children and I will keep the Abulafia Bakery closed during the week of Pesach without charging you for it. I no longer want money for doing this."

Reb Shlomo Zalman asked him to explain.

"Mr. Shlomo," Saeed replied, "I want to tell you something. Since I began closing my bakery six years ago during Pesach, I have seen a tremendous increase in business in my bakery during the rest of the year. We have been the recipients of great blessing in our bakery. That is why I am planning to close my bakery during Pesach from now on without charging you for it — just because I feel it's the right thing to do."

Reb Shlomo Zalman was taken to his heavenly rest twenty-one years ago, in 2001.

His neighbor, Mr. Abulafia, also passed away and is no longer alive. Today the Abulafia Bakery is managed by his children. And every year, come Pesach time, a very large sign is hung on the front of the bakery.

"The Abulafia Bakery blesses the entire Jewish people with a Chag Kasher V'sameach!"

Beneath their good wishes to Klal Yisrael, the Abulafia family has written the story of how their bakery came to be closed for Pesach.

Reb Shlomo Zalman Stauber was a prime example of the way a Yid is supposed to live his life, doing *chesed* for Klal Yisrael without fanfare and without telling anyone about it. All he cared about was saving his fellow Yidden from the transgression of eating *chametz* on Pesach. He didn't form a committee to deal with the issue. He didn't call a meeting or take out an ad in the local newspaper. Instead, he asked himself one simple question: "What can I do to make this situation better?"

And then he did it.

This is the power of one Yid, the impact that a single individual can achieve — even today, fifty years later!

Yehi Zichro Baruch.

יָדֶיהָ שִׁלְחָה בַכִּישׁוֹר, וְכַפֶּיהָ תָּמְכוּ פָלֶךְ
*She stretches out her hands to the distaff,
and her palms support the spindle.*

Always Busy

Keep Busy

Once our *eishes chayil* feels that she has been successful enough — either because she doesn't want to utilize her future reward in the World to Come, or because she has made a lot of money and can afford to be more relaxed about making a living — she now reaches the point of יָדֶיהָ שִׁלְחָה בַכִּישׁוֹר, "she stretches out her hands to the distaff." (A *kishor*, distaff, and a *palech,* spindle, are tools for spinning threads.)

Earlier we wrote of the many different types of work that a woman can be occupied with, such as working with flax, selling merchandise in the market, waking in the middle of the night to work by candlelight, or planting a vineyard.

Our *eishes chayil* no longer needs to do any of these. Yet even so, she still keeps herself busy with weaving wool. As mentioned before, this is the one task that the halachah requires of a wife, as the Mishnah (*Kesubos* 59b) states: A husband can obligate his wife to keep busy by weaving wool.

Why can he do this?

Answers the Mishnah:

Every person, even an *eishes chayil*, needs to keep busy. Idleness is a terrible thing, because a person who doesn't work ends up bored, and boredom leads people to sin. And even if they don't end up sinning, it can actually impact their mental health.

So her hands keep busy with the *kishor*.

The reason this instrument for weaving is referred to as a כִּישׁוֹר (*kishor*) is because the word implies that by keeping busy, she is ensuring that she remains "kosher" — in top shape, spiritually. She will be active and busy and will avoid all the negative outcomes that stem from boredom and idleness.

וְכַפֶּיהָ תָּמְכוּ פָלֶךְ — "And her palms support the spindle."

The *eishes chayil* makes sure that whatever work she is doing is done in the most modest manner. She is careful not to let the spindle or the threads fall to the ground, because then she would have to bend down to pick them up. This reminds us of how Rus was careful when she bent down to gather the fallen sheaves of wheat.

(In our day and age this would apply to how she comports herself while working in an office with men.)

Zera Shimshon continues:

By now the *eishes chayil* and her husband are financially solvent. They have invested years of work and have done well for themselves.

וַתָּקָם — For years, she rose in the middle of the night to do extra work.

זָמְמָה — They purchased properties for investment.

They have now reached a point where they can afford to take it easy.

The *eishes chayil* can now work less. She contents herself with weaving wool and nothing else. But the *avodah* of weaving wool is something she will never give up. Because the *eishes chayil* knows how damaging it is for a person to do nothing.

There are people who are happy to relax and do not feel the constant urge to get up and accomplish, and there are those who are driven and always need to be doing something productive.

During the Covid era, I received many emails from different people asking me to participate in various initiatives that they had established or were in the process of establishing.

Over and over I found myself impressed with those people — for their drive and desire to help those around them, and for the fact that they considered time a gift and something to be used wisely.

Like our *eishes chayil*, they could not stop doing good things — and no, they are never bored — because they are constantly busy serving Hashem with all their resources and ingenuity.

In September of 2020, I received an email from a girl I didn't know. She introduced herself, explaining that she had established an organization called "Hashem First" and that she would really appreciate it if I spoke for them.

I found myself amazed by this girl, not only because she had launched such an incredible initiative (which has actually grown into something phenomenal), but also because she had chosen to remain anonymous while doing it.

Shortly afterward, she sent me a follow-up email so that I would really understand what she was trying to accomplish.

This is what I read.

> *Dear Rabbi Seltzer,*
>
> *As each girl signed up, she received this email:*
>
> *Welcome to Hashem First! You are now part of a tremendous zechus for yourself and for Klal Yisrael. As you already know, the goal of this group is to be marbeh kavod Shamayim and bring ourselves closer to Hashem by fine-tuning our middos, bringing meaning to our everyday actions, and of course, putting "Hashem First" in everything we do. We are going to improve ourselves and our relationship with Hashem, one step at a time. This year, prepare yourselves for awesome speakers! Get excited by our incredible collection of inspirational quotes to motivate yourselves! Look out for our monthly project cal-*

endar with a personal plan, positive peer pressure, and an overflow of inspiration and berachah. "Hashem First" is an ideal that's going to change your life. Thanks for taking the "First" step!

I hope that our theme will keep this all positive and motivational. It's not a "Don't do" program, it's a "Do" program. How CAN we come closer to Hashem??? Now we can look forward to Rosh Chodesh when we can reflect on all the things we have accomplished and move on to a new concept. We will never fall short, only move up with each success. There are no rules, but there are suggestions and goals. We will learn a lot this year, and we will love it.

Each month, we will choose a new path toward achieving more Hashem orientation. I'll offer some insights about the topic of that month, and set specific goals for ourselves toward that end. These aren't commitments as much as suggestions. Each girl can tailor it to her own life. Take the topic... and run with it; make it your own.

When I present the new topic, I'll also offer some reflection on the previous month. Please send in your own stories — the victories and also the defeats — as we work on this together.

Some of us might have come to past Rosh Hashanahs feeling like a long list of mistakes. But let us realize that we are not such messes; we're all under construction, works in progress. Next year we can enter the new year with months of accomplishments behind us so that Rosh Hashanah is actually exciting. It will become a point in time when we can reflect on the past, and motivate ourselves with a vision for the future that will keep us going, building a little more each day.

If anyone has any suggestions or quotes or ideas for a theme of the month that you want to cover, or just any feedback, please email me at hashemfirsthost@gmail.com. — I would also love to hear how this program is impacting all of you, so please, let me know! Or if any one of the names on the Zechus sheet has improvement or a yeshuah, please keep me updated. I'm davening for everyone.

This program is for you, for me, and for Klal Yisrael. With

YOUR help, we can bring Mashiach!!! May Hashem give you only good, and may you see that good in everything you set out to do. Only berachah!!! Looking forward to a great year of growth!!! Inspired by Mindel Kassorla's article in the Family First on Rosh Hashanah.

Please forward the original email that introduced you to Hashem First to all your friends and contacts. If even ONE person gets inspired or signs up because of you, you will get tons of schar every time they do a mitzvah because of the decision they made to join Hashem First.

I ended up speaking for Hashem First and was happy that I did. It is not every day that you run into people who are trying so hard to work on themselves and to do the *ratzon Hashem*. And, of course I was very careful not to reveal the true identity of the founder of Hashem First — as per her instructions.

In June 2021, I received an email from the founder — I will call her Chana just to give her a name — with a story that she wanted to share with me.

"A while ago," she wrote, "I sent out a song to all the members of Hashem First to listen to."

Chana happens to write songs that contain positive and uplifting messages, and she wanted to share this particular song with the girls of Hashem First. Here she ran into a slight technical challenge, because the song had been sent out in an M4a format, and the majority of those who received it needed it in an MP3 format instead. *Baruch Hashem,* one of the girls was very helpful and offered to change the format and send it back to her as an MP3 file. She took care of it right away and sent it back. Now everyone was able to enjoy the song.

"A month later," Chana continued, "an organization called Special Sister's Corner (a support group benefiting girls with special-needs siblings) contacted me, asking if they could use the song — Modeh Ani — for their hotlines. They felt it would give their listeners *chizuk* and would be of great benefit for all concerned. I sent them the song and offered to send my other songs as well, since they are all full of *chizuk*. They thanked me for my offer and told me that they would love to receive them.

I sent them all my songs and they wrote back to say that the songs were in an M4a format, and they needed it sent in MP3. Since I still didn't know how to change the format, I thought about who I could ask to do it for me. And then I remembered that, a month earlier, a girl had kindly offered to change my song from M4a to MP3. I contacted her right away and asked if she could do me a favor and change the format of all the songs. She graciously agreed and sent them back right away.

Six months passed. One day I received an email from a girl in Hashem First.

This is what she wrote.

I was debating whether or not to send this...

Baruch Hashem, my mother had a beautiful baby boy 3 weeks ago with Down syndrome. Someone told me about the hotline called Sister's Corner, for girls with special-needs siblings. I was listening to the music and came across a few songs written by you. (I only know that because you had asked me to convert them to mp3 files.)

I just want to tell you how meaningful those songs are to me, especially the song "Fly."

As a side note, I will not ask the girls who run the hotline for the author of those songs, as I know you don't want your name out there. Thank you for your inspiration through Hashem First and through the beautiful songs you have written!

I was a little speechless, thinking about our whole interchange and the way everything played out.

It was such *Hashgachah.* Such an example of the concept of *"Refuah Kodem L'makah."* When I asked her to convert the songs for me, she had no idea why or what I needed them for.

I wrote back.

"OH MY GOODNESS!!!

First of all, MAZEL TOV!

I am tearing up as I write this. Hashem is so incredible, I have no words. Only G-d could orchestrate events like this.

I know this is going to sound crazy, but I want to tell you something.

The reason I asked you to convert the songs into an MP3 format... was because someone contacted me through Hashem First, asking to convert the songs into MP3 for them. Since I remembered that you did this for me in the past with my Modeh Ani song (without my even asking you to), I decided to reach out to you and ask if you could do it again. You so kindly did, and I sent on the songs to the person asking for them in MP3. Who was it?

Sister's Corner.

Because of YOU, Sister's Corner has the songs that are now inspiring you.

Full circle.

Months ago, you provided your own chizuk.

Hashem has everything under control. Hashem is literally carrying you in His hands. This is not normal. I am actually blown away. I am so happy to be a part of this!"

At the end of the day, we live our lives without realizing how the *hishtadlus* and help that we give others can often rebound back onto our own lives with startling and beautiful results.

Of course, all women and girls reading this should feel free to contact Hashemfirsthost@gmail.com or sign up through Hashem-first.com if you want to participate in the beautiful magic that is constantly happening in the group that Chana established. You never know what being a part of this will do for you. In all seriousness — it may just change your life...

The Segulah of the Zera Shimshon

Like that special young lady, there are so many people going out of their way for Klal Yisrael, each in the area that interests and excites them. Everyone is doing their part and everyone is needed. And while there are many incredible initiatives going on, it's always nice to know that you have the *Zera Shimshon* on your side...

In 5777 the *Zera Shimshon* teams decided that they wanted to do something major in honor of that year's *hilula*. (*Hilula* is the *yahrtzeit* of a *tzaddik*; the *Zera Shimshon's yahrtzeit* is the 6th day of Elul.) They decided to print a special pamphlet that would be distributed worldwide. As can be expected, such a project is expensive, especially since they planned on printing tens of thousands of copies. Turning to one of the donors who had long been paying the printing costs for the pamphlet that was distributed in tens of shuls and public places in his city, they told him about the plan for the special pamphlet and asked if he would be willing to undertake the costs of this project.

He got back to them a few days later to let them know that he was willing to cover the entire cost. He transferred the money and they went to work. At the same time, the donor let the *Zera Shimshon* team know that he was experiencing a personal challenge: one of his sons was having a very difficult time. He did not have children and had been undergoing this challenge for quite a few years.

"I am paying for this project," he told them, "with the hope that it will serve as a *zechus* to change my son's situation."

A little later, he sent them a note with the names of his son and daughter-in-law, describing his hopes and dreams for a positive change in their lives. The names were sent to the members of a *Zera Shimshon* kollel which learns Rav Shimshon Chaim's Torah every Thursday night, leading into Friday morning. The kollel members began davening for the couple to merit a *yeshuah* and to be the recipients of the *Zera Shimshon's berachah*: "Your — וְעֵינֵיכֶם תִּרְאֶינָה בָּנִים בְּנֵי בָנִים כִּשְׁתִלֵי זֵיתִים סָבִיב לְשֻׁלְחָנְכֶם eyes shall see children and children's children, like olive shoots around your table."

A year passed, and the team received a phone call from the donor, who was calling them a few minutes after his grandson was born. He was filled with a sense of uplift, joy, and gratitude. And so were they.

כַּפָּהּ פָּרְשָׂה לֶעָנִי, וְיָדֶיהָ שִׁלְּחָה לָאֶבְיוֹן
She spreads out her palm to the poor,
and extends her hands to the destitute.

When With Your Palm and When With Your Hand

Two Questions

The *pasuk* begins with the words כַּפָּהּ פָּרְשָׂה לֶעָנִי — "She spreads out her palm to the poor." In the second part of the *pasuk* we find a different description, וְיָדֶיהָ שִׁלְּחָה לָאֶבְיוֹן — "She extends her hands to the destitute." *Zera Shimshon* raises two questions on this *pasuk*.

Question one: What is the difference between the word פָּרְשָׂה (spreads out) and the word שִׁלְּחָה (extends)?

Question two: Why does the *pasuk* begin with the word כַּפָּהּ (her palm), and not "her hands"? And why does the *pasuk* begin by writing "palm," in the singular, one palm, when later it says וְיָדֶיהָ — "her hands," in the plural?

The Evyon and the Ani

Zera Shimshon writes:

The primary mitzvah of *tzedakah* is to give to a poor person who has nothing at all, and this is the *evyon* (destitute person) referred to in the Torah (*Devarim* 15:7), "If there shall be a destitute person (*evyon*) among you." The source of the word "*evyon*" stems from the root "*to'evah*," desire, in the sense that he wants everything since he has nothing. According to *Chazal*, we are referring to a truly poor person, and there is a Torah obligation to support him and give him charity. (If an *evyon* asks for food, we give it to him immediately, without any investigation. However, if he asks for clothing or other amenities, we may investigate first.) And he who gives charity to the *evyon* will receive great reward.

On the other hand, there are poor people who have enough money to fall back on, and others about whom we are in doubt. In these cases, there is no halachic obligation to support them. However, someone who does give such a person charity is still fulfilling the mitzvah of *tzedakah*. We are therefore told to give this type of poor person at least a smaller amount of *tzedakah*.

When the *pasuk* says she "spreads out her palm" to the poor man, this is referring to the second type of poor person. The *eishes chayil* therefore gives him a smaller amount of *tzedakah*, offering it with one hand and not two.

Not only does she give him a smaller amount of *tzedakah*, she also waits until he is actually standing on her doorstep, because she doesn't know whether he will want to accept *tzedakah*. After all, he's not destitute, and he might have come to the house for a different reason altogether. She therefore waits until he is close by and she actually sees that he wants the money — and then she extends the palm in which she is holding a coin or some food, showing him that he can have it if he wants it.

This is why the *pasuk* uses the term "her palm." She is not extending her hands, merely opening her palm, and giving the poor person the opportunity to accept the charity.

Now we arrive at the end of the *pasuk*. Here we are talking about an *evyon*, a truly poor person, a person who desires everything because he has nothing. To such a person, the *eishes chayil* will give *tzedakah* with both hands, and she will give him a larger donation — because he is really in need and there is a halachic obligation to support him.

This is why the *pasuk* uses the word "her hands" in the plural — since she is giving a larger donation, she needs both hands. This also explains why the Torah uses the term "hands" and not "palm"; since he's an *evyon*, she will not wait until he comes close to give him *tzedakah*. Rather, she will send it to him with a secure heart, knowing that he will accept the *tzedakah*. And we now also understand why the *pasuk* uses the word "extends" to describe how she goes out of her way to send him money, and doesn't wait for the poor person to come to her.

A Very Valuable Gift

Zera Shimshon now discusses the idea that *tzedakah* serves as protection for a person. He explains that by giving *tzedakah*, a person acquires a protection that will help him avoid a *gezar din,* a harsh judgment — and even protect him from death!

How to achieve this kind of merit? *Zera Shimshon* explains:

If you want this *zechus*, the merit of giving *tzedakah* to an *evyon* before the time of a *gezar din* has arrived, a person should make a habit of dispensing *tzedakah* on a regular basis, even if the person that you are giving to is not an *evyon*.

A person should also remember that if Hashem has put the idea of giving *tzedakah* to a particular *evyon* in his mind, it's for a good reason, as it says (*Mishlei* 11:4): לֹא יוֹעִיל הוֹן בְּיוֹם עֶבְרָה — "A treasure will not help on the day of wrath," וּצְדָקָה תַּצִּיל מִמָּוֶת — "[but] charity saves from death."

Zera Shimshon then discusses a quote from the *Zohar* about Avraham and Sarah. It comments on the verse (*Bereishis* 18:11), וְאַבְרָהָם וְשָׂרָה זְקֵנִים בָּאִים בַּיָּמִים — "Avraham and Sarah were old, well on in years." It was at that time that the angels came to tell Avraham and Sarah that they were going to have a child — which is the best gift in the world.

The *Zohar* (*Bereishis* 104a) continues to discuss the idea of gifts from Hashem. "When Hashem loves a person, He sends him gifts. And what is the gift that Hashem sends the person? None other than a poor man." Why this gift? So that the person whom Hashem loves will have the merit of *tzedakah*. And if, Heaven forbid, there is a harsh judgment on this individual, the merit of the *tzedakah* will protect and save him — so that the *middas hadin* will have no power to affect him.

Give Tzedakah Before the Judgment!

Zera Shimshon explains that the *Zohar* is telling us that for the merit of *tzedakah* to protect a person, it must be given before the judgment is decreed. Once a person gives *tzedakah*, the harsh judgments have no power. However, if a person gives *tzedakah* after judgment has already been passed, the merit will no longer help.

Why not?

The Mishnah (*Avos* 4:23) says: אַל תְּרַצֶּה אֶת חֲבֵרְךָ בִּשְׁעַת כַּעֲסוֹ — "One shouldn't try to appease someone while he is angry." Just as one should not try to appease another when he is angry, so too, after harsh judgment has been decreed, showing that Hashem is angry with a person, *tzedakah* cannot help. We see this in *Mishlei* (11:4) where it says: לֹא יוֹעִיל הוֹן בְּיוֹם עֶבְרָה — "A treasure will not help on the day of wrath," which means that even if a person gives a fortune to charity, it will not help once there is harsh judgment against him.

However, the *tzedakah* that he gave earlier will provide salvation, as it says (ibid. 10:2), וּצְדָקָה תַּצִּיל מִמָּוֶת — "[but] charity will save from death." The word תַּצִּיל, "will save," is written in future tense. *Tzedakah* will help when given before the judgment.

Zera Shimshon brings another example (ibid. 11:5): צִדְקַת תָּמִים — Someone who makes a habit of giving *tzedakah* — doing this even when he doesn't know whether the poor person is a true pauper or not; תְּיַשֵּׁר דַּרְכּוֹ — will be sent genuine *evyonim* before he needs them.

On the other hand, the *pasuk* continues, וּבְרִשְׁעָתוֹ — the evil person, who does not habitually give charity; יִפּוֹל רָשָׁע — will not merit to find a poor person to whom he can give *tzedakah*, even when he wants the merit of *tzedakah* and goes searching for someone to give to!

צִדְקַת יְשָׁרִים תַּצִּילֵם — But after a person has merited to give *tzedakah* to an *evyon*, says the next *pasuk,* he will be saved and the judgment will not be able to work against him.

To sum up:

Tzedakah must be given *before* a judgment in order for it to help save a person.

If a person gives *tzedakah* regularly, even to those who are not destitute, he will merit to give *tzedakah* to *evyonim* who truly need it.

The fact that he merited to give *tzedakah* to an *evyon* will grant him the merit he needs to be saved from harsh judgments.

Back to the Eishes Chayil

Zera Shimshon continues:

Since the *eishes chayil* opens her palm and gives at least a small amount of charity to the poor man, never turning him away empty-handed — even though she isn't sure that he truly warrants it — her charity will bring other mitzvos in its wake. She will see that *mitzvah goreres mitzvah* — "one mitzvah leads to another," and Hashem will put the idea into her mind to send a generous amount of money to an *evyon* who genuinely needs the money, before any harsh judgment against her is decreed.

There is no question that giving *tzedakah* is one of the most beloved mitzvos in Klal Yisrael. Whether on Purim to a group of *bachurim*, at the Kosel or other holy sites, or to collectors knocking on doors, millions of Yidden are constantly dipping into their pockets to help those who are less fortunate than they are.

In the following story, told by Mrs. Sylvie Gutwirth-Davidovici, we learn about just such a story — and how one act of *tzedakah* and *chesed* led to another.

Along with several friends, my late husband, Pinny Gutwirth, *z"l*, established an organization in Belgium with the idea of helping many of the sick people who found their way to our corner of the world to deal with their medical emergencies. Pinny decided to call the organization "Yad B'Yad." The goal was to help alleviate hardships for the many people — mostly Israeli — who come to Belgium for heart or liver transplants. The help came in a number of forms.

First of all, the organization went out of its way to translate the medical inquiries addressed to the Israelis and to help them understand what the hospital needed from them. Then there was the question of food. Here, too, Yad B'Yad stepped up. The organization became involved in the preparation and transporting of kosher food to the hospital in Brussels, along with reading material in Ivrit, so the patients would have something to do while awaiting their surgeries.

There were other important things to be dealt with as well. The organization went out of its way to lobby the hospital team of directors to agree to give some priority to visitors who were non-Belgian and non-European. It took a great deal of work, but eventually the hospital agreed to give them some priority on their waiting lists. Even so, it could take many weeks or even months until a compatible organ was found.

In those days, Israel was not yet providing organs for transplant, nor helping to cover the huge costs of surgery done outside the country. Consequently, after the surgery was over and the patients given permission to return home, there were cases when the patients were simply unable to afford the astronomical fees being demanded of them, and ignored the hospital's repeated requests for payment. In those cases, the hospital turned to Yad B'Yad and requested that we cover the costs. Although this was extremely challenging, we would always agree since it was very important to us to avoid a *chillul Hashem*. We also very much wanted to protect the good name of the organization for future transplants.

One day, I was participating in one of our numerous brainstorming meetings, where we tried to come up with different ideas to raise money for the organization. The people at the meeting were mainly communicating with one another in Yiddish. Although I understand the language, I was not exactly fluent when it came to expressing an opinion. Which meant that, instead of participating in the discussion, I sat at the table and spent my time looking at two women at the meeting sitting next to me, whom I didn't recognize. I'd come late and had missed the "meet and greet" part of the meeting. While I was listening to all the talk at the table with one ear, at the same time I was trying to figure out where our unexpected guests had come from.

Twenty minutes into the meeting, the two women stood up. They excused themselves, saying they had to leave early. They turned to me. One of the women opened her handbag and pulled out a very thick envelope, which she handed to me.

"This is what we managed to collect in Brussels for the organization," she said.

Not having expected to receive money from people I didn't even know, I was completely taken aback and just managed to ask her name.

"Mrs. Kapouia," she replied.

When they left I opened the envelope. There was a lot of money inside and everyone at the meeting was extremely happy with the welcome surprise that had come our way. We hadn't even known the women who showed up — and yet, they had come to the meeting and provided genuine support.

I knew I would never forget the moment when the woman reached into her handbag and gave me that envelope. I also knew that I would always remember her name, despite the fact that we had met on all of one occasion.

One day, I received a phone call from someone who identified herself as *Miriam. She called me on a Friday morning. After telling me her name, she asked if she could come to us for Shabbos.

"Where are you?"

"I am studying in a local school," she replied.

Since I like having Shabbos guests, I was about to tell her that she could come, when I suddenly remembered that it might not be the best idea since my parents, who were living in Paris at the time, were planning to come to us in Antwerp for that very Shabbos. I still remember standing there, phone in hand, as I tried to figure out what to do. My husband possessed an exceptional love for the mitzvah of hospitality and *kiruv*. This meant that hosting guests was a frequent occurrence for us. Because there were always people coming and going, and because of all the *kiruv* activities we were involved with, whenever my parents came to us for Shabbos it was always difficult to find private time to spend with them.

"Listen," I said to Miriam, "unfortunately, this Shabbos doesn't look like it's going to work. But I would be very happy to have you a different week."

Just before I got off the phone, I casually asked Miriam where she had received my name and telephone number.

"A woman named Madame Kapouia gave them to me."

When I heard who had recommended that Miriam come to me for Shabbos, I suddenly felt that I couldn't turn her away. It had been Madame Kapouia who had given my husband's organization such a beautiful donation. In my mind, having Miriam for Shabbos was a way to repay her just a little bit for the care and concern that she had exhibited for Yad B'Yad.

"Do me a favor and call me back in five minutes," I told Miriam. "I'm going to try and arrange for you to come to us for Shabbos. I just need to make a phone call first."

I then called my mother, Edith Davidovici. My mother was a Holocaust survivor who had received the Legion D'Honneur from President Jacques Chirac via Rav Sitruk, *z"l*, for her amazing educational work with youth in Paris. A smart woman, it didn't take her long to grasp my dilemma.

"Would you agree to allow me to host Miriam, even though we are having the pleasure of your company this week?"

I explained that I especially wanted to have Miriam because she had been sent by Madame Kapouia.

"Of course she can come," my mother said. "What's the question?"

When Miriam called back a few minutes later, I told her that she was welcome to come, and gave her our address.

So Miriam came to us, and it turned out to be a very interesting Shabbos. She had not had the opportunity to experience an authentic Shabbos before and had an incredible number of questions. Everything she saw was the catalyst for another question, which we were of course happy to answer. Miriam was in her mid-thirties and thinking seriously about settling down and getting married, now that she had finished her education and was working in her chosen career.

Despite the fact that I had agreed to host Miriam, I still wanted to have some time just with my mother. I asked my younger daughter, Nechama, if she could take Miriam for a walk after candle-lighting.

"Do me a favor," I told Nechama. "Introduce her to some of the neighbors. Spend some time in their homes and give them all a chance to get to know her."

Meanwhile, I sat at home and enjoyed a conversation with my mother. My daughter and Miriam returned in time for the *seudah*, and we had a wonderful time that night.

On Motzaei Shabbos, I received a call from one of my neighbors, Mrs. Israel, telling me that she had a fantastic *shidduch* for my friend, whom she'd met during that Friday-night walk.

I was completely taken aback. I hadn't been expecting any *shidduch* ideas to come about from Miriam and Nechama's Friday-night outing. I told Mrs. Israel that she should feel free to jump right in.

My neighbor went straight to work, picking up the phone and making all the inquiries needed to see her idea through. Miriam ended up going out with the person she had in mind, and it wasn't long before we found ourselves at a beautiful wedding organized by the Satmar *kehillah* of Antwerp. Nobody knew any of the people involved — the *chassan* was from one end of the world, the *kallah* from another — but, if anything, that was even more of a reason for everyone to help put it all together.

As I watched the dancing at that wedding, I couldn't help but reflect on the chain of events that had taken me from standing outside an elevator and receiving an envelope filled with *tzedakah* money, to being introduced to a young woman who I just "had" to host for Shabbos, to watching as a *shidduch* was made, to standing at her wedding a short while later.

לֹא תִירָא לְבֵיתָהּ מִשָּׁלֶג, כִּי כָל בֵּיתָהּ לָבֻשׁ שָׁנִים
She fears not snow for her household,
for her entire household is clothed with scarlet wool.

Afraid of the Snow

Snow: Mercy or Judgment?

T he *Shach* quotes the *pasuk* (*Shemos* 4:6): הָבֵא נָא יָדְךָ בְּחֵיקֶךָ וְגוֹ׳ — וְהִנֵּה יָדוֹ מְצֹרַעַת כַּשָּׁלֶג — "Bring your hand to your bosom ... and behold, his hand was leprous, like snow." This is referring to when Hashem told Moshe to place his hand into his shirt and it emerged with *tzaraas* — white as snow.

We also find the word snow used to describe the *tzaraas* that afflicted Miriam when she spoke *lashon hara* about her brother Moshe. These are the only times in the Torah that the word snow is used to describe *tzaraas*.

Zera Shimshon tells us a very interesting fact about snow. Snow, he says, does not come from *din*, judgment. Instead, it comes from *rachamim*, mercy. Though snow does contain some aspects of *din* — it is very cold and has the potential to cause harm — it is primarily *rachamim*, since it waters the ground and provides sustenance. It is very much a form of mercy.

Zera Shimshon continues:

Afraid of the Snow ◆ 141

The *Shach* seems to be alluding to the opinion of Rav Nosson Shapira in his *Sefer Nitzotzim*. There, he writes that snowflakes are *oros*, lights, surrounded by *kelipos*, shells, and even so they are considered mercy that is just tinged with judgment — since they are only falling to sustain the world.

Now let us bring these ideas back to our *eishes chayil*.

The *pasuk* says, לֹא תִירָא לְבֵיתָהּ מִשָּׁלֶג — "She fears not snow for her household." Our *eishes chayil* is not afraid of the *dinim*, the judgments, and the *kelipos* that come with snow. Why is she not afraid? כִּי כָל בֵּיתָהּ לָבֻשׁ שָׁנִים — "Because her entire household is clothed with scarlet wool."

The Word "Shanim"

Let's look at the word שָׁנִים (*shanim*, "scarlet wool"). The word is discussed in a Gemara (*Shabbos* 89b) that is speaking about the *pasuk* (*Yeshayah* 1:18), אִם יִהְיוּ חֲטָאֵיכֶם כַּשָּׁנִים כַּשֶּׁלֶג יַלְבִּינוּ — "If your sins are like scarlet, they will become white as snow."

The word "*shani*" refers to a red thread. The Gemara asks why our *pasuk* in Eishes Chayil uses the word "*shanim*," which is the plural form and implies many threads, when it could have written it in the singular, "*shani*."

Rabbi Yitzchak answers that the word *shanim* has two meanings: "red threads" and "years." In the *pasuk* in *Yeshayah*, Hashem is telling Klal Yisrael: אִם יִהְיוּ חֲטָאֵיכֶם כַּשָּׁנִים — "[Even] if you will do as many sins as all the years combined [since the six days of Creation]," כַּשֶּׁלֶג יַלְבִּינוּ — "[I, Hashem,] will turn everything white as snow."

Zera Shimshon now revisits the Gemara's question of why our *pasuk* in Eishes Chayil uses the word *shanim* (years) in the plural when it should have used the word *shanah* (one year). After all, the *pasuk* uses the word *sheleg* (snow), which is singular. For the *pasuk* to be consistent it should have used a singular term, *shani*, and not *shanim*.

Zera Shimshon concludes that the *pasuk* is coming to hint that the *eishes chayil* is not afraid of the *dinim*, the harsh judgment. Why not? כִּי כָל בֵּיתָה לָבֻשׁ שָׁנִים — Because the way she lives her life, all her years (shanim) bring her much merit, merit that is like beautiful clothing for her neshamah, her soul. And since the word shanim also means colorful clothing, it reinforces the idea that everything our eishes chayil has done through the years has created a magnificent "spiritual wardrobe" for her.

We can find support for this idea in the Zohar's explanation of the pasuk (Bereishis 24:1): "Now Avraham was old, well on in years, and Hashem blessed Avraham with everything." Says the Zohar (Bereishis 224a): A person who lives his life with Torah merits to see his days turned into מַלְבּוּשֵׁי כָּבוֹד — beautiful and impressive garments to use in the World to Come. The opposite is also true; if a person doesn't have Torah and mitzvos, he will come to the next world without the appropriate clothing.

The Zohar (ibid.) writes:

Just as a person's clothing protects him from the cold and snow of winter, so too, the clothing created by his mitzvos will protect him in the World to Come from the mazikim (harmful spiritual forces).

The Children Too!

This pasuk describing the eishes chayil uses the word בֵּיתָה, "her household," making the point that the eishes chayil's merits will not only help her, but will also help her children, the members of her household.

The Gemara (Shabbos 151b) states that a person should always pray not only to be blessed with financial stability, but that his children too should be protected from poverty — it shouldn't afflict him or his children or grandchildren. From here we see that it is not sufficient to daven for ourselves; we need to daven for future generations too.

Our eishes chayil does this well. Through her לָבֻשׁ שָׁנִים — the spiritual clothing that she created with her mitzvos — she provides protection for her household, for her children and grandchildren. This protection shields them from the "snow" — from harsh judgment, and from poverty and from mazikim.

Wintertime: Stay at Home!

No one likes to go outside during the freezing winter days. The commentators on the *pasuk* (*I Divrei HaYamim* 11:22, *II Shmuel* 23:20), הוּא יָרַד וְהִכָּה אֶת הָאֲרִי בְּתוֹךְ הַבּוֹר בְּיוֹם הַשָּׁלֶג — "He [Benayahu ben Yehoyada] went down and killed a lion in the middle of a well on a snowy day," explain that even though it was wintertime and most people want only to curl up in a warm place, even so, Benayahu fought with a lion and vanquished the beast.

Here, too, the *pasuk* is telling us that our *eishes chayil* is not afraid of the cold of winter and doesn't become lazy because of it, as it says, לֹא תִירָא לְבֵיתָהּ מִשָּׁלֶג — "She is not afraid of snow...," which the *pasuk* is using as a term to denote cold. The *Zera Shimshon* mentions a few more *pesukim* that all use the word "snow" as a way of expressing the idea of cold.

Cold does not disturb the *eishes chayil*. Why not? כִּי כָל בֵּיתָהּ לָבֻשׁ שָׁנִים — For her entire household is clothed in scarlet wool. She knows how to bundle up well against the frigid winter weather, giving her the warmth she needs to get things done.

As the Gemara (*Yerushalmi Sanhedrin* 10:5) writes on the *pasuk* (*Tehillim* 147:17), "Who can stand before His cold?": יַתִּיר חַד כִּסוּ וְצִינְתָא אָזְלָא — If it is very cold, put on another sweater and the cold disappears.

So here is still another reason why the *pasuk* uses the word *shanim* in the plural and not in the singular: Because in the winter she needs *shanim* — she must wear more layers of clothing than when it is warm outside.

Adds *Zera Shimshon*: Not only does she make sure to wear enough clothing to deal with any type of weather, she also goes out of her way to purchase clothing that is colorful and appealing.

She has nice clothing, sufficient clothing for her needs, and she never forgets to take the weather into account and dress accordingly, as it says (*Mishlei* 22:5): צִנִּים פַּחִים בְּדֶרֶךְ עִקֵּשׁ שׁוֹמֵר נַפְשׁוֹ יִרְחַק מֵהֶם — which can be translated as:

צִנִּים — The cold

פַּחִים — brings challenges

בְּדֶרֶךְ עִקֵּשׁ — to someone who isn't careful.

However, the wise man שׁוֹמֵר נַפְשׁוֹ יִרְחַק מֵהֶם — will guard himself from the cold and the frost.

From all this we see that the *eishes chayil* is never lazy. She protects herself from the weather, and knows that her exalted behavior in this world will provide her with a beautiful and extensive "wardrobe" in the World to Come.

In the following story we will read about a woman who takes care of herself and her health, while doing her best at the same time to make sure the spiritual components of her life are not overlooked. In the process, Mrs. Leah Ausch learns a priceless lesson.

It was a day I have a feeling I won't be forgetting in a while. As a teacher, I have a pretty intense schedule — and that's without having to deal with medical emergencies. But on the morning of the day in question, I woke up to my tooth throbbing with a powerful pain. I knew that I had to get to a dentist as soon as humanly possible. I ran over to a nearby dental office, davening that they would agree to see me quickly, that they would be able to soothe my pain, and that the whole procedure would be done rapidly enough to allow me to make it to my next class.

That was the hope.

I entered the dentist's office and approached the receptionist's desk.

It was eleven o'clock in the morning when I walked in and told the woman behind the desk that I needed to be examined by a dentist immediately.

She looked at me doubtfully and replied, "I'm very sorry, but the next available appointment is at four o'clock this afternoon."

"You have nothing until then? I'm in terrible pain!"

"Both of our dentists are busy now. Both of them just started with a patient that will take at least an hour, and by the time they are finished, there will be other patients. Like I said, there is nothing free until four."

I knew that it was going to be a real challenge to sit around and deal with the pain I was experiencing until four in the afternoon. Besides, I really needed to get to my classes, which I hated missing! But the receptionist had told me in no uncertain terms that there was no way in the world anyone was going to have the time to help me until four. Which meant that maybe Hashem wanted me to sit in the office and wait until that time — and miss my classes. Bottom line, it wasn't my place to worry about Hashem's calculations. And there was no way I could possibly leave the office without taking care of the pain.

"I will wait," I said.

"No problem," she countered. "Take a seat."

"I will. But you should know, I have a feeling that I'm not going to be sitting here until four in the afternoon."

The receptionist heard what I said and didn't like it. Instead of replying, "I hope you're right," she became a little agitated. "What do you mean? I already explained to you that both of our dentists have started working on their patients and that they are going to be inside for at least an hour each. And when they are finished, other patients will be arriving for their appointments. You're going to be here until four, no doubt about that. But don't worry, we have plenty of chairs and you are invited to sit here for as long as you like…"

It wasn't the nicest response in the world, but she honestly believed that I was going to be waiting there until four.

And so, I found myself a seat and settled in to watch Hashem do His *chesed*.

I didn't have long to wait.

Opening my pocketbook, I removed a copy of my *techinos* and started davening. I was still hoping that the dentist would find the time to take care of my tooth in record time and that I would still be able to make it to my next class. I recited two *techinos*, which took all of five minutes. In my thoughts, I told myself, "I know that Hashem is going to make sure I don't have to wait. There are full classrooms, with girls waiting for me to arrive so I can teach them Torah. I have a feeling that everything is going to work out beautifully."

As I was thinking this, I suddenly heard a loud commotion coming from the back of the office. It was the sound of two people disagreeing with one another at the top of their voices. Not the kind of noise you usually associate with a dentist's waiting room. I couldn't help but wonder what was going on.

A few seconds later, two women emerged into the waiting room — doctor and patient. The patient was loudly insisting that she wanted to go home immediately!

"I didn't know it was going to take so long!" she cried. "When I made the appointment, I thought it was going to be much shorter!"

"How could you have thought that?" the dentist responded, her own voice rising. "You came in for a procedure, and that's the amount of time it takes."

"I thought it was supposed to be a simple thing. But the way you just described it, you were talking about drilling for, like, an hour straight!"

"Of course I'm going to drill your teeth," the dentist yelled at her. "You came in for a root canal! What do you expect to happen when you sit down in the dentist's chair for a root canal?"

"I'm not stupid," the patient shouted back at the dentist. "I understand that you have to drill for a root canal. But when I sat down in your chair and you started telling me what you planned on doing — well, let me just say that no dentist ever put it quite that way before..."

"So what do you want?"

"What do I want? I'll tell you exactly what I want. I want my money back and I want to go home! I'm afraid of the way you described the procedure, and I'm not ready to continue doing this right now!"

"If you cancel on me now," the dentist said, "I can promise you that not only will you not be coming back here for your root canal, you won't be coming back here for treatment ever again!"

Having delivered her final ultimatum, the dentist turned on her heel and returned to her office. The woman went up to the receptionist.

"Listen," she said, "you know me. I've been coming here for a while. But I'm not comfortable with this particular dentist. She's not my regular dentist and I don't like her style. That's why I'm leaving in the middle of the procedure, even though I'm already numb! Do me a favor and reschedule me with my regular dentist. Don't worry, I'll pay for my session here."

The receptionist didn't have anything to say. The woman thanked her for her time before turning to make her way out of the office, numb mouth and all. On her way to the door, she happened to pass my seat.

As she passed by, I could see that she looked very uncomfortable. As if she felt silly for having come in and started a serious procedure — and then leaving in the middle. I stood up and approached her.

"I want to tell you something," I said.

"Yes?"

"There's something I feel you should know."

"Yes?"

"Hashem made you schedule this appointment weeks ago with this very thing in mind. For whatever reason, the dentist decided to walk you through the procedure, instead of just jumping in like everyone else does. Her words made you nervous, which is why you decided to leave in the middle of the treatment, even though you know that the work wasn't finished, and even though your entire mouth is numb.

"I just want you to know that Hashem has a plan for every single person, and that my plan included waking up today with an incredible toothache and the knowledge that I needed to come here right away. For whatever reason, the Master of the World made you feel the urge to get up and leave just when I need to see the dentist. I don't know why, but I know that it's the truth. Perhaps it is because I have several classes with girls who are sitting and waiting for me to teach them Torah. I can't speak for Hashem, but there's no question that He just moved everything around so that I will be taken care of and can go do what I need to do."

The patient listened. When I finished speaking, she smiled at me. It was obvious that she was fine with the way things had worked out.

There's no question in the world that Hashem has a plan for every person. I had come in at eleven. Guess what? By 11:18 that morning, I was already taking x-rays in preparation for my treatment.

"I have only one thing to say to you," the receptionist said when I was done.

"Yes?"

"Hashem loves you!"

I thought about the entire chain of events, how I had been in so much pain, and how I had come into the office hoping that I would be taken care of relatively quickly. I thought about the receptionist's response and how she had basically told me that there was no way in the world I would be taken care of before four o'clock in the afternoon — which was hours away — and how I hadn't been convinced. I thought about the patient who had come in for her appointment and suddenly decided to change her mind and leave for no apparent reason. I knew that it was all part of the incredibly intricate and fantastic way that Hashem runs His amazing world.

And I appreciated it.

Oh, by the way, I made it to class that day.

מַרְבַדִּים עָשְׂתָה לָּהּ, שֵׁשׁ וְאַרְגָּמָן לְבוּשָׁהּ

She made herself luxurious bedspreads,
her garments are linen and purple.

Clothes Make the (Wo)man

The *pesukim* (*Mishlei* 7:16-17) speak of a woman who tempts a youth: "I have decked my bed with spreads (*marvadim*)... I have perfumed my bed with myrrh, aloes, and cinnamon..." In contrast, the *ishah kesheirah*, the *eishes chayil*, makes herself luxurious bedspreads (*marvadim*), seeing to it that her husband wishes to be close with her, for the sake of Heaven. Her modest behavior is described in the Gemara (*Nedarim* 20b). When the *eishes chayil* succeeds in fostering this sort of atmosphere, she will be blessed with children who would have been outstanding even in the time of Moshe Rabbeinu!

שֵׁשׁ וְאַרְגָּמָן לְבוּשָׁהּ — "Her garments are linen and purple." The *eishes chayil* has a robe made of *sheish*, linen, which is delicate and enjoyable to wear. She wears *argaman* as well, which can refer to various types of perfume.

(*Rashi* explains [*Shabbos* 90a] that someone who carries quality *argaman* from one domain to another domain on Shabbos will have to bring a *korban chatas*, even if he just carried a tiny quantity. The reason is that even a minuscule amount of *argaman* is sufficient to provide a delicious fragrance.)

Sheish and Argaman: Another Definition

Zera Shimshon now gives another explanation of the words *shesh v'argaman*. Here, *sheish* is a delicate garment, and *argaman* are colorful garments appropriate for women. *Sheish* is an undergarment worn next to the skin, and *argaman* is outerwear.

As proof, *Zera Shimshon* quotes a *pasuk* (*II Shmuel* 1:24) in which David HaMelech eulogizes Shaul: "Daughters of Israel, weep over Shaul, who would clothe you in scarlet with linen." This refers to the fact that Shaul provided Jewish girls with colorful outerwear, and linen garments to be worn next to the skin, called *adanim*, which are soft and pleasant to the touch. (The Gemara [*Kesubos* 66a] notes that this is a tribute to Shaul, who took care of the girls' needs so that they could make good marriages.)

From the ideas presented here by the *Zera Shimshon*, we can see how important it is for a woman to dress appropriately and to have the proper wardrobe for every season and need that may arise. Of course the *eishes chayil* is just as concerned that the members of her family have all the clothing that they need as well — and will go to great lengths to make sure they are taken care of and provided for.

Please consider the following...

If any of you reading this have ever spent time in the magnificent state of Arizona during the summertime, you will most probably remember that it was hotter there than pretty much anywhere else you have ever been. This is why some residents of Arizona like to leave "The Grand Canyon" state for cooler destinations during the days when the sun blazes most strongly.

One summer, we decided to take a vacation in northern

California. A friend arranged for us to stay at an empty house for Shabbos. We had never met the house's owners, but they very graciously extended the offer for us to use it, and we were glad to take them up on it.

We arrived at the house on Friday afternoon and immediately began preparing for Shabbos. After my three daughters had finished getting dressed, it was time to help my nine-year-old son get ready for Shabbos. I took advantage of his being in the bath to go through his suitcase and lay out his Shabbos clothing for him. I found his suit jacket and tie, his shirt, socks and shoes. Unfortunately, there was one item missing, an item whose importance cannot be over-emphasized.

To my chagrin, I saw that although I had remembered to pack everything he needed for Shabbos — I had forgotten his pants. No Shabbos pants!

This was a problem.

Hoping that I had somehow missed them, I emptied the entire suitcase and went through every item of clothing, wishing I would find them folded up in a corner somewhere. But no such luck.

Now, I know that there are certain children who would not be fazed by this turn of events. Their mothers would tell them that they had somehow forgotten their Shabbos pants at home, and those boys would shrug their shoulders and wear their weekday pants without thinking twice about it.

That, however, is not my nine-year-old son.

I knew that the moment he grasped that I had forgotten to bring his Shabbos pants, he would feel very bad, especially since he takes Shabbos Kodesh and dressing for Shabbos very seriously.

Not knowing what to do, I continued combing through the suitcase, absently musing that maybe the owner of the house had a son close in age to my son, and that perhaps I could look in that hypothetical son's closet to find some Shabbos pants for my son to borrow.

"There's really no way for you to justify rifling through your host's closets," I told myself, and put the idea out of my mind. It was one thing for them to give us permission to use their home, and quite another to start browsing through their children's clothing to see if I could possibly save the day for my son.

At that moment, in the midst of my dilemma, I looked up at the wall and noticed a little sign I hadn't seen before.

It was a plaque that had been hung above the dresser. Written on the plaque was a beautiful poem, entitled "Welcome to Our Home."

I read the poem in fascination, filled with gratitude and admiration for the wonderful people who had allowed us to use their home. But when I arrived at the last line of the poem, I suddenly understood that perhaps my troubles would be solved after all.

This was the last line in the poem:

"If there is anything you need — just ask."

"That's very generous of you," I said, thinking of my hosts. "Especially because there *is* something that I need. I need a pair of Shabbos pants for my son!"

I was rather overwhelmed by the poem on the wall — not only because it seemed to have come to address the very point I was grappling with at that moment, but more, because it gave a special welcome and an offer of assistance to any guests who might be staying in their home.

There and then, I pulled out a piece of paper and a pen from my purse and copied down the sweet poem, intending to display it in my guest room back in Arizona.

I was still in the middle of copying it when I heard my husband open the front door and speak with someone who had come over. Since we were not expecting anyone, I walked out of the room and down the hall to see who had come over, and why. To my surprise, I saw a young boy — about my son's age — standing in the doorway.

"This is Moishy," my husband said. "Moishy lives here, but decided to remain at a friend's house this Shabbos while the rest of his family went out of town. Moishy came home because he wants to take a shower and get ready for Shabbos."

"Moishy," I said, "can I ask you a question?"

He nodded seriously.

"How old are you?"

"I'm ten years old."

"That's very good news," I said. "I want to ask you a favor."

He waited to hear where I was going with this.

"We have a little boy here with us who is nine years old. Right now, he is taking a bath *l'kavod* Shabbos. I packed his suit jacket and his shirt, tie and shoes, but unfortunately I forgot to pack his Shabbos pants."

Before I could say another word, Moishy was on top of the situation.

"Would you like to borrow some Shabbos pants?" he asked me in a very mature and grown-up way.

Without waiting for an answer, he ran to his room and returned a minute later with three pairs of dress pants. He then went to take his own shower and prepare for Shabbos, before returning to his friend's house leaving us completely stocked in the pants department.

When my son was ready to get dressed, I pulled him aside and said, "Rory, let me tell you what happened. I packed your jacket, shirt, tie, and even shoes, but I forgot your Shabbos pants."

He stared at me.

"Guess what?" I said. "Hashem loves you and He just performed a Shabbos miracle for you."

"What do you mean?"

I told him how I really hadn't known what I was going to do for him, and how I had seen the poem on the wall offering us help and encouraging us to ask if we needed anything.

"I had just finished reading the poem when there was a knock on the door. Do you know who was there?"

"Who, Mommy?"

"A boy about your own age. His name is Moishy, and this is his house. The reason he isn't here right now is because his family went away for Shabbos and he decided to stay at a friend's house. But he came home to get ready for Shabbos, and that's why he was suddenly knocking on the door. When I saw him, I asked if he would mind lending you a pair of Shabbos pants. And he was so happy to help that he brought me three pairs instead of one!"

My son was staring at me with his big, wide blue eyes.

"Is he skinny like me?"

I smiled at him and replied, "Try the pants on and let's see."

Even though my little guy usually wears a size 8 slim, somehow Moishy's size 10 slim pants fit him perfectly.

It was the perfect end to a sweet Erev Shabbos miracle — just when I needed one for a boy who really cares about looking his best for the Shabbos Queen.

Author's note:

I might as well finish the story with a poem of my own.

Before we left for our vacation I was ready to dance,
Yet who would have imagined I'd forget my son's pants?
But with a poem on the wall and a surprise knocking sound,
The Master of the World turned everything around...

The Segulah of the Zera Shimshon

"One morning," one of the *Zera Shimshon* team related, "the phone rang in my home at a very early hour, waking me up. I was surprised by the call, and slightly apprehensive. I wanted to know who was calling. Glancing at the caller ID, I saw the number of a donor who helps with the spreading of the Rebbe's Torah on a regular basis.

*Reb Shlomo was a person who had made learning *Zera Shimshon* an integral part of his life and had even helped with the publication of the *Toldos Shimshon*, which Rav Shimshon Chaim had written on *Maseches Avos*. Before the *sefer* was published I had been in frequent communication with Reb Shlomo, but since its release we hadn't spoken much. I couldn't help but wonder why he was calling me at such an hour.

"*Mazel tov*, Reb Yaakov," he exclaimed. "I wanted to let you know that my wife just gave birth to a baby boy!"

While part of my brain wished him a hearty mazel tov, another part was wondering what was going on. After all, I had seen him with children on numerous occasions. This wasn't his first son, which would have explained his calling so early in the morning. Obviously, he was calling me because he connected this particular child to the merits he had garnered for his enthusiastic support for the *Zera Shimshon*. So what was the story?

"I want to tell you something, my friend," he said. "I know what you're thinking. You are probably saying to yourself, "Doesn't Shlomo already have children?"

"The answer is, yes, this is my fourth child, *baruch Hashem*. However, this child was born after a break of ten years. A year ago, I was *mekabel* on myself to learn *Zera Shimshon* and to help with the publication of the *sefarim* that you are releasing on a regular basis. It's been less than a year since I started getting involved, and I have merited to bring a brand-new baby boy into the world!

"I felt an obligation to call you immediately and personally let you know what happened — even at such an early hour of the day — because you were the one who introduced me to the world of the *Zera Shimshon* and you have a portion in my *simchah*. *Baruch Hashem*, since I started learning *Zera Shimshon* I have seen many *yeshuos* in the realm of *parnassah*. But this is so much greater — because now I have the *zechus* to welcome my son into the *bris* of Avraham Avinu!"

נוֹדָע בַּשְּׁעָרִים בַּעְלָהּ, בְּשִׁבְתּוֹ עִם זִקְנֵי אָרֶץ

Her husband is known in the councils,
when he sits with the elders of the land.

Wife in Lakewood,
Husband in Brisk?

Eretz Yisrael or Bavel?

Zera Shimshon asks two questions on this *pasuk*:

Question one: Why is the word *aretz* ("the land") men-tioned here? Couldn't the *eishes chayil's* husband sit and learn Torah with the *zekeinim* anywhere in the world?

Question two: Why is her husband being known in the councils contingent on the idea of sitting with the *ziknei aretz*?

Zera Shimshon explains:

The Gemara (*Yoma* 72b) discusses a verse (*Tehillim* 19:10): יִרְאַת ה׳ טְהוֹרָה עוֹמֶדֶת לָעַד — "The fear of Hashem is pure, enduring forever."

Rabbi Nechunia[2] explains that the *pasuk* is referring to a person who studies Torah in purity, which will enable him to reach the point where the Torah becomes very familiar to him and he will not forget it.

---

2. Our text of the Gemara reads "Rabbi Chanina."

And how does a person come to learn Torah in purity? Through getting married and learning Torah as a married man. Once he is married, his thoughts will be purer and his Torah will stand steady for all eternity.

The Gemara (*Kiddushin* 29b) describes the following discussion on the age-old question — marriage first, or learning first?

Rav Yehudah said in the name of Shmuel: "The halachah is that a man should marry and then learn Torah."

Rav Yochanan didn't understand this. Here he is getting married so that he can study Torah in purity, but how will he be able to learn? After all, now that he is married he is financially responsible for his wife, which means that his mind will be occupied by other considerations that will detract from his Torah learning.

The Gemara explains that it depends where the *chassan* lives. People who live in Eretz Yisrael conduct themselves one way, and people who live in Bavel do things another way.

Rashi explains further:

The people who lived in Bavel would travel from their homes to go study Torah in Eretz Yisrael (kind of what is still done today). And since they are away from their homes (presumably their wives moved back into their parents' homes as long as their husbands were away) they do not have any financial responsibilities on their minds and can focus on their learning to the exclusion of everything else. They can therefore get married and go learn Torah with a pure mind, without having to worry about earning a livelihood.

The people living in Eretz Yisrael, on the other hand, are learning close to home, and the moment they marry, their brand-new financial responsibilities fall on their shoulders. They therefore studied first and then married.

We will now return to our original questions.

The *eishes chayil* provides her own jewelry and adornments. We saw this idea previously in the words "she made herself… bedspreads." Just as she made her own bedspreads, she can make her own jewelry, and does not demand that her husband purchase jewelry for her even though he is obligated to do so according to the *kesubah*.

Because the *eishes chayil* is so self-sufficient and undemanding, her husband can marry and continue learning Torah with a clear and pure mind.

When a person studies Torah in such a pure manner, it remains with him forever, and he will be "known in the councils." Whether he lives abroad and has to leave home to go study in Eretz Yisrael, or whether he lives in Eretz Yisrael and is therefore close to home, he will learn Torah without distraction. He will be able to learn Torah in purity (since he is already married) and with a mind that is not burdened by financial worries, since his *eishes chayil* does her best to help him learn.

That's fine when it comes to her jewelry and clothing; she manages to make it herself. But what about the food they will need? If he has to make sure that she has enough food to eat then he still has financial obligations. How can he concentrate on his learning?

Therefore the very next *pasuk* tells us, "She makes a cloak to sell, and delivers a belt to the peddler." The *eishes chayil* finds ways to make money — all because she wants her husband to learn and to grow in the best and most effective way possible.

The *Zera Shimshon* is teaching that when a wife and husband are truly dedicated to Torah learning, Hashem will take care of them.

Dovy's story is a classic example.

There are some people who are close to Hashem, and it seems to me that because they are so close to Hashem certain kinds of things happen to them. My brother Dovy is such a person. From the time I was a kid, I always knew that if I wanted to become a real *ben Torah*, all I needed to do was follow Dovy's example and I'd find myself on the right path. Dovy always did the right thing: learning when it was time to learn, doing mitzvos when it was time to do mitzvos, and generally bringing our parents tremendous *nachas*.

Now, some of you may think that I'm exaggerating. How good can a *bachur* be, right?

Aware of what's going through your mind, I want to give you an example of something Dovy did that really impressed me. It all started when he was traveling from Eretz Yisrael, coming back home for our sister's wedding. When he boarded the plane he saw that he was seated all the way at the back. Under ordinary circumstances that would have been fine with him, but that day the seating arrangements made him anxious. The El Al flight was scheduled to land fairly late the next morning, and Dovy was afraid that since he was sitting at the back of the plane and would be getting off last, he would not be able to catch Shacharis with a *minyan*.

This possibility had Dovy worried. He was a boy who was scrupulous about davening with a *minyan* whenever possible, and the idea that he might miss that opportunity just because he had been assigned a seat at the back of the plane really didn't sit well with him.

Was there anything he could do about the situation? Dovy thought about it, and concluded that his only option was to wait until things had settled down and then ask a stewardess whether moving closer to the front of the plane was an option.

In the meantime, he sat down in his seat and opened a Gemara. After all, there was no reason to waste time while he waited. When the cabin was fairly full and the luggage stowed up above, Dovy stopped a passing stewardess and asked his question.

"Excuse me?"

"Yes?"

"I was wondering whether it would be possible to see if there are any seats available near the front of the plane. If there are, I would like to switch nearer to the front."

"Any particular reason, sir?"

"Yes. The moment the plane lands in America, I will have to get off as soon as possible so I can get through passport control and take a taxi to the nearest shul. The closer I am to the front of the plane, the sooner I'll be able to disembark and the better chance I have of getting to shul in time to daven with a *minyan*."

The stewardess listened carefully.

"I will see what I can do," she promised.

She returned a few minutes later.

"I found an available seat for you. Are you ready to move?"

"Yes."

Dovy took down his bags from the overhead bin and made his way to his new seat, which was noticeably closer to the front of the plane. The fact that he would be able to get off much faster relaxed him, and he settled into his new seat happy and filled with anticipation at seeing all the family back home.

It wasn't long before they were taxiing down the runway and lifting into the sky. Five minutes into the flight found Dovy with his Gemara out again, busy reviewing the last *suyga* that he'd learned.

Time passed, everyone was settled in. The lights in the plane were dimmed, as most people began to doze. It soon became difficult for Dovy to see the words in his Gemara.

Looking at the console beside him, he found the button to switch on the overhead lamp and pressed it. His seat was bathed in light. With a sigh of pleasure, he resumed learning from his Gemara. That is, until he noticed the person sitting two seats away from him. From the way the passenger's eyes were squinting as he closed them, it appeared that the light from Dovy's seat was shining into his eyes and disturbing him.

Not wanting to learn Torah while causing discomfort to someone else, Dovy reached over and shut the light, making the decision to continue learning in the semi-darkness even though he had every right to use his light.

He had been learning for a good twenty minutes when a stewardess passed by. She glanced down at the boy peering into the *sefer* and was unhappy with what she saw. Leaning closer, the stewardess let Dovy know in no uncertain terms how she felt.

"*Kasheh l'einayim* — this is bad for your eyes," she told him in an authoritative tone.

"The passenger near me is sleeping," Dovy replied. "That's why I had to shut the light. I don't want to disturb him."

"You can't learn like this," she repeated. "It's bad for you!"

Reaching over, she turned on his light.

Dovy didn't bother to respond, especially since her actions

stemmed from concern for him. Instead, he waited until she had returned to the galley before shutting the light again. While he appreciated the fact that she cared so much, at the same time he really didn't want to keep someone else from their hard-earned rest.

The stewardess passed by again a short while later. The same story repeated itself, with her telling him to turn on his light and Dovy letting her know that he didn't feel comfortable doing so on someone else's account. She scolded him, but he held his ground. He was grateful that at least this time she didn't reach over and switch the light back on.

And then came the big surprise.

"I see that you're not going to give in, right?"

He nodded.

"Well, then," she said, "come with me."

"What do you mean?"

"Take your stuff from the overhead bin and come with me."

Dovy removed his belongings from over the seat and followed the stewardess down the aisle and out of economy, and into a spacious seat in First Class.

"You will stay here for this flight," she said. "Here you will have plenty of light to learn by and you won't be disturbing anyone else."

After Dovy told me the story of that flight, I couldn't resist sharing it with a couple of friends. It was just another example of my *tzaddik* brother going out of his way for other people — and Hashem showing how much He appreciated Dovy's behavior.

"I guess I'd better bring along my Gemara next time I get on a plane," my friend Shuey said lightly after I finished relating the story.

"You're missing the point," I told him. "With Dovy, it was never just about the learning. It was about the entire package of what it means to be a Yid. He had his Gemara with him and learned as much as he could throughout the flight.

"That was Torah.

"He asked the stewardess if he could move to a seat closer to the front of the plane because he wanted to be able to catch a *minyan* for Shacharis.

"That was *avodah*.

"Last, but not least, he went out of his way to learn in semi-darkness because he didn't want to disturb another Yid's sleep.

"That's *gemilus chasadim*.

"With such behavior, I don't think there's any question at all why the Ribbono shel Olam gave my brother Dovy a seat in First Class..."

The Segulah of the Zera Shimshon

Just as learning *lishmah* — purely for the sake of Torah — sent Dovy to First Class, so, too, for a mother who decided to do some serious learning, and her son...

"My sister's son was an older single when she was first introduced to the *Zera Shimshon's* beautiful *peirush* on Eishes Chayil," *Mrs. Chaya'le Landau said. "Many ideas were suggested, but nothing was happening and his parents were growing frantic with worry. One day, someone told my sister about the *segulah* of learning the *Zera Shimshon* and about his wonderful *peirush* on every *pasuk* of Eishes Chayil, which he wrote at the beginning of *Parashas Chayei Sarah* in *Zera Shimshon*. My sister decided to start learning this *sefer* as a *zechus* for her son to find a *shidduch*.

"She didn't waste any time. Soon she had purchased the *sefer* and started learning it. Not long afterward, a very good *shidduch* was suggested for her son. Every *shidduch* has its own pace, and this one took some time to conclude — but eventually they were celebrating their son's engagement! In a fascinating turn of events, the *vort* took place on the day my sister made a *siyum* on the *sefer*. Thus, the day that she finished learning the *sefer* was also the day that she finished dealing with the challenge she'd been living with for so long. She couldn't help feeling that the *shidduch* actually moved along according to the pace at which she learned the *sefer* — starting when she started, and ending when she finished.

"When I came to wish her *mazel tov,* my dear sister whispered in my ear, 'I know that you are also dealing with a *shidduch* challenge and that you need to marry off your daughter. I am telling you with my entire heart to learn the Torah of the *Zera Shimshon* and you will see *berachos* and *yeshuos!*'"

סָדִין עָשְׂתָה וַתִּמְכֹּר, וַחֲגוֹר נָתְנָה לַכְּנַעֲנִי
She makes a cloak to sell,
and delivers a belt to the peddler.

Time Management

The Eishes Chayil Business Strategy

*I*n the previous *pasuk* we discussed the idea of an *eishes chayil* making her own jewelry and clothing, thereby allowing her husband to learn with a clear mind.

As we saw, *Zera Shimshon* asked: What about food and other basic necessities that he is still required to provide? How will he be able to learn when he has so many responsibilities on his head?

He explained with the words of this *pasuk*, "She makes a cloak to sell." The *eishes chayil* is so determined for her husband to maximize his potential that she finds ways of doing business, thereby allowing her husband to learn Torah with a clear mind, even if they live in Eretz Yisrael.

Zera Shimshon now raises a question:

The first part of the *pasuk* states that she makes a cloak and sells it, implying that the *eishes chayil* interacts with her clients herself, without a middleman. However, the second part of the *pasuk* says she "delivers a belt to the peddler," which seems to be saying that she sells through a middleman.

Why the switch from managing her business on her own to using a salesman?

Zera Shimshon explains: When the *pasuk* is talking about selling a cloak, it is referring to the type of clothing — such as flowing robes — that were used by everyone and which are made more or less in a one-size-fits-all kind of style. Because nobody has to spend time trying on the clothing, and they are able to just pay and leave, the *eishes chayil* deals with that part of her business on her own, without a salesman or middleman. It doesn't take up a lot of her time and there is no reason to delegate this to someone else.

However, when it comes to the second part of the *pasuk,* she is dealing not with a cloak but with a belt. *Zera Shimshon* brings *pesukim* to show that a *chagor* (belt) is used by both women and men. Moreover, unlike the *sadin* (cloak), which can be purchased without anyone trying it on, the *chagor* has to be measured and tried on to ensure it is the right size. This makes it a much more complicated and time-consuming business.

The *eishes chayil* therefore does not busy herself with this part of the business, but instead she simply manufactures it, letting a middleman take care of selling it. The salesman purchases different sizes and sells everything that people need, but the *eishes chayil* is not involved in this aspect of the business.

In addition to not wanting to waste time, she prefers not to deal with men's clothing, and would rather the middleman take care of that, because of the question of *tznius* (modesty).

Bottom line, the *eishes chayil* is an expert at time management and has too many important things to do to get sidetracked — and modesty is one of her great values.

And this is one of the secrets of her success.

While we are on the topic of time management I want to share a beautiful story that just happens to be about a watch — which belongs to an *eishes chayil* — who was able to learn a timeless lesson from the timepiece on her arm.

It was before Pesach 5779 (2019) when my husband asked me if there was something I had in mind for a Yom Tov present. As a matter of fact, there was. It was expensive, it was beautiful, and I knew that it was something I would treasure for many years to come. I had seen that particular watch while browsing through a store that we frequented on a regular basis, and it had caught my eye. It had dark hands and clear, large Roman numerals that would be easy for me to read even if I wasn't wearing my glasses. I told my husband the name of the brand and described the watch to him as best I could.

My husband purchased the watch and I received it in time for Yom Tov. As you can imagine, I was very grateful to him for going out of his way to buy me such an expensive gift, something that I knew I would be happy to wear for years to come. Since the watch was automatic, I understood that I wouldn't even have to change the battery. The company, however, did advise me to have the watch serviced every three years.

The watch came with a two-year warranty. Because it was such an expensive timepiece and had been manufactured by such a famous company, I had been sure that it would continue to work without any problems for decades. However, that was not to be. In the days after Pesach 5780 (2020), my watch began to lose time. At first, I didn't really pay attention. I didn't make a big deal about it, merely adjusting the time in the hope that it would soon start behaving itself. Unfortunately, it was consistently slow — which, being a watch, meant that it was basically worthless.

I put it away in a drawer. From time to time, I would take it out and give it another chance, hoping that it would work. To my great disappointment, however, the watch did not, and eventually I gave up trying to use it. In all honesty, it was difficult to understand how such an expensive timepiece could give me so much trouble. But even the best companies sometimes manufacture "lemons," and it seemed like this was one of those times.

Finally, I decided that the time had come for me to call the company and see if I could make some headway to try and heal my watch. I dialed the number and spoke with a representative.

"Good morning, *Charles speaking. How can I help you?"

"Good morning, Charles. My name is Mrs. Neiman, and I'll tell you how you can help me. Recently my husband bought me one of your watches as a gift. Unfortunately it has stopped working and I was hoping that you would be willing to fix it for me."

"First of all, ma'am, thank you for calling us about the watch. We take our responsibility to our customers very seriously. The first thing you should do is bring the watch to the store closest to where you live. I'm assuming that they will be able to fix it on the premises."

"And if they are unable?"

"If they are unable, which is highly unlikely, they will send it to the company to be dealt with by our best watchmakers. Rest assured, the problem will be dealt with promptly!"

"Well, that's very good news," I said.

I was all set to bring in my watch when I suddenly had another idea for how to fix it. It was something I had read in the name of Rav Avigdor Miller.

Just the previous week, I had come across a weekly *parashah* booklet containing Rav Avigdor Miller's Torah thoughts. This particular *shiur* pertained to the mitzvah of *bikkurim*. There he wrote that absolutely everything in the world belongs to the Ribbono shel Olam, Who is the *Koneh Hakol* — the One Who created everything and to Whom everything belongs. One of the ways we show our gratitude to Hashem for everything He gives us is by making *berachos*. Rav Avigdor went on to give an example of a person who goes shopping in a supermarket and fills a huge wagon with goods he wants to buy.

"Once you pay for everything in your wagon, you think it all belongs to you," he wrote. "That, however, is not true. The entire shopping cart still belongs to the Master of the World, as do the rest of the goods for sale. And even though we have paid with the swipe of a plastic card or some pieces of colored paper, we must remember that our money is His as well."

I read the words of Rav Avigdor Miller with avid interest. As always, he had summed up his thoughts succinctly and presented deep ideas in a way that anyone can grasp.

The words I'd read prompted me to say something to Hashem on one of the following mornings. Out of the blue, I said, "Ribbono shel Olam, I want to thank you for everything You have given me so generously until now! Thank you for the beautiful watch that You gave me. It still belongs to You, and for reasons that I do not know You have decided to make it go slow. At the same time, I know that You can make it work perfectly if You want, since You, Hashem, are a *Kol Yachol*. I am going to put the watch back on my wrist, and if it starts working accurately again, I will make sure to publicize Your kindness."

I wore the watch all that day, and by the time I took it off that evening I noticed that it worked to the minute. I hadn't even brought it into the store for repairs. Hashem had straightened out the glitch without anyone's help or assistance. I was very grateful to Him for having caused the watch to stop working in the first place, thereby giving me the opportunity to comprehend how Hashem hears every word that we say and think!

I do not have the words to adequately express the feelings that course through me every time I think of how the watch was repaired. It has brought me to a level of *Kirvas Elokim*, closeness to Hashem, that I had never experienced until this time.

I wish I could say that every time I make a *berachah* today I remember to sense Hashem listening to the words coming from my mouth. I also wish that every word I use during davening would be filled with complete *kavanah*. However, I am human and imperfect. What I *can* say, though, is that this story has greatly impacted the way I say the word "*Atah* — You" when reciting *berachos* and during davening. Thanks to the incident with the watch, I have merited to openly see that Hashem is with us all the time. And for that, I am grateful beyond measure.

עוֹז וְהָדָר לְבוּשָׁהּ, וַתִּשְׂחַק לְיוֹם אַחֲרוֹן
Strength and majesty are her garments,
she joyfully awaits the last day.

What's Mine Is Yours...

A Spiritual Wardrobe

*T*he *eishes chayil* gives her husband her full consent to go
to learn Torah. She is reminiscent of Rochel, the wife of
Rabbi Akiva, who sent her husband away to learn Torah for
twenty-four years. In this way she shared in the merit of her husband's Torah learning, as Rabbi Akiva famously said to his *talmidim*
(*Nedarim* 50a), שֶׁלִּי וְשֶׁלָּכֶם שֶׁלָּהּ הִיא — "My [Torah learning] and your
[Torah learning] are hers."

From here we learn that when a woman encourages her husband to learn and gives him permission to focus on his learning to
the exclusion of other activities, she receives a share in his Torah
as well.

Furthermore, the Gemara (*Berachos* 17a) states, "In the merit
of sending their husbands and sons to learn Torah and waiting for
them to come home from the *beis midrash*," they can be calm and

sure that they will have reward in the World to Come.

Chazal also comment on the verse (*Tehillim* 127:2), "... for you who rise early." They say that it refers to the wives of Torah scholars who wipe the sleep from their eyes in this world, for which Hashem rewards them with *Olam Haba* and allows them to bask in the glory of the *Shechinah* (*Yoma* 77a).

Clearly, the *eishes chayil* who encourages her husband to learn Torah can be confident in her reward from the One Above.

Zera Shimshon continues:

We know that all the mitzvos that a person does in this world become spiritual clothing for his *neshamah* (soul). This is what this verse in Eishes Chayil is talking about when it says, "Strength and majesty are her garments." The word עוֹז (*oz*, strength) is referring to the merit of Torah study, as it says (*Tehillim* 29:11), "Hashem gives His nation strength (*oz*)...," referring to the Torah that Hashem gave His nation.

The word הָדָר (*hadar*, majesty) is a reference to the mitzvos, as it says (*Bava Kamma* 9b): הִדּוּר מִצְוָה עַד שְׁלִישׁ בְּמִצְוָה — "When it comes to beautifying a mitzvah, one should spend up to a third of the sum spent on the mitzvah itself." The word *hadar* is used when the Torah is discussing mitzvos that one is supposed to do with extra beauty.

So we have the word עוֹז (strength), which means Torah.

We have the word הָדָר (majesty), which means mitzvos that we beautify.

And we have the word לְבוּשָׁה (*levushah,* her garments), which refers to the idea that her actions will turn into the "clothing" she will wear in *Olam Haba.*

Who's Laughing Now?

Now we are left with the second part of the *pasuk,* וַתִּשְׂחַק לְיוֹם אַחֲרוֹן — "She joyfully awaits the last day."

Zera Shimshon explains this beautifully:

In this world, he says, the *eishes chayil* endures a certain degree of suffering because she starts her life living under her father's authority, and after she marries, she is under the authority of her husband. The *eishes chayil* also suffers because she isn't obligated in all the mitzvos, and even though there are some mitzvos that she is obligated to do, her primary reward comes from her partnership with her husband.

All this, however, is just in *Olam Hazeh*, in this world.

After she passes on, the *eishes chayil* will have the last laugh, because she will not have to return to this world as a reincarnation, a *gilgul*, like so many men. The reason men find themselves being sent back to this world to have another chance is due to the fact that they are obligated in so many mitzvos, and if they don't do the mitzvos properly, they are sent back again to get them right. So while she may be sad at times in *Olam Hazeh* — both because she isn't obligated in all the mitzvos and because she is under other people's authority — she will laugh on the last day, in *Olam Haba*, where she will come to the end of her journey, receive her reward, and not have to return to this world as a reincarnation. For the *eishes chayil*, it is really the final day. She has finished her job and will not have to return. Instead she will go to her restful place, as discussed in *Sefer HaGilgulim,* written by Rav Chaim Vital, the renowned student of the Arizal.

The *eishes chayil* lives her life to the best of her abilities and when it is over, she finds herself the proud owner of a beautiful wardrobe of the finest spiritual clothing — eminently suitable for the World to Come. And because every additional mitzvah is yet another article of clothing, it's heartbreaking when we miss the opportunities that come our way to "purchase" yet another incredible suit or outfit.

Consider the following thought-provoking stories.

Those of you who live outside of Lakewood may not be familiar with the concept of the "January Jolt." Those who do live in Lakewood, however, will unquestionably know what I am referring to. Let me explain.

There is a Judaica store in Lakewood called Judaica Plaza that came up with a brilliant idea to ensure that they have a steady flow of customers even during the month of January, when business is typically slow. January is when Judaica Plaza runs a promotion that brings streams of customers to the store. The idea is simple and very effective. They send you a scratch-off card bearing an undisclosed discount ranging from 10% to 100% off that day's purchase. When you present yourself to the cashier who rings up your purchases, you find out what your discount is. You might be lucky and receive an incredibly fantastic discount — turning your purchase of a *chassan Shas* into the best buy ever. Or you might be only moderately lucky with a ten-percent discount.

Most people find themselves the recipients of a 10% discount. Those who are a little luckier receive 15% discounts, and the rare few find themselves on the receiving end of a 50% discount — or even a whopping 100%!

In need of a couple of items, I decided that I might as well buy them during the month of January, since this would doubtless save me at least a certain amount of *gelt*. When I arrived at the store, I was chagrined to find that they didn't have the set of *sefarim* I was primarily looking for. However, I found some other items I needed and waited patiently on line to make my purchase.

Guess what?

The cashier rang up my purchase. I saw a big smile cross his face as he announced, "Your discount is…100%!"

I guess receiving a 100% discount is a pretty rare occurrence, since everyone on line began oohing and aahing in my general direction.

From behind me, I heard a guy call out, "You could have bought the whole store!"

Now, that is actually not true, since the store has a five-hundred-dollar limit in place for that very reason, and I didn't even come close to that figure. My bill had come to a mere $146. I was suddenly filled with a certain emotion. It took me a few minutes to recognize that it was the very human, "You could have gotten more and missed the boat" feeling. Who would have thought that such a feeling could eat a person up for days?

Not I.

And yet, I found myself bothered by the fact that I had been in a position to make a significant purchase for free and had missed the opportunity. In a way, it felt as if I had chosen lottery numbers for a ticket and changed one number at the last second — the number that spelled the difference between winning ten dollars and a billion dollars. Imagine how that would make a person feel! Although what had happened to me was not even close to that kind of situation, the feeling of having missed out on an incredible discount really rankled.

I'm going to be honest with you. After all, that's the whole point of writing this. If I don't tell the truth, what have we accomplished here? The feeling of having missed the financial boat really did eat me up inside for some time. It was an example of true mental anguish. You might think it odd that I reacted that way, but that's what happened. I had been given a 100% discount and squandered it on a small $146 purchase! Then, after a couple of days, the truth hit me. And the concept that I suddenly understood was the kind of realization that gave me incredible peace of mind.

This is what I came to understand.

When we come up to *Shamayim* after 120 years on earth, we will be shown all the potential mitzvos we could have done. All the potential Torah we could have learned. All the potential merits we could have acquired for the day of our ultimate *Yom Hadin*.

Yet here's the thing, my friends.

Our ticket has already been swiped. There's no going back and nothing to do about all the missed opportunities. Can you imagine the mental anguish our *neshamos* are going to have when they realize how much they missed? I can only imagine how powerful and painful a realization that will be. And I hope that by sharing my story with you all, my realization can wake us up to become better Yidden in our personal lives, and to try our best to stop passing up the many opportunities that Hashem gives us each and every day to utilize for the good of our eternal lives.

After reading this story sent me by a friend from Lakewood, I realized that I had been touched by his message and that he had really tapped into something. And I knew that what he had just sent me had everything to do with a story I had heard from my friend and neighbor, Rav Aharon Pessin, during his Shabbos Ha-Gadol *derashah* the previous Shabbos.

It was a story that happened to a man named Reb Shlomo Reichenberg, the father-in-law of Rav Druck, rosh yeshivah of Yeshivas Nesivas Olam in Bnei Brak. It wasn't a long story, but it contained a message that I knew would resound throughout the ages. In a sense, Reb Shlomo's story was the alter ego of the January Jolt, showcasing the crux of my Lakewood friend's realization in the truest and most profound sense of the word.

Shlomo Reichenberg lived through the Holocaust, suffering like so many members of Klal Yisrael. At one point, he was sent to a relatively small concentration camp with a population of some three thousand inmates. There he tried to stay under the radar as best he could.

One day, as he was walking outside his barracks, he was suddenly set upon by a Jew he didn't know — a man he had never spoken to, a total stranger to him. Inexplicably, and without warning, this stranger began punching and beating him, to the point where he literally caused him to bleed! Shlomo couldn't understand why he was being attacked, but there was no question that the inmate was intent on causing him real physical damage.

"What are you doing?!"

The man continued hitting him with his fists.

"Stop hitting me!" he cried.

But the Jew carried on, beating Shlomo with all his might.

It took a while, but the beating finally came to an end. Shlomo was beaten, bruised, and terribly hurt. Blood was flowing from his wounds, and he was in agony. What was worse than the physical pain, however, was the fact that he didn't have a clue as to why the stranger had chosen to inflict the pain in the first place!

"Why did you hit me?" he demanded. "I don't even know you!"

"That doesn't matter," the other replied.

"It does matter! I don't understand. Why did you lift up your fists and hit me?"

"You will now come with me to Barrack 10," the stranger said. "There we will learn the truth about you, and why I just beat you up."

It was obvious that he wasn't being given a choice. Shlomo Reichenberg followed his attacker to Barrack 10, wondering what lay in store for him.

It didn't take Shlomo long to understand why they were going to Barrack 10. One of the prisoners housed there was the Jew who served as the unofficial arbitrator of all disagreements, arguments, and fights within the camp. Shlomo's attacker was leading him to this man, to be judged — for what, he still did not know.

They were allowed into the barrack and brought before the judge.

"What is the nature of your disagreement?" he asked them.

Shlomo spoke first.

"I was walking outside my barrack this morning," he began, "when this man" — he pointed at his attacker — "began beating me up for no reason. He punched me and slapped me and made me bleed… and I don't even know why! I have never seen him before and have certainly never exchanged two words with him. Yet he decided to attack me unprovoked and for no obvious reason!"

The judge turned to the attacker.

"What do you have to say for yourself?"

"I had a very good reason for hitting this man," the attacker said.

"Yes?"

"I saw him smiling to himself as he stood outside his barracks. Not once, but twice."

"So what if he was smiling?" the judge asked. "Why is that a reason to attack him?"

"Let's analyze the situation," the man said. "Everyone in the camp is slowly starving to death. The Nazis barely give us enough food to keep body and soul together. Now, you and I both know that people who are starving do not smile. And yet, I saw this man smiling — as I said, not once, but twice. Let's take a minute to understand what that means.

"If he is smiling, then it stands to reason he isn't starving, because starving people do not smile. Yet how is it possible that he isn't starving when every single inmate is suffering from not having enough to eat? The answer is simple. The reason he isn't starving is because he is working with the Nazis, who are giving him extra rations as a reward for his collaboration.

"I am sure you will agree that a Nazi collaborator deserves to be beaten even worse than the beating I gave this man! That is why I attacked him."

The judge turned back to Shlomo Reichenberg and said, "He makes a strong argument, or at least raises a solid question. How do you respond?"

Shlomo Reichenberg looked at the judge and at his attacker and made the decision to tell them the secret that lay behind his smile.

"You have just accused me of being a Nazi collaborator," he told the attacker. "You made the erroneous calculation that, seeing me smile, I must be working with the enemy since only then would I have enough food. Moreover, you posited that a person who is starving cannot possibly smile, and that the only way someone in our position can smile is if he has a full stomach. With this calculation you decided to beat me until I bled, because you were sure that I did something wrong and deserved what I received.

"What if you were wrong? What if a person *can*, in fact, smile for reasons that have nothing to do with having enough food? What if a person can smile because he is satisfied with his lot in life for different reasons and in other ways that have nothing to do with the world of food or physical gratification?

"I will explain what I am talking about.

"A few months ago, I and a few of my friends were somehow able to get hold of a pair of *tefillin*. I cannot go into the details of how we managed to do this, but since that great day, I have been able to don a pair of *tefillin* every morning. When you saw me smile, I was thinking about the fact that I have had the merit to wear *tefillin* even here, in this terrible place, and how my connection with the Ribbono shel Olam is still intact, even here, in this form of Gehinnom.

"That is why I smiled, not once, but twice. It had nothing to do with food, and everything to do with the satisfaction I receive from my ongoing connection with Hashem. I am so lucky. I have a pair of *tefillin* to put on every morning. As a Jewish man who has been granted such incredible good fortune, how can I *not* smile?"

Needless to say, the judge ruled in favor of Reb Shlomo Reichenberg.

This was the story that came to my mind when I read the email about the "January Jolt" and the powerful lesson that my friend learned from what happened to him. He came to understand the power of the concept of regret, and how we will feel when we finally comprehend just what we missed out on.

The story of Reb Shlomo, and the beating he received for a smile, is a sterling example of a person who didn't miss the boat and who never allowed the truth to slip away from him. It didn't matter where he was or what was happening around him. To Reb Shlomo, the fact that he was able to put on *tefillin* in the middle of a concentration camp was the biggest privilege in the world, because it meant that he would never have to look back at his life and say, "if only I didn't miss out on a mitzvah"— because he hadn't missed out.

Can there be a better reason to smile than that?

The Segulah of the *Zera Shimshon*

"We moved into a new home not long ago," Reb Yechiel said, "and in the very first week, before we'd even had a chance to unpack, my wife found out that she was sick and was suddenly faced with what could be a real uphill battle. This was a really tough thing to hear. And while the doctor's prognosis was positive, it was still obvious that the journey would be long and challenging. All this was compounded by the fact that it was happening just after the move, to which everyone had been looking forward and which was supposed to be a happy time. The scary news caused us to rethink our decision to move, as we asked ourselves if maybe we should have remained where we were.

"On the second Shabbos after the move, I was sitting in shul, when I happened to notice a Torah *parashah* sheet filled with beautiful *chiddushim* from the *Zera Shimshon*. I was especially excited when I saw that the author had written that learning his Torah helps bring *yeshuos* to a person בְּבָנֵי חַיֵּי וּמְזוֹנֵי — with children, life, and *parnassah*. I had never heard of this *sefer* until then, but for some reason I was struck by everything the *Zera Shimshon* had written and filled with an inexplicable hope that matters were going to work out in the best possible way. I felt as if I had been sent to the shul that night (or maybe to our new neighborhood) so that I would be introduced to the *Zera Shimshon* and his lofty Torah, and through this merit a *yeshuah*.

Suddenly I realized that my fears about the move were incorrect. I had been afraid that perhaps our *mazel* had changed for the worse with the move. Now I understood that in fact the opposite was true. The move had been for our benefit and was an example of the medicine having been prepared before the illness. It goes without saying that I brought the *Zera Shimshon* sheet home, and over the course of our Shabbos *seudah* my wife and I learned the Torah together. We were *mekabel* on ourselves to learn the *Zera Shimshon's* Torah thoughts on a regular basis.

We were in the hospital a short while later, when we saw a Yid walking through the halls with a copy of *Zera Shimshon* in his hands.

"Look," my wife said. "Hashem sent us the *Zera Shimshon* again! It must be a sign that we should purchase a copy of the *sefer* for ourselves! That way we can learn it inside."

I immediately ran out to buy the *sefer*. As soon as I held it in my hands, I found Rav Shimshon Chaim's emotional introduction, with his rare promise and blessing, and I undertook to learn from the *sefer* every day as a *zechus* for my wife to have a complete recovery. In retrospect, when I looked back at the way the entire sequence of events played out, I felt that Hashem had made sure we were in the right place at the right time, helping us move to another home so that we would be introduced to the Torah and the *segulah* of the *Zera Shimshon*.

In an incredible display of *siyata d'Shmaya,* my wife went through a series of treatments with a minimum of hardship and suffering. Somehow, she felt astonishingly good throughout her ordeal. Less than six weeks later, we were given the wonderful news that she was done and now had a completely clean bill of health. The doctors were astounded by how rapidly they had been able to deal with the illness. They made it extremely clear that, in their minds, there was no question that the whole situation was nothing less than a miracle. And since I felt that the power and the merit of the *Zera Shimshon* had accompanied my wife and me throughout our challenge, I wanted to publicize our story so that everyone will understand what a treasure we have in our midst.

פִּיהָ פָּתְחָה בְחָכְמָה, וְתוֹרַת חֶסֶד עַל לְשׁוֹנָהּ
She opens her mouth with wisdom,
and a lesson of kindness is on her tongue.

Beruriah's Mussar Schmooze

Women's Wisdom

Zera Shimshon begins with a question:

The Gemara (*Berachos* 48b) says that נָשִׁים דַּבְרָנִיּוֹת הֵן — "Women are talkative." It explains that women enjoy talking, and they talk a lot.

Zera Shimshon continues with a proof that those who talk a lot are generally more foolish than those who do not, by quoting a *pasuk* (*Koheles* 5:2) that states: וְקוֹל כְּסִיל בְּרֹב דְּבָרִים — "The voice of a fool [is evident from] his abundant speech."

In addition, we find another *pasuk* (ibid. 10:14) that says: וְהַסָּכָל יַרְבֶּה דְבָרִים — "It's the foolish person who speaks much."

Above and beyond all of this, *Chazal* relate (*Shabbos* 33b) that נָשִׁים דַּעְתָּן קַלָּה — "The minds of women are easily swayed," a statement that seems at odds with the idea of women being filled with wisdom.

Yet Shlomo HaMelech describes the same women who talk excessively with the words, פִּיהָ פָּתְחָה בְחָכְמָה וְתוֹרַת חֶסֶד עַל לְשׁוֹנָהּ

— "She opens her mouth with wisdom, and a lesson of kindness is on her tongue."

The answer?

The *eishes chayil*, says the *Zera Shimshon*, does not talk a lot. She does not open her mouth to speak for no reason and for no purpose. On the contrary, regarding the *eishes chayil*, פִּיהָ פָּתְחָה בְחָכְמָה — "She opens her mouth with wisdom," and as everyone knows, most wise people use their words sparingly.

Zera Shimshon continues:

Not only does the *eishes chayil* not talk a lot, she also encourages others to keep their conversations with her to a minimum. This is why she is referred to with the words וְתוֹרַת חֶסֶד עַל לְשׁוֹנָה — "And a lesson of kindness is on her tongue."

As the Gemara (*Eiruvin* 53b) states:

Rabbi Yose HaGlili was traveling and he encountered Beruriah, the wife of Rabbi Meir.

"Which is the best road to take into the city of Lod?" he asked her.

"You foolish person from the Galilee!" she replied. "Didn't the Sages say אַל תַּרְבֶּה שִׂיחָה עִם הָאִשָּׁה — 'Avoid having lengthy conversations with women'? You should have kept your question to a minimum and asked, 'Which road to Lod?'"

This, then, is what *Chazal* mean when they write וְתוֹרַת חֶסֶד עַל לְשׁוֹנָה. Not only does the *eishes chayil* herself keep conversation to a minimum and treat her words with reverence and care, she is also able to teach others to do the same, instructing them in the art of talking less and not more.

Some people talk a lot. They feel as if the only way they can make their point is if they repeat themselves over and over. Other people are like our *eishes chayil* in the sense that while they specifically do not talk a lot, when they finally do say something it makes a major impression.

Our *eishes chayil* wields her words with tremendous wisdom and uses her mouth with true *chochmah*. And at the end of the day, sometimes a few powerful words can make all the difference in the world. In the following powerful story, told over by Mrs. Erika Salczer, you will see how one line — one line! — can change a person's life in the most profound way.

Shmuel Beller was raised in a city called Auschwitz. It had never been a particularly well-known city, but it was destined to become one of the most infamous cities in Jewish history. As a child, Shmuel never dreamed of what lay in store for him and his family. But the day arrived when the neighboring German hordes crashed over the border and invaded. It didn't take them long to conquer Poland, especially since the Germans were fighting with tanks and planes, which the Poles greeted with the pride and might of Polish horse-flesh.

When he was twelve years old, Shmuel was taken from his home. Through the traumatic years that followed, the young boy forgot everything he had seen in his parents' home. He had been taken before his bar mitzvah. He hadn't even had the opportunity to don a pair of *tefillin* while standing beside his father in the local shul. The challenge of remaining alive was a daunting one and it left no room for anything else for many of the prisoners.

And so, while there were heroic Yidden who risked their lives on a daily basis to avoid any taste of *treife* food, to keep Shabbos or to bury the dead, Shmuel spent his days and nights merely trying to survive. Somehow, he succeeded. It took many years, but eventually the Allied planes were flying overhead, dropping their payloads of bombs on the cities of the enemy. Winter turned into spring and spring into fall, and another year passed bringing more hope in its wake. Soon the Nazis were no longer as self-assured as they had been. They were growing more nervous. And then, one day it was over. The Nazis had fled.

They were free.

For some, freedom meant the ability to return to the ways of their fathers. For Shmuel Beller, being free meant that he was able to walk outside, gaze at a sunset, and buy a drink in a grocery store. No thought crossed his teenage mind about candles on a Shabbos table or the feel of a tall, sturdy *lulav* in his hand. Others, yes, but not Shmuel. He was just happy to be free.

It was Shimon Salczer who would make all the difference in Shmuel Beller's life. It was one thing for a Yid to act a certain way when his life was in constant danger. But they were in the D.P. camps now, and there was no longer any reason to simply survive. It was time to return to the ways of their fathers.

One day, they were sitting together in the dining room. Shimon was eating kosher food, while Shmuel consumed a *treife* sandwich. Shimon looked at the young man with compassion. While there were some people who might have raised their voices at the sight of a Jewish teen eating whatever he wanted, Shimon didn't see the point of that. In his mind, the only way he would ever be able to make a dent in the wall that encased the teenager sitting across from him was by speaking softly and with genuine empathy.

Looking into Shmuel's eyes, Shimon Salczer said softly, *"You are free now! How much longer...?"*

The words were deceptively simple.

"You are free now. How much longer... ?"

A simple line, but there was no denying the depth of the message.

Shimon's words flew out of his mouth, across the table and into Shmuel's heart, where they sank into the moist earth and laid down roots. The words reverberated through Shmuel's mind: *"You are free now, you are free now, you are free now... How much longer...?"*

Soft yet powerful, the words succeeded in entering Shmuel's soul and shifting him ever so slightly. But Shimon didn't stop there. He took it upon himself to introduce Shmuel Beller to Rav Yekusiel Yehudah Halberstam, the Klausenberger Rebbe. This was the beginning of a relationship that would last for the rest of Shmuel Beller's life.

Many decades passed. I was introduced to Shimon Salczer, and the two of us married and raised a beautiful Yiddishe family. Shmuel

Beller did the same. Neither of them knew what had happened to the other. It was as if they had had one reason to meet, and now that the crucial words had been uttered and the message received, there was no longer any reason for them to see one another again.

Shimon never told his family the story of what had occurred on the benches of the D.P. camp dining room. A humble man, it wasn't his style to talk about himself.

One day, a relative of the Salczer family was listening to an interview on Kol Halashon. The subject of the interview was a man by the name of Shmuel Beller, and he was telling a fascinating story of survival during the war and what came later. During the interview, they touched upon the years after the war and his state of mind when everything had finally settled down.

"The truth is," Beller said, "I wasn't holding by religion at that point. I hadn't kept anything in the camps, and I didn't even consider returning to the ways of my parents and grandparents when the war was over."

"So what happened to turn things around for you?"

"What happened was this. One day I was sitting and eating a sandwich in the dining hall. The sandwich was not kosher. I didn't even pay attention to that. I had been eating whatever came my way for so long that keeping kosher wasn't even a factor.

"But then a man whom I didn't even know made a comment to me that changed everything."

"What was his name?"

"Shimon Salczer."

"What did he say?"

"He looked at me and said in a soft, almost pleading tone, 'You are free now.' Then, using the same soft tone, he asked me how much longer I would live that way.

"There was something about the way he spoke to me… something about the sound of his voice that made an impression. He didn't yell at me. He didn't take me to task. He simply reminded me that I didn't have to live that way anymore. That I could do whatever I wanted now and return to the life I had been living before the entire world went insane."

"Was that all?"

"No. Then Shimon introduced me to the Klausenberger Rebbe. And I never looked back."

My relative called me up when the interview was over. He was very excited. When I answered the phone, he told me the whole story. He said that a man named Shmuel Beller had just credited my husband with saving his spiritual life.

Naturally we were all very happy to hear such a story. I would have loved to ask my husband about it, but he was no longer among the living. Still, the idea that a few words on his part had altered the course of another Jew's life was something that inspired me beyond all measure.

In 2019, my daughter-in-law recommended me as a participant for a Holocaust program taking place at Magen David Yeshiva in Flatbush. The program was called "Names Not Numbers" and had been in existence for fifteen years. Holocaust survivors would participate, and I agreed to be interviewed. Although I am not and never was much of a public person, I felt it was vital that today's teenagers have the opportunity to interview and meet people who witnessed the worst atrocities mankind has been able to devise.

The interview took place at the school, where I was asked questions by six articulate and empathetic young people, all of whom were well prepared and familiar with the subject at hand. The interview was being filmed. I spoke with them for as long as they wanted, and then they told me that footage of my interview was going to be shown at an upcoming dinner along with the interviews of an additional four survivors.

The night of the dinner arrived. I sat in my seat and ate the delicious meal that was served. But my mind was far away — in the years of the war, and the memories that had resurfaced (not that they had ever truly disappeared).

I watched the interview of one of the other survivors in the darkened ballroom.

He told his story.

How he was born in Auschwitz.

How he was twelve when the war broke out.

How he didn't keep any mitzvos.

How he was eating a sandwich when a man saved his life with a few well-chosen, yet simple words.

It was Shmuel Beller, and he was telling the story of how my husband saved his life.

I found my son in the hall and whispered in his ear, "That's Tatty's story!"

My son approached Mr. Beller and introduced himself. It was a very satisfying moment. Something akin to the closing of a circle. For years, Mr. Beller had been telling his story, crediting my husband for saying the right words at the right time. Now we were finally together.

Recently I decided the time had finally arrived for the two of us to talk. I tracked down his number and called him up.

"It's Erika Salczer," I said, introducing myself.

"Your husband was my good friend," Shmuel Beller said to me. "A good friend in the sense that he saved me from living a *goyishe* life…"

I thought about what he said for a long time after the conversation was over. He was right. My husband had been a good friend to him. Maybe the best friend a person could have. *Baruch Hashem*, he was there at the right time and didn't hesitate to speak when he felt there was something important to say.

I was proud of my husband, and proud of his friend.

Two Yidden who did what they could to live the right way.

The Segulah of the Zera Shimshon

Sometimes one line is all it takes to change a situation. That's what happened with Shmuel Beller. And that's what happened when someone else gave his friend a timely piece of advice.

I sell the work of the special Yidden who spend their days writing *tefillin, mezuzos, Megillos* and Sifrei Torah. Not long ago, something interesting happened — something that I can't comprehend.

This is the story.

I was involved in a deal between a *sofer* and a Jew who wanted to purchase a Sefer Torah and make a *hachnasas Sefer Torah* in the shul where he davens. Part of my job is to stay in touch with the *sofer,* to make sure that he is making progress on the Sefer Torah and ensure that it will be ready at the agreed-upon deadline. I also check his work, because I want him to know that I expect the writing to be done on the highest level. Every month I receive the work that has already been finished and send it to be checked, making sure that everything is as *mehudar* as possible.

The *sofer* sent me the final pieces of the Sefer Torah a few days before I was supposed to give it to the buyer, which gave me enough time to assemble the whole thing. But when I arrived home, I was unable to find the final pieces. I looked everywhere — to no avail.

I had been in many places that day and had no idea where I might have left the lost *yerios* (sheets of parchment). They could have fallen down near the Mir — or across the city. I was truly at a loss. I cannot describe how upset I was at the thought that the holy pieces of parchment might have fallen down somewhere and were lying in a disrespectful manner in the street. It wasn't about the money — though the loss was potentially huge. I was terribly disturbed at the idea of holy pieces of Torah in a state of disrespect. I was unable to fall asleep that night.

I updated the buyer about the possibility of a delay and indicated that we might have to hire the *sofer* to write the lost pieces again. Even if they were found, there was a good chance that they would be *pasul,* having lain on the wet pavement. The buyer was understandably distraught, and that caused me more pain on top of everything else. What can I say? It was a very challenging time for me.

♦♦♦

The next day I decided that I had better let the *sofer* know that he should begin rewriting the end of the Sefer Torah. But just before I gave him a call, I happened to tell the story to a friend of mine.

"Before you take the next step," he said, "I want to give you a little piece of advice."

"What are you talking about?"

"You are part of a group of people who learn the *sefer Zera Shimshon* on a regular basis, right?"

"Yes."

"So why don't you promise to make a significant donation toward the publication of the *Zera Shimshon's* Torah, and ask Hashem to find the missing *yerios*, in the *zechus* of the regular learning that you do and in the *zechus* of the *tzedakah* that you are now giving for the public's Torah learning?"

I liked the idea. Wasting no time, I immediately promised to give a respectable amount of money to spread the *Zera Shimshon's* Torah if I found the missing *yerios*.

A few hours after I made my promise, I was walking down the street when I suddenly noticed a small sign hanging on a wall. The sign explained that someone had discovered a package of *yerios* in a place where I would have never thought to look for them.

"Please be in touch with *simanim* (identifying details), so that the *yerios* can be returned to their proper owner."

I had plenty of *simanim* to give the finder, and I called the number. Within the hour, the *yerios* were back in my house. I was overjoyed to discover that nothing had happened to them and that they were still kosher and *mehudar*. There was no question that the *Zera Shimshon* had come through for me in the greatest way!

צוֹפִיָּה הֲלִיכוֹת בֵּיתָהּ, וְלֶחֶם עַצְלוּת לֹא תֹאכֵל
*She anticipates the ways of her household,
and does not partake of the bread of laziness.*

One *Breakfast* Coming Up

A Good Start

*C*hoshen Mishpat (337:19) states that a worker may not refrain from eating or sleeping properly, even after working hours. The reason this is forbidden is that it will cause a loss to his employer, since the worker will be unable to do his job properly if he is weak.

The Mishnah (*Demai* 7:3) discusses a worker who receives his food from his employer. What should the worker do if he suspects that his employer hasn't taken *maaser* from the food? The first Tanna in the Mishnah says that the worker should take *maaser* from the produce and then he may eat of it. But he should not eat the first fig, which would have been given to the Kohen as *terumas maaser* [i.e., ten percent of the Levi's *maaser*, which is given to the Kohen], since the prohibition of eating *terumas maaser* is very serious.

Rabban Shimon ben Gamliel, on the other hand, argues with the first opinion, saying that the worker should eat that fig, since if he does not he will be hungry and unable to work in the best possible way.

Once again, we see proof that a worker who doesn't eat as much as he needs to be satisfied and full will be unable to accomplish all that he needs to do.

The Gemara (*Bava Kamma* 92b) tells us that the Sages say, "Make sure to eat breakfast every day. In the summer, the bread you eat will protect you from the heat, and in the winter it will save you from the cold."

There is another well-known saying: "Even if a person runs around a lot and is used to moving quickly, he will not be able to equal the quickness and agility of someone who eats breakfast every morning."

All this brings us back to our *eishes chayil*, who epitomizes the words צוֹפִיָּה הֲלִיכוֹת בֵּיתָהּ. The word צוֹפִיָּה means "she looks ahead" — in other words, she looks ahead at the day in front of her — and she takes note of everything she needs to accomplish for her household.

And because there are so many things on her to-do list, וְלֶחֶם עַצְלוּת לֹא תֹאכֵל — "She does not partake of the bread of laziness." That is, she makes sure not to be lazy about eating breakfast, so that she will have the necessary strength to do everything on her list and won't feel any weakness throughout the course of her long and arduous day.

Eating breakfast every morning has long been recognized to be a smart move. It gives a person strength for the day ahead of him, and is highly recommended by our *Chachamim*, as well as health and nutrition experts of every stripe. And while the idea behind a good breakfast comes from the recognition that a body needs fuel to sustain itself, it's a known fact that offering people something delicious as an incentive is a true and tried recipe when it comes to filling a hall at an event, or at a *shiur*.

The story of Reb Peretz Chaim Levin and the Coolatta incident is a prime example of how using food for the right reasons can help a person achieve maximum results. Like anything in life, food, when used correctly, is an incredible motivator and can help a person reach the stars. I will now turn the floor over to Rabbi Levin so he can tell you all about it in his own words.

I am a proud member of MDY. That stands for Mercaz Daf Yomi, a *daf yomi shiur* given by Rabbi Eli Stefansky, who lives in Ramat Beit Shemesh and delivers a live *daf shiur* every day. This *shiur* is viewed by close to eight thousand people on a daily basis.

The Flatbush members of MDY were initially getting together every Motzaei Shabbos Mevarchim to watch the *shiur* on Zoom. (We can watch it Motzaei Shabbos, since it's given in RBS at 7:15 a.m. on Sunday mornings!) At a certain point, we decided to try and see if we could get together every Motzaei Shabbos and make learning together a weekly thing. Unfortunately, attendance was not as strong as I wanted it to be. Due to the time difference, the *shiur* takes place very late at night in Flatbush. I found myself thinking about what I could do to help make our Melaveh Malkah/*daf shiurim* stronger.

One Motzaei Shabbos, I decided to purchase a Coffee Coolatta at Klein's Ice Cream House on Avenue M before heading over to the *shiur*. My reasoning was simple. I knew that if I had myself a nice large cup of java, I would find it a lot easier to stay awake during the *shiur* — something that can be difficult at times, since I am very involved with running Pirchei groups on Shabbos and am usually fairly exhausted by the time Shabbos is over.

I picked up a drink for myself and headed over to the *shiur*. When I arrived and found a seat, one of the group took a look at my Coolatta.

"That looks really good," he said.

I couldn't argue. It did look really good — and it tasted even better than it looked. In an interesting twist, his observation bore fruit. Later that night, after the *shiur* was over, I found myself thinking about the fact that we couldn't seem to get the *shiur* off the ground on a weekly basis, and tried to come up with ideas for making it happen.

Suddenly, I had a brainstorm.

"Just tonight, you came into *shiur* holding a specialty drink and someone commented on how enticing it looked. What can we learn from this?" I asked myself. "Simple. We can infer from that conversation that people get excited about a nice plate of food and a delicious drink. What if I channel our normal desire for good food into a way to convince people to attend the *shiur*?"

At that moment, I decided that instead of just picking up something delicious to help me stay awake, I would offer refreshments to anyone who made an effort to attend the Motzaei Shabbos *shiur*.

And so it began.

I decided that I would supply Coffee Coolattas and pizza as an inducement for the *chevrah* to show up. During the days that followed, I reached out to many members to let them know what the menu was going to be on the coming Motzaei Shabbos. I got some positive feedback and was hopeful that we would have a larger crowd than before.

When Motzaei Shabbos came around, I figured I would call up the Ice Cream House and the pizza shop and ask them to prepare my order to be picked up at around 11:30 p.m., which would give me enough time to have everything ready and set up by 11:45 p.m. (As I said, the *shiur* takes place late at night. That's why strong coffee is so important…)

Both culinary establishments are located on Avenue M, just a short distance from one another. This was very convenient for me, since I knew I would be in a rush to get to the *shiur* with enough time to set everything up before the others arrived. I called the pizza shop and successfully placed the order. When I called the Ice Cream House, however, things did not go as smoothly.

"Hi, I would like to make an order for ten Coolattas," I told the person at the other end of the line.

"I'm sorry," he replied. "We have a long line of people here right now and I can't take your order. Please come in and we'll prepare the drinks then."

This threw a bit of a monkey wrench into my plans. It was already close to 11:00 p.m. and I still needed to get to the store, place the order, wait until it was ready, and then go set up at the *shiur*.

At the same time, I couldn't blame the worker. There were many customers in the store and he needed to focus on them.

I quickly got into my car and drove over to the store. To my great relief, by the time I arrived everyone who had been waiting on line earlier had been served and I was able to give my order right away. I ordered my drinks and waited for them to be served.

A few minutes later, another customer walked into the store and ordered an ice cream. As he stood beside me, I saw him looking at the counter where my ten Coolattas were lined up in a row, waiting for me to pick them up and take them away.

"Can I ask you a question?"

"Sure," I replied. "What's on your mind?"

"Why do you need so many drinks?"

"I'm bringing them to a *daf yomi shiur* that I attend."

"Why are you learning the *daf* so late? Shabbos ended hours ago!"

"Our group is participating in a live Zoom *shiur* being given by a *maggid shiur* in Eretz Yisrael."

"Is the *maggid shiur* Reb Eli Stefansky?"

"Yes, it is."

"I listen to his *shiur* every so often," he said. "If this is what these drinks are for, then I want to pay for all of them!"

The next thing I knew, he took his credit card out of his wallet, gave it to the cashier and told him to put all ten Coolattas on his bill. I was floored that someone whom I had never met would do such a thing!

"What's your name?" I asked him. I wanted to offer the appropriate gratitude for his beautiful gesture.

"I don't want to tell you my name," he replied. "But my mother passed away a few months ago and I want to do this as a *zechus* for her *neshamah*.

"What was her name?"

"Regina bas Simcha."

He then became very emotional.

"This is real *hashgachah pratis*," he told me.

"What do you mean?"

"Over Shabbos, I wanted to encourage my son to learn in his grandmother's *zechus*, and I promised him that after Shabbos I would reward him by giving him a treat from the Ice Cream House. I came here tonight to fulfill my end of the bargain — and was just given another opportunity to bring merit to my mother!"

Now it was my turn to be overcome with emotion, and we both hugged.

"*Mi k'amcha Yisrael*," I thought. "Can you imagine if I had been able to place the order over the phone? None of this would have occurred! *Baruch Hashem* for the long line in the store when I made the call!"

We said goodbye a few minutes later and I left to make my next stop at the Persian Pizza Place on Avenue M, to pick up the three pies I had ordered.

It was 11:30 p.m. I was back on schedule.

When I reached the store, the man behind the counter was also curious as to why I needed three pies of pizza so late at night. I couldn't help thinking, "Here we go again…"

"I need the pizza for a group of guys who are about to watch a live *daf yomi shiur* via Zoom. It's late at night, and I know that they are probably tired and want to go to bed, so I'm buying some pizza to make the *shiur* even more enjoyable."

"You know something?" he said. "I always wanted to start doing *daf yomi*. I just never got around to it. Can you recommend a good *shiur* for me to join?"

Of course, I immediately launched into my MDY pitch, explaining what the *shiur* is, how many people watch it around the world, and how many lives have been altered for the good because of their newfound commitment to Torah and daily learning.

He heard me out. After I was finished he asked, "How do I join?"

Before I left the store, I gave him all the info he needed to sign up, so that he, too, could bring the true *simchah* and *geshmak* of learning into his life.

Talk about a productive night!

קָמוּ בָנֶיהָ וַיְאַשְּׁרוּהָ, בַּעְלָהּ וַיְהַלְלָהּ
Her children stand up and praise her;
her husband, and he lauds her.

Like Mother, Like Son...

A Tribute to Mom

Children are a living testimony to the essence of a woman.
The Gemara (*Yoma* 47a) tells the story of Rabbi Yishmael ben
Kimchis. Kimchis was a woman who merited to see two of
her sons serve as the Kohen Gadol on the same Yom Kippur, and
the rest of her sons serve as Kohanim Gedolim as well.

"Why do you think you were *zocheh* to such a thing?" the Rabbis asked her.

She explained that she attributed it to her care in covering her
hair.

From this story we can see that the way children act is a tribute
to the integrity, behavior, and overall merit of the mother.

This is what the words קָמוּ בָנֶיהָ וַיְאַשְּׁרוּהָ are coming to teach
us.

When קָמוּ בָנֶיהָ — "her children stand up," that is, when they
have grown up and have become great people in their own right;
וַיְאַשְּׁרוּהָ — they show the "*yashrus*" (integrity; similar to the word

"*vaye'ashruha*" that is used here) and the unique and special characteristics of their mother by the way they turned out.

We find a similar idea in *Yalkut Shimoni* (*Bereishis* 135). The *Yalkut Shimoni* asks why the Torah describes Yitzchak Avinu's passing but not Rivkah's. The Midrash answers: So that no one should hear the news and curse her, saying, "Woe to the womb that bore a son like Esav!"

(Author's note: There are always exceptions to the rule, and nowadays in many cases children behave in ways that have little or nothing to do with the parents — who did everything right...)

The "Crown" of His Wife

Zera Shimshon now moves on to the next words in the *pasuk*, בַּעְלָהּ וַיְהַלְלָהּ — "her husband, and he lauds her."

A *pasuk* (*Mishlei* 12:4) states: אֵשֶׁת חַיִל עֲטֶרֶת בַּעְלָהּ — which means, says the *Metzudas David,* that a husband takes great pride in the actions of his wife.

The Midrash (*Bereishis Rabbah* 47:1), when discussing the *pasuk,* "Your wife, Sarai; don't call her name Sarai..." (*Bereishis* 17:15), says: בַּעְלָהּ נִתְעַטֵּר בָּהּ וְהִיא לֹא נִתְעַטְּרָה בְּבַעְלָהּ — "A husband wears his wife's behavior like a crown, but a wife does not do the same."

Where do we see this?

We find that Avraham Avinu took great pride in the fact that Sarah Imeinu was a prophetess. Says the *Zera Shimshon*, every husband who has the good fortune to be married to an *eishes chayil* takes great pride in her actions and is justifiably proud of his wife.

But then he raises a question: Do you want to say that Sarah Imeinu had greater merits than her husband, Avraham? Could it be that she was on a higher level than Avraham Avinu, who was tested with ten *nisyonos* and passed them all?

And since we know that Avraham Avinu was so great — why would Sarah Imeinu not take pride in her husband?

He finds a possible answer in a *Tosafos* (*Kesubos* 2b, s.v. "*matzi amrah*") that says that a wife is called the "field" of her husband, but the husband is not referred to as the "field" of his wife. So while she can very well have pride in her husband, she cannot refer to him as her crown, since he is not called "hers" — while she can be called "the crown and pride" of her husband.

The *Zera Shimshon* makes a beautiful point: We can tell how special an *eishes chayil* is by the children she has raised. When we see a child — or an adult, for that matter — acting with *derech eretz* and concern for others, chances are there is an *eishes chayil* who raised him and taught him well. The following story is a classic example of a child who was raised to make the perfect move — for his mother — and did so.

In the final analysis, she succeeded in her mission.

I first met *Sruly when he showed up at the yeshivah in Eretz Yisrael where I teach. Since this yeshivah is for boys who are in the process of making changes in their lives, he wasn't wearing a white shirt when I met him. But there was something about him that made me feel he had a good chance of turning things around and going the distance. Whereas some guys that come to yeshivah choose to spend a lot of their time hanging out and manage to avoid the *beis midrash*, Sruly did come to *shiur* and we had many conversations — talks that resonated for their honesty, and for his willingness to take on things from which the other boys were shying away.

But there was something weighing on him — and had been from the first minute he stepped into the yeshivah. I only learned about it a few weeks into the year, when he asked me if we could talk.

"Sure," I said. "When?"

"Tonight, after night *seder*?"

"No problem."

When the time came, we sat down together for a long talk.

"What's up?" I asked him.

He was silent for a minute. There was a serious look on his face.

"Sruly, what's going on?"

"Rebbe, I have a friend back home. His name is Eliyahu."

"Yes?"

"Eliyahu is sick. He's been sick for a while. We speak pretty often, even though he's in America and I'm here. I wanted to know if you could daven for him."

I was touched by his care and concern for his friend.

"Of course," I said. "What's his and his mother's full names for *Tehillim*?"

Sruly told me the names and I wrote them down.

"Keep me posted," I said.

"I will."

And he did. Every few weeks, I'd get a report on the friend's condition and how his treatment was progressing. It wasn't always bad. Sometimes it sounded like there was a chance that his condition was improving. But that was just once in a while. In general, the situation was pretty bleak. So it went through the long Yerushalayim winter, with Sruly learning and growing and keeping in touch with his friend back home.

It was after Pesach when he came over to me one night.

"Rebbi?"

"Yes, Sruly?"

"I think I have to go home this week."

"What happened?"

"Eliyahu's condition is worse. Much worse. The doctors think he isn't going to be around much longer."

I didn't say anything. I have long found that when there isn't anything to say, saying nothing is a good idea.

"Anyway, I need to go home and spend some time with him before he goes. It's not just me. There's a whole group of our old *chevrah* who will be getting together to spend time with Eliyahu at the hospital."

I told Sruly to keep me posted, and he promised that he would. I had been davening for his friend for more than half a year by now, and I wanted to know what the future held in store for him. Sruly left a few days later and we said an emotional goodbye to one another.

"Call me with the news. Whatever it will be."

"*B'ezras Hashem.*"

Sruly called me a few weeks later.

"Sruly, *meine teiyere bachur*, it is so nice to hear your voice!"

"It's good to hear your voice, too, Rebbi."

"So what's the good word?"

"I have so much to say."

"And I have all the time in the world to hear you say it."

"Great."

Then Sruly told me a story that I have never forgotten.

After I got back to America, I spent most of my time with Eliyahu, he began. Not just me. Like I said, the whole *chevrah* was back together. We had been apart for most of the year, so it was really nice to be with one another. It wasn't long before the staff at the hospital developed a soft spot for us. After all, they could see how much we cared about our friend and how much time we were spending with him, trying to make him laugh and lifting his spirits.

One afternoon, we were sitting with Eliyahu when he told us something.

"I have a wish," he said.

"What kind of wish?"

Some patients want to go scuba diving. Others want nothing more than to be visited by a famous singer or personality. Every person with their own heart's desire.

"I want to give my mother a present."

We were utterly silent.

"You know, to thank her for being such a great mom and for taking such wonderful care of me."

It was difficult for us to speak. Boys are not supposed to get all emotional, but he was talking about his mommy — and we all have a mommy...

We got it. He wanted to give her a gift. Of course he did.

"I don't want to give her something simple or standard. No balloons or flowers. None of that."

"So what?"

"Something unique. Something special. I was wondering if you had any ideas."

Here's the thing. Unique and special presents usually cost a lot of money — which none of us had. Still, we promised to keep the question in mind and to let him know if we came up with anything.

A week later, we had to leave Eliyahu in the afternoon because we had managed to swing a job for all of us.

"Sorry to leave you, buddy," I said, "but we are all going to the Hatzolah Auction tonight. We have jobs setting up and cleaning up."

"Great."

"So we'll see you later, okay?"

"Sure."

We were about to leave, when Eliyahu said, "This auction? Are there good prizes there?"

We thought about his question for a few seconds. Were there going to be good prizes? Probably.

"It makes sense that the prizes are great."

"Well, then, do me a favor and buy a ticket for something really nice. Maybe I'll win a special present for my mother."

"You got it, buddy."

Then we left.

The hall was all lit up when we arrived. It was going to be quite a party. There was a major food situation, along with music and entertainment of the highest order. But that's not what caught our attention. That went to the prizes, which were fantastic. Vacation packages. A new dining room set. A brand-new minivan. A trip to Eretz Yisrael. Really nice stuff.

And then we saw the necklace.

It was super-special. Super-unique. Very large. Very tasteful. Classy. A diamond necklace lying on a bed of black velvet, glittering under the sparkling lights. I'm no expert on jewelry, but if I had to guess, it probably cost somewhere in the region of twenty-five thousand dollars. It was the real deal.

"If we're buying a ticket for anything, that's the one, right?"

Everyone agreed, and we purchased a ticket for the necklace.

Then we received our orders for the night and got to work.

It was a long night. There were speeches extolling the greatness of Hatzolah and the vital service it provides for Klal Yisrael. There was singing and jokes, stories and laughter. And the food was over the top. We were busy from the beginning of the night till the end, cleaning up and making sure that the hall remained fresh and appealing for all the guests.

Finally, it was time for the actual auction to begin. One by one, the MC began picking out the tickets and announcing the names of the lucky winners. There were shrieks of excitement from different corners of the hall as people learned that they were heading off to Florida or to Eretz Yisrael for Succos.

Then they reached the necklace.

It was held up in the air for everyone in the hall to get a good look at. It really was a magnificent piece of jewelry.

The ticket was pulled out of the box. Our group of friends didn't move. We were frozen in place. This was it: the culmination of our stay together. The reason we had returned from all over to be with Eliyahu at the end.

Was he going to win a super-special present for his mother?

The MC announced the winning name.

For a few seconds, I couldn't breathe. Then my group of friends all began jumping up and down in the air, ecstatic with the happiness of having been able to help our friend with his dearest wish.

"Guess what," we told Eliyahu the next day when we returned to his bedside.

"What?"

"Your dream came true!"

"My dream came — what?"

"Yes! You wanted to give your mother a real present. Well, it doesn't come realer than this!"

We showed him the necklace. He was overcome. Couldn't speak. His eyes were shining with unshed tears.

"Help me write her a note," he said at last.

We did.

"When are you going to give it to her?"

"Not yet. I'll know when it's the right time."

"Rebbi," Sruly said, "the right time came the next week, when Eliyahu began sliding in and out of consciousness. Knowing that the end was near, he gave his mother her dream present. We weren't there when he gave it to her. It was a private moment. But our hearts were filled with the joy that giving brings a person.

"Eliyahu passed away shortly after that," Sruly said, "but he passed away having shown his *hakaras hatov* to his mother. And we had been given the opportunity to be the best friends we could be."

We hung up the phone a few minutes later. Even though Sruly told me this story about fourteen years ago, I can still remember every word and every nuance of that conversation. That's how powerful it was.

It taught me the meaning of a child's love.

What it means to want to say thank you to someone with all your heart.

What levels to aspire to when it comes to friendship.

And I wanted to share those lessons with you.

רַבּוֹת בָּנוֹת עָשׂוּ חָיִל, וְאַתְּ עָלִית עַל כֻּלָּנָה
Many daughters have amassed achievement,
but you surpassed them all.

Teaching by Personal Example

The Power of Siyata D'Shmaya

*I*n the previous *pasuk*, *Zera Shimshon* explained that successful and good-hearted children are a sign of a true *eishes chayil*. In this *pasuk*, however, he goes on to say that sometimes children turn out incredibly well, yet the reason for that is not clear.

Chazal tell us (*Yoma* 47a) the story that we previously related about Kimchis, who merited to see two of her sons serving as the Kohen Gadol on one Yom Kippur, and all seven of her sons serving as Kohanim Gedolim at different times.

Seven Kohanim Gedolim! Certainly a world record!

When the Sages asked her to what she attributed her success in child-rearing, she explained that she was so careful when it came to *tznius* that the beams of her house never saw any strands of her hair.

To this the Sages replied that many other women also did great things, but it did not serve as a *zechus* for them as it did for her. So while רַבּוֹת בָּנוֹת עָשׂוּ חָיִל — "Many women have seen great children,"

שֶׁקֶּמַח קְמְחִית עָלָה לַגַּג — וְאַתְּ עָלִית עַל כֻּלָּנָה — "you surpassed them all," וְאַתְּ עָלִית עַל כֻּלָּנָה — "because Kimchis's flour rose to the surface."

Flour is a reference to Kimchis's children; children who were more special than everyone else around them, and who "rose up," as it were.

The Sages are making the point that while it is possible that her sons turned out so well because of Kimchis's scrupulous care for modesty, it is also possible that she was the recipient of special *siyata d'Shmaya* for reasons known solely to Hashem.

Torah Above All

Zera Shimshon now offers another understanding of the *pasuk*.

רַבּוֹת בָּנוֹת עָשׂוּ חָיִל — Many women have done great things, taking upon themselves to eagerly perform every mitzvah that comes their way.

However, וְאַתְּ עָלִית עַל כֻּלָּנָה — our *eishes chayil* has risen above everyone else. Because in addition to the seriousness with which she does every mitzvah, she is also *zocheh* to Torah learning, making certain to learn all the halachos that pertain to her and to her life.

The Mishnah (*Peah* 1:1) tells us: וְתַלְמוּד תּוֹרָה כְּנֶגֶד כֻּלָּם — "The benefit of Torah study is equal to all the mitzvos," which is why, when an *eishes chayil* also studies Torah, in addition to all the other great things that she does, she cannot help but rise above everyone else.

Zera Shimshon now asks a question.

Why does the *pasuk* say רַבּוֹת בָּנוֹת ("many daughters") and not רַבּוֹת נָשִׁים ("many women")?

The answer?

The Gemara (*Sotah* 20a) writes: חַיָּב אָדָם לְלַמֵּד אֶת בִּתּוֹ תּוֹרָה — "A father is obligated to teach his daughter Torah." The fact that the *pasuk* uses the word "daughter" is an allusion to the idea of women learning Torah.

And even if רַבּוֹת בָּנוֹת עָשׂוּ חָיִל — "Many daughters have merited to study Torah," אַתְּ עָלִית עַל כֻּלָּנָה — our *eishes chayil* outdoes them all, because she not only learned Torah herself, she also taught Torah to her children as well.

As the *Zera Shimshon* wrote, רַבּוֹת בָּנוֹת עָשׂוּ חָיִל — Many women have done great things, and have taken on themselves to eagerly perform every mitzvah that comes their way.

Other women perform as many mitzvos as possible, and also teach their children Torah.

In the following story, you will read about a mother who taught her son the right way to act and treat other people — her personal example, the kind of behavior that a child never forgets.

Because it's just so right. And so like an *eishes chayil...*

The reason I was so happy to finally get some "new" beds for my guest room was because the old beds were ones I had brought with me from America to Eretz Yisrael years and years earlier, and they were quite ancient. If I wanted my married kids to come for Pesach, I needed to be able to offer them a comfortable place to sleep. *Baruch Hashem*, I found some great beds that someone from Kfar Saba (of all places) was literally giving away — and they even boasted storage space underneath. I called the person giving away the beds and told her that I wanted them. It was just a question of how and when to get them to me.

I figured out that renting a vehicle large enough to transport the beds would cost about three hundred shekel for the day, plus gas, time and labor. I decided that it made more sense to hire a mover. I sent the mover a picture of the beds. He gave me a quote for five hundred shekel and told me that he could do the job the next day.

I booked him without further ado and thought no more of the matter.

In the morning, Shirley (the giver of the beds) called to tell me that Gil the mover had arrived. We confirmed that I didn't want the mattresses. My daughter helped me empty out the guest room to make space for the new furniture. Soon it was totally empty, for the first time since the day we moved in. I assumed that it would take the mover an hour, at most, to reach us from Kfar Saba. That's why I was so surprised when it was almost one o'clock in the afternoon and he still had not put in an appearance.

Finally, I called him.

"Gil," I said. "How's everything?"

"Good."

"When should we expect you with the beds?"

"Well, we got stuck in Givat Shmuel."

"What do you mean? How did that happen?"

"We spent the morning filling up the truck with different items that needed transporting from one location to another, and now we are spending the afternoon emptying out."

"So when should I expect to see you?"

"Probably around 3:30."

"Okay, I'm not in a rush. 3:30 sounds fine."

At five o'clock in the afternoon, Gil emailed me a picture of his Waze screen. Estimated time of arrival: 5:33.

At eight o'clock that evening, I finally called him to ask what was going on.

"I thought Modiin Illit is right next to Modiin."

"You thought right. It is."

"Here's the problem. Modiin Illit is situated in the *shtachim* (the territories)."

"So?"

"So I got held up for two hours by an army *machsom*." (There are military *machsomim*, or checkpoints, usually set up between parts of the country that are primarily populated by Arabs.)

"I don't understand," I told Gil. "There are no checkpoints from Kfar Saba to Kiryat Sefer unless you went through the Arab towns."

"We did, and my Arab worker got caught."

"I don't understand," I said again. "Don't you know that it's not a good idea to try and bring a Palestinian worker through an army checkpoint?"

"Of course I do. But the fact is, my worker actually has a work permit."

"If he has a work permit, what's the problem?"

"The problem is that his work permit is only valid in the Gush Dan area of the country and not for Modiin. That was my mistake."

"So what happened?"

"I explained to the army, and I explained to the army, and I explained to the army — and finally they let my worker go with a warning that, if such a thing happened again within the next year, I would be given a retroactive fine of 2,000 shekel. My worker, who is supposed to know that he cannot enter certain areas," continued Gil, "had his work permit suspended for 48 hours, along with a warning that if such a thing happened again, he would lose his work permit altogether.

"The truth is," Gil continued, "I could have abandoned my worker on the highway and let him find his own way home after our ordeal, which was his fault. But I didn't want to do that. Instead, I drove him home — which is why I still haven't arrived."

"Okay," I said. "I get the picture. Bottom line, where are you right now?"

"Chawaj."

I laughed. Really, there was nothing else to do at that point but laugh.

"Are you still coming tonight, or first thing tomorrow morning?"

"I'm coming tonight. I promised you that I would deliver the beds today and I am going to keep my word! I don't have a worker right now, but I'm going to do it anyway."

"Gil, I really do not mind if you go home and get some rest. You can deliver the beds tomorrow."

"No, I'm coming tonight."

Knowing how exhausted Gil must be after his long and arduous day, I went to put a Pepsi Max in the freezer, so that he would have a refreshing, cold drink waiting for him when he arrived. That long-awaited delivery finally occurred at around 9:30 that night. My son Yitzchak went out to greet him.

"Yitzchak," I said, as I handed him the soda, "tell Gil that, after a day like this, we are sure he can really use a nice, ice-cold bottle of Pepsi."

I cannot tell you how much Gil appreciated that cold drink. Even more, how much he appreciated the thought that went into the small act of placing the bottle in the freezer so that it would be ready when he arrived.

After Gil had recovered a bit from his intense journey, Yitzchak helped him shlep the beds into the guest room. Watching Gil, I found myself very impressed. I saw that he had separated the headboards from the beds and was now putting it all back together. I was pretty sure that most movers would have asked for money for doing that, but he didn't. Not only did he take it all apart and put everything back together again, he had made sure to bubble wrap everything so that none of the parts got damaged during the trip.

When everything was done, I gave Yitzchak the money to pay him, thanked him and went back inside. When Yitzchak came in, he handed me 300 shekel.

"What's this?" I asked. "I specifically remember that the price was 500 shekel."

"When I gave him the money," Yitzchak told me, "Gil would only agree to accept 200 shekel and no more. I reminded him that we had agreed on 500 shekel, and that we were not upset by the fact that he had arrived so late since we knew that it was all out of his control."

"What did he say then?" I asked my son.

"I'll tell you, Ma. He was close to tears."

"What do you mean, close to tears?"

"I mean he was literally holding himself back from crying!"

"Why?"

"I asked him the same question. This is what he told me:

"'I am in the moving business for about a year, and this was the first time anyone treated me like a person. Not only didn't you yell at me for being so late, you greeted me with an ice-cold drink and helped me shlep the stuff into the house!

"'This is not the way it is anywhere else. People yell at me if I come late. Nobody helps me shlep anything in. Forget helping me — they would have demanded that I give them a discount for having to wait so long! That's why I will accept 200 shekel for this job, and no more. Two hundred will cover my expenses and pay for my gas and the bubble wrap I used. I don't want any more.'

"But you earned the money," my son protested. "We don't want the discount. We want to pay you for the job you did! You deserve to get paid!"

But Gil wouldn't listen. Instead, he got into his truck and drove away — still holding back his tears. Still overcome by the fact that we had treated him like a human being instead of a human shlepper.

So that's the story, my friends. It's not some outlandish tale with a fantastic twist. It's a simple story of how we treated a person whom we hired to do a job, and how he responded to our actions. It's a story about taking the time to calm down and not overreact, and how it's okay if things don't go exactly the way we want.

More than that, it's a story about people, and how the people we hire to do jobs for us deserve our patience, understanding, and respect. Sure, maybe sometimes they aren't perfect. At the same time, we need to remember something important. If they aren't perfect, neither are we.

The Segulah of the Zera Shimshon

This lesson in the *Zera Shimshon* is devoted to the importance of teaching others Torah. While it refers to the children of the *eishes chayil*, there is no question that anyone who is able to teach others Torah should do so. I can tell you that the *Zera Shimshon* definitely feels this way and is even ready to lend his assistance to Yidden who teach others Torah. Read on, and see if you agree.

Rav Yisroel Moshe Samson is a *Zera Shimshon maggid shiur* in Yerushalayim. I'll let him tell the story:

A Jew named Shloimy asked the *Zera Shimshon* team to help arrange a *shiur* at his shul in Talpiot. He told them that, in his opinion, all they needed was a good *maggid shiur* and he was sure that many people would come to hear the *shiurim*.

I was told about Shloimy's request and decided to volunteer.

I began delivering *shiurim* there, even though it is a good half-hour from my house. The *shiur* began with two participants and now, a few months later, there are over twenty who attend on a regular basis. The shul where the *shiur* is given is closed throughout the day, and is only opened toward evening for Minchah, Maariv, and the *shiur*.

One day, the man who opened the shul arrived his usual half-hour before the *shiur* to prepare the room. On his arrival, he saw that the lock was broken. Turning the key in the lock did nothing, since the mechanism was not working and the key just turned itself around and around. He tried with the key for a while before admitting defeat. In the end, he understood that the only recourse was to bring a locksmith who would be able to take apart the lock and put in a new one. While all this was going on, the members of the *shiur* kept on arriving — including me — but all of us had no choice but to stand outside.

Nobody wanted to even consider the possibility that the *shiur* would be canceled, but nobody had any good ideas for where to hold it either. The assembled all put on their best thinking caps and tried coming up with original and out-of-the-box solutions, but nothing was right. One of the group wanted to offer his house, but was unable to do so because they were having a *simchah* there that night. The closest shul in the neighborhood was locked and we were unable to reach the *gabbai*. Everyone was upset about the situation, but nobody had any ideas.

A minute before the group was about to give up and disperse, each in his own direction and each saddened by the cancelation — a sudden thought raced through my mind.

"We have to do something," I heard a little voice say. "What about all those stories of *tzaddikim*, where Hashem was waiting for just a little more effort on their part? Should we take on a *kabbalah*? Maybe that would be the right thing to do to break through the door?

"*Rabbosai*," I spoke up. "The *kochos* of our rebbi, the *Zera Shimshon*, are huge and we shouldn't leave the area without another try. I want us to undertake a commitment. If the door should open and we are able to have the *shiur*, then we will go out of our way to make sure a new member joins our *shiur*, so that yet another Jew will have a connection with Rav Shimshon Chaim and have the opportunity to learn his Torah!"

After saying those words, we again put the key in the lock. We turned it. And, to the astonishment of every single person standing there, the door simply opened! We felt as if the *Zera Shimshon* himself had taken apart the shul's lock for us, and had even gone out of his way to save us the cost of hiring a professional locksmith. It was suddenly crystal clear that our fierce desire to keep the *shiur* going, and the *kabbalah* that we made to bring *nachas* to the *Zera Shimshon*, had managed to accomplish what we had not been able to do earlier.

From the events that occurred that day, we understood the level of *nachas ruach* that Rav Shimshon Chaim receives from our *shiur* in his Torah. I am therefore calling everyone who lives in the neighborhood to come and attend the *shiur*, which takes place every Tuesday at 108 Derech Chevron Street at eight in the evening. And we should all merit to share in the tremendous *yeshuos* that the *Zera Shimshon* promises to those who learn his Torah...

שֶׁקֶר הַחֵן וְהֶבֶל הַיֹּפִי, אִשָּׁה יִרְאַת ה' הִיא תִתְהַלָּל
Charm is false and beauty is vain,
a woman who fears Hashem — she should be praised.

Eternal Beauty

True or False?

hy does the *pasuk* use the word שֶׁקֶר (*sheker*, falsehood) when describing a woman's *chein* (her natural charm)? Why is it false?

Furthermore, why is יֹפִי (*yofi,* beauty) being described as הֶבֶל (*hevel,* vain)?

And what do either of these things have to do with the end of the *pasuk*, which states that a woman who fears Hashem should be praised?

In *Tehillim* (103:17), David HaMelech tells us, וְחֶסֶד ה' מֵעוֹלָם וְעַד עוֹלָם עַל יְרֵאָיו — "The kindness of Hashem is forever and ever for those who fear Him."

Regarding this, the *Yalkut Shimoni* (*Tehillim* 859) tells us that "it is known that a person who possesses the element of *chein* (charm) possesses fear of Heaven."

Wait a second. One can make such a statement regarding men, because what you see is what you get. Women, on the other hand, are adept at using cosmetics and jewelry to enhance their natural appearance and to give themselves a dose of extra charm when needed. Since that is the case, how can you consider *chein,* charm, a yardstick by which to measure a woman's *yiras Shamayim*? Maybe she is just very adept with lipstick, blush and mascara?

Keeping all of this in mind, says the *Zera Shimshon,* the *pasuk* wants to make something very clear. Charm that results from wearing cosmetics and beautiful clothing is *sheker* — falsehood. It is transient. Temporary. An illusion.

Why?

Because the moment the makeup and jewelry are removed, the real face of a person is exposed — and the artificial *chein* disappears.

Even if a woman is blessed with *yofi* (natural beauty) that makes people think she is charming, it is *hevel* (vain) and without authentic value.

On the other hand, when an *eishes chayil* is an אִשָּׁה יְרְאַת ה' — a woman who possesses an honest fear of Hashem — then Hashem will gift her with real *chein.* Then הִיא תִתְהַלָּל — she will have something of which she can be truly proud.

Oy, to have *yiras Shamayim*....

Who doesn't dream of being in possession of such a lofty and priceless reality? *Yiras Shamayim* is one of the elements that turns our *eishes chayil* into the queen that she is.

Yet unlike the *eishes chayil,* a woman who exudes *yiras Hashem,* there are other people in the world who strike us as not having any *yiras Hashem* at all. And yet sometimes the reality of a situation may be the exact opposite of our initial impression, because so many of our brothers and sisters have hidden depths where *yiras Hashem* can be found. And maybe it is our task to try and uncover those depths.

I bring you the case of The Atheist's Dvar Torah as an example.

I work at a law firm in Tel Aviv where most of the lawyers are not religious. At the same time, they are in almost every case unfailingly polite to me when it comes to matters of Torah observance, and sometimes some of them are even interested in finding out more.

There was one particular lawyer who identified himself to me as an atheist. Since our relationship was confined purely to the business realm, we didn't discuss the reasons why he considered himself an atheist. At the back of my mind, however, I was fairly certain that I would be hearing more about his connection with Hashem at some point down the line.

And so it was.

One afternoon, this lawyer — I'll call him *Benny — walked into my office with a request.

"David?"

"Yes?"

"Can you do me a favor, please?"

"What do you need?"

"I was wondering whether you could give me a *dvar Torah* on this week's *parashah* for my kids?"

This is Israel, which means that when a self-identified atheist asks you for a *dvar Torah* for their kids, you take it in stride. But try as I might, I couldn't come up with a nice *dvar Torah* on the spot. Finally, in desperation, I told him about how Sarah Imeinu passed away when she heard the news of the *Akeidas Yitzchak*. It was far from a solid *dvar Torah*, but it was all I could think of at the moment.

Benny thanked me for the *vort*, but I felt bad knowing that I'd missed an opportunity to make more of an impact — one that would have had a stronger bearing on his life.

The next day, Friday, I received a *dvar Torah* from Rav Nissan Kaplan (I'm a *talmid* of his) which arrives in the form of a weekly email. Still feeling ashamed that I hadn't had something more substantial to tell Benny, I clicked on the *shiur* and listened to what Rav Nissan had to say.

He explained in his inimitable style that, according to Rabbeinu Yonah, Avraham Avinu's tenth test was having to purchase Sarah's burial spot from Efron — and not the *Akeidah* at all.

Why, Rav Nissan asked, should this be the case?

Wasn't the purchase of a burial spot a relatively small thing for Avraham Avinu to have to deal with?

Rav Nissan answered that sometimes overcoming a major *nisayon* is easier than a simpler one. Why? When the challenge is big, everyone knows what the person is doing. Everyone is talking about the test he confronted and what a *tzaddik* he is to have succeeded. The person is accorded a great deal of honor.

A small *nisayon* is much harder. Nobody knows what the person is doing and it's easy not to take it seriously since it's just a small thing and easy to overlook. He gave the example of getting up for Shacharis, explaining how that is a relatively easy thing, yet sometimes it can become a person's most difficult challenge.

After listening to Rav Nissan's *vort*, I was excited since I now had something solid to tell Benny. I sent him an email telling him that I had another *dvar Torah* for him from the week's *parashah*. He replied that he was looking forward to hearing it. On Sunday morning, I went into Benny's office when I arrived at the firm and told him the *dvar Torah*. Then I went back to my office and got to work.

An hour later, Benny came to my office. I was on the phone. He left.

When I finished my conversation, I went to see him.

"What did you want to tell me?"

Benny "the atheist" was very serious. He looked into my eyes and said, "I want to tell you something personal about myself."

"I'm listening."

"I don't know if you know this, but a while back I was in a serious car accident."

"I didn't know."

"Yes, it was a very bad accident and it had terrible repercussions."

"In what way?"

"It caused me to become blind in one eye."

I was shocked. I had not known this.

"But you're not blind anymore, correct?"

"Yes."

"What happened?"

"I made a deal with G-d."

Now, there are times in life when we hear people tell us that they made deals with Hashem for all sorts of things. This is something that the *poskim* discuss. There are those who say that one is not allowed to do this, and others who write that it is a good thing to do in certain cases. For me, that was all beside the point at that moment, because how often do you hear an "atheist" telling you that he made a deal with Hashem?! I didn't feel like pointing out to him that making deals with Hashem was a pretty glaring contradiction to his self-avowed approach to life...

Instead, I asked him a question.

"What was the deal you made with Hashem?"

"It's a funny deal."

He told me that he had always loved to eat pork — which, as everyone knows, is *tereifah*. But Benny was so far away from *Yiddishkeit* that he never even thought twice about it, and ate pork whenever he was able to.

"Now that I was faced with such a serious health challenge," he said, "I turned to Hashem and told Him that if He gives me back my complete eyesight, I will stop eating pork. I said, 'Give me back my sight and I will never eat a piece of *chazir* again — even though it's my favorite food in the world!'"

"Then what happened?"

"I got my sight back!"

"And?"

"And I kept my side of the deal. From that day on, I never touched a piece of pork again. Hashem had given me back my sight and I stopped eating pig."

I was truly fascinated by his story. It was yet another proof of the fact that every personality is composed of so many layers and components and belief systems. Imagine... A self-professed atheist making deals with Hashem. And keeping them!

"Anyway, David," he went on, "this is where we get to the latest part of the story."

I waited, knowing it was going to be good.

◆◆◆

"Recently I was getting ready to go on vacation. I had booked a hotel for my wife and myself in Greece and was already imagining how much fun we were going to have there. I was especially looking forward to the delicious gourmet meals at the hotel and local restaurants. Suddenly, a thought occurred to me.

"Maybe my deal with Hashem could be reworked so that it only applied in Eretz Yisrael? 'Yes,' I told myself, 'that makes sense.' While in Eretz Yisrael I would continue to stay away from pork. But maybe, when I was out of the country, the deal didn't apply.

"I was all set to accept this argument — which meant that I would have been eating whatever I wanted in Greece in just a few days. Then you walked into my office this morning and told me that Torah idea — about how sometimes the smallest challenges in life are the most difficult ones for us to fulfill. You stood in my office, and you said that the hardest tests are the ones that nobody knows about. The tests where nobody is clapping when you overcome them.

"Your words were an exact definition of the test that would be facing me in Greece in a few days' time. The test that I had been planning on failing.

"When I heard your *dvar Torah*, I knew that I could not do what I wanted. I could not break my deal with Hashem. I could not eat any pork. I had to remain faithful to the promise I had made. Bottom line, I knew that I had to keep my word..."

As I watched Benny leave my office, I could not help but remember what *Chazal* tell us about how every Jew, even the smallest among us, possesses numerous merits.

And I said to myself, "*Oy*, Benny, what a *frum* atheist you are..."

The Segulah of the Zera Shimshon

How amazing it is that even a Yid like Benny, who claims to be an unbeliever on the outside, is really deeply connected to Hashem on the inside. And if that is the case with people who aren't even religious, how much more so when it comes to people who believe in Hashem and in the power of the *tzaddikim*.

◆◆◆

"My daughter was in *shidduchim* for a very long time," *Mrs. Silver said, "but no matter what we tried, nothing worked. There was no movement. Needless to say, the situation caused the entire family tremendous anguish. I had heard about the *segulah* of the *Zera Shimshon* long before, but because the Torah is very deep and not exactly the kind of material that women generally learn, I hadn't felt able to fulfill the *segulah* and learn the words of the *tzaddik* in the way I would have wanted to.

One day, a friend of mine told me about a beautiful *peirush* she had seen brought down in the *Zera Shimshon* on *Parashas Chayei Sarah*, where he goes through the *pesukim* of Eishes Chayil one by one and gives a unique and precious explanation for each. She told me that the *Zera Shimshon* team had published a *sefer* that explained everything Rav Shimshon Chaim wrote about Eishes Chayil, with clarity and in a way that was easy to grasp.

Now I was excited.

I purchased the *sefer* and started learning it for the *zechus* that my daughter should merit to meet her *zivug*. I also took it upon myself to distribute the *sefer Zera Shimshon* to people who hadn't heard of the *sefer*, because I knew how important this was to Rav Shimshon Chaim. Throughout this period, I had a very powerful feeling that the *yeshuah* would come after I'd given away the tenth set of *Zera Shimshon*. I don't know why I felt this way, but I did.

I didn't have the funds to purchase ten sets at once, nor did I have people to give them to. This meant that the process took time. But whenever I had the occasion to give someone a nice gift, a bar mitzvah boy, for example, or a neighbor, the rebbi of one of my kids, or even just a Jew in need, I would purchase a set of *Zera Shimshon* and happily give it to that person as a present.

I had just finished learning the *Zera Shimshon's* Eishes Chayil and, in the same week, given away the tenth set of *sefarim*, when a *shidduch* was suggested for my daughter. Ten days later, she was a *kallah*."

תְּנוּ לָהּ מִפְּרִי יָדֶיהָ וִיהַלְלוּהָ בַשְּׁעָרִים מַעֲשֶׂיהָ
Give her from the fruits of her hands,
and they will praise her actions at the gates.

The Outcome

Rewards

*I*n the end, it works out very well for the *eishes chayil.*

The Gemara (*Sotah* 21a) tells us that while it is true that women are not commanded to learn Torah, they merit reward for bringing their children to learn Torah and for waiting for their husbands to return from the *beis midrash.* Shouldn't their devotion to Torah earn them half of their husband's reward?

Of course they deserve half the reward, says the *Zera Shimshon.*

And that is why the *pasuk* writes תְּנוּ לָהּ — "give her" half of her husband's reward מִפְּרִי יָדֶיהָ — as "the fruits of her [intensive, lifelong] labor."

Now we arrive at the last words of the *pasuk.*

וִיהַלְלוּהָ בַשְּׁעָרִים מַעֲשֶׂיהָ — "They will praise her actions at the gates."

Zera Shimshon raises a few questions. Why will they praise her actions specifically at the gates and not in other places? Also, why doesn't the *pasuk* say וִיהַלְלוּהָ מַעֲשֶׂיהָ בַּשְּׁעָרִים ("Her actions will be praised at the gates") rather than וִיהַלְלוּהָ בַשְּׁעָרִים מַעֲשֶׂיהָ ("Praise at the gates her actions")? That would have been a more grammatically correct way of writing the same thing, in Hebrew.

The answer?

Because it appears in the middle of the phrase, the word בַּשְּׁעָרִים (the gates) can be connected to the words on either side of it. It can be connected to the word וִיהַלְלוּהָ (they will praise her) or it can be connected to the word מַעֲשֶׂיהָ (her actions).

What does this mean?

וִיהַלְלוּהָ בַשְּׁעָרִים — "They will praise her at the gates" is referring to the gates of the *beis midrash*. This is how the Gemara (*Berachos* 8a) explains the word "gates" in the *pasuk* (*Tehillim* 87:2), "Hashem loves the gates of Tzion"; it says that this refers to the "gates designated for the study of halachah." And it is there, beside the gates of the *beis midrash*, a place that is steeped in the study of halachah, that she will be praised for all the sacrifices she made for her husband when it came to his Torah learning.

This is what Rabbi Akiva was referring to when he praised his wife to his students, saying (*Nedarim* 50a), שֶׁלִּי וְשֶׁלָּכֶם שֶׁלָּה הִיא — "Yours and mine are hers."

High praise indeed!

Now we will discuss the second way of phrasing the end of the *pasuk*: בַּשְּׁעָרִים מַעֲשֶׂיהָ — "at the gates, her actions."

A kosher and modest woman can be the catalyst for her sons to become *talmidei chachamim*, as we saw previously when discussing Kimchis, and how her sons all served as Kohanim Gedolim, rising above everyone due to their mother's *tznius*.

The same message can be learned from the words of the *Chumash* (*Bereishis* 49:25): בִּרְכֹת שָׁדַיִם וָרָחַם — "blessings of the bosom and the womb," which means that the mother is blessed through her children. It is in her merit — since she fed them kosher food and acted in a modest manner — that they developed wisdom in Torah learning.

The outcome is this: The *eishes chayil* receives two types of rewards: a reward for the Torah study of her husband, and a reward for the Torah study of her sons. And this is the meaning of the words: וִיהַלְלוּהָ בַשְּׁעָרִים — people praise the *eishes chayil* in the gates of the *beis midrash* on account of her husband's learning, and בַשְּׁעָרִים מַעֲשֶׂיהָ — and they praise her also for her actions, which were the catalyst for her children to become *talmidei chachamim*.

After learning so much about the *eishes chayil*, we have come to the final verse, where *Mishlei* repeats once again the *sechar*, the reward that awaits her — both because of what she did for her husband and also for her children. Why is she so deserving of reward? Because she caused great things to happen through her behavior. And at the end of her life she will take her seat in Gan Eden and reap the benefits of all her hard work.

The following story, the tale of Rav Chaim Kanievsky *ztz"l* and his Erev Shabbos *chavrusa*, is a story about yet something else that Rav Chaim did for someone he didn't know and to whom he had no obligation. And yet, that didn't stop the Sar HaTorah from changing that young boy's life and turning him into a person who would go on to make a major difference to Klal Yisrael.

Who can even fathom the reward for such a thing?

And now... the story of Rav Chaim and his young *chavrusa*.

I was still a *bachur* learning in yeshivah in Yerushalayim when I visited my cousins in Petach Tikvah for Shabbos. Sitting around the table that Friday night, my cousin Reb Michoel Lipsky *z"l* told me something I hadn't known about his new son-in-law.

"Meir learns with Rav Chaim Kanievsky every Friday afternoon," he said.

"Really?"

"Yes, they've been learning together for years."

That was something. How many people were able to boast of such an achievement? I was impressed.

I had spent Shabbos with my cousins many times over the years. Reb Michoel and his wife Esty built a beautiful family of *talmidei chachamim* and *ovdei Hashem* who are also fun to be around. I had met the Lipsky family shortly after moving to Eretz Yisrael with my family. At the time, their oldest was just a teen and I enjoyed spending time in their home.

Decades passed.

The Lipsky children got married one after the other. So did I. Reb Michoel and his wife were in attendance. In the years to come, my wife and I would continue getting together with the Lipsky family for *simchahs* and Shabbosim. By this time, Meir Arava, the Lipsky's oldest son-in-law, was the father of many children and our paths didn't usually cross. But he visited his in-laws one Chanukah evening when we were all there for a beautiful family gathering. Handing me a copy of his latest *sefer*, Reb Meir explained that every time he published a *sefer*, he was blessed with another child.

"How many *sefarim* are you up to now?"

"Nine."

"And children?"

"The same," he replied with a smile.

We left later that night, brand-new *sefer* in hand.

I should have realized there was a story there. The moment Reb Meir mentioned that they had a child every time he wrote a *sefer*, I should have asked him to clarify what he was talking about. But I didn't. It was only a few years later that more of the puzzle pieces fell into place and I was able to fill in the blanks. His story was exceptional, and filled with incredible lessons for every Jew.

The time has finally come to write it down.

Menachem Arava (Meir's father) was a top-ranking officer in the Israeli Air Force when he first became interested in *Yiddishkeit*. Although he wanted to spend more time figuring things out for himself, this was not easy to do given the environment in which he lived. And then a possible opportunity appeared. The Air Force arranged for officers who had served for a specific number of years to take paid leave while going for a university degree — usually one designed to help them further their military careers.

"What if," Menachem asked himself, "instead of the military supporting me while I study for a degree, it supports me while I study in yeshivah instead? Could such a thing work? Would the military agree to such a concept?"

He approached his commanding officer and shared his idea.

"I don't have a problem with you going to a yeshivah for a 'degree' in Talmudical study, instead of a regular university," he replied. "But it will obviously have to be cleared by the Ministry of Defense first."

Menachem was not surprised when he was informed that the Ministry of Defense was not in favor.

Now what?

He wanted to learn Torah. He wanted to investigate the new world he knew so little about. How was he going to be able to do that? He wasn't sure. All he knew was that he did not plan to give up the dream.

The Arava family spent Shabbos in the city of Bnei Brak not long afterward. During the hours spent in a religious home, Menachem utilized the opportunity to ask his hosts many of the questions that were on his mind.

"Tell me," he asked at one point. "What is the name of the greatest Torah scholar in Bnei Brak today — the accepted leader of the yeshivah world?"

"That's an easy question," his host replied. "The name you're looking for is Rav Elazar Menachem Mann Shach, rosh yeshivah of Ponovezh."

"Would it be possible for me to talk to the rosh yeshivah myself?"

"Why don't you go over to the Ponovezh campus and try?"

So Menachem Arava, a Lieutenant Colonel in the Israeli Air Force, made his way through the congested streets of Bnei Brak until he reached the sprawling campus of the yeshivah on top of the hill.

Ponovezh.

He was directed to the rosh yeshivah's apartment and knocked on the door.

"Come in."

Rav Shach was home and welcomed him.

"What can I do for you?" the world-famous rosh yeshivah asked the officer.

Seconds later, Menachem Arava was unburdening his heart to Rav Shach. He told the rosh yeshivah how he had begun to be more and more interested in living a life of Torah and mitzvos, but being a top-level military officer, he had no way of turning his dreams into a reality.

"But then I had an idea," he said, and proceeded to describe his brainstorm about using his time at university for Torah study instead.

Rav Shach heard him out.

"What happened to your idea?"

"My commanding officer was in favor, but it was not cleared by the Ministry of Defense."

In the next few minutes, Menachem Arava was treated to a scene that he would never forget. It was then that he understood that just as there are generals sitting in the "pit" in Tel Aviv coming up with brilliant campaigns and giving orders, so too was there a general sitting in a simple apartment in Bnei Brak coming up with brilliant campaigns and giving orders.

The rosh yeshivah asked his *gabbai*, Rabbi Yecheskel Eschayeg, to call Rabbi Shlomo Lorincz, who was then serving as a member of the Knesset for Agudas Yisrael, and ask him to come see the rosh yeshivah. Before long Rabbi Lorincz presented himself to Rav Shach.

"Reb Shlomo," the rosh yeshivah said, "at this point in time, Agudas Yisrael is engaged in coalition-building negotiations with the upcoming government, correct?"

"Yes."

"I would like you to add another clause to our agreement."

"What should it say?"

"It should say that any army officer who would prefer to use the university degree that the army normally encourages and pays for to go and learn in yeshivah, should be able to do so while being supported by the army, just as if he were enrolled in the Technion or Tel Aviv University. It will state that a sabbatical year will be funded whether it is spent at a university or a yeshivah."

"I will take care of it immediately," Reb Shlomo promised the rosh yeshivah.

And so, Menachem Arava became the first officer in the Israeli Air Force to be fully supported by the Ministry of Defense when he enrolled in a yeshivah for *baalei teshuvah*.

It wasn't long before the Arava family had left the neighborhood where they had been living and relocated to an apartment in Bnei Brak. Menachem was learning in kollel, studying day and night to make up for lost time, and his children were making strides at their new schools as well.

All but Meir.

When they'd first moved to Bnei Brak, Meir had been known as Zohar, the name he'd received at his *bris*. After being introduced to Rav Chaim Kanievsky, however, things changed.

"You need to change your name," Rav Chaim told him.

"Why?"

"Zohar is the name of a *sefer*, not the name of a person."

"What should I call myself, then?"

"You should change your name to Meir."

It might have been more difficult for him to make the change. However, having witnessed firsthand the power of Rav Chaim's *berachos* (he'd experienced a personal *yeshuah* after turning to Rav Chaim for a *berachah* a short time before), Meir trusted Rav Chaim implicitly and was willing to do whatever the *gadol* asked.

And so it was that Zohar became Meir.

Meir was fourteen years old and having a lot of trouble figuring out how to read the Gemara. While the rest of his class seemed to breeze through the *sugyos* of *Bava Metzia*, Meir couldn't figure it out. Where learning Gemara seemed to come naturally to everyone around him, he was having no success at all. He confided his worries and fears to his father.

Reb Menachem Arava listened to what his son told him, and said, "Meir, why don't you visit Rav Chaim and tell him how difficult learning Gemara is for you?"

But Meir didn't feel comfortable bothering Rav Chaim.

"Thousands of people stream to visit Rav Chaim," his father protested.

"I don't want to."

"So what are you going to do?"

"I'm going to write a letter to Rav Chaim instead."

Meir wasted no time. He sat down and wrote a letter to Rav Chaim detailing all his challenges. Rav Chaim replied — penning his reply on the same letter that Meir had sent, as was Rav Chaim's way.

Meir read Rav Chaim's reply, but he didn't understand what he was being told to do. In the end, he decided to follow his father's advice and returned to the home of Rav Chaim Kanievsky on Rashbam Street, just adjacent to the Lederman Shul.

He presented himself at the Kanievsky home on Friday afternoon, a volume of *Bava Metzia* under his arm. To his great happiness, Meir soon found himself sitting with Rav Chaim. He told the venerable *gadol* all about yeshivah life and how he wasn't making it. Rav Chaim listened as Meir Arava poured out his heart. Eventually the stream of words and tears came to an end. That was when Meir Arava, fourteen-year-old *baal teshuvah*, made the request that would change his life.

"Would I be able to learn with the Rebbi?"

Rav Chaim stared at the young boy for a moment.

"I don't really have time to learn with new *chavrusos*," he replied. "You know how busy I am. The number of people who come here every day…"

But Meir — perhaps even surprising himself — reiterated his request, begging the *gadol hador* with pleading eyes to learn with him, to share his wellsprings of Torah with a boy who was trying his best.

"Okay," Rav Chaim said at last. "Let's learn."

Meir opened his Gemara and the two of them — the fourteen-year-old boy and the celebrated *talmid chacham* — sat side by side and learned together, studying the wisdom of the ages like any pair of scholars at any time in history.

They learned for an hour. When they finished, Meir looked at Rav Chaim.

"Rebbi?"

"Yes?"

"Can I come and learn with Rebbi next week, too?"

It was difficult for Rav Chaim to agree. Who knew better than he the myriad commitments that he already had on his shoulders, both to the general public and to his own learning?

There is no way to know what went through Rav Chaim's mind at that moment. All we know is what he answered.

"You can come back to learn with me next Friday."

And so it began. Once they had learned together twice, it became a weekly commitment, with Meir arriving at Rav Chaim's home every Friday afternoon for their weekly session.

Time passed. A year, and then another. Meir finished *yeshivah ketanah* and it was time for him to transfer to a *yeshivah gedolah*. His father wanted him to learn in a small yeshivah, where the rebbeim would have the time, patience and inclination to give him the attention he needed.

Rav Chaim, however, had other plans for his *chavrusa*.

"Meir is going to Ponovezh," he told Reb Menachem.

"But it seems to me that my son still needs the kind of attention he will only be able to receive in a smaller place…"

"Reb Menachem, I know your son better than you do. He is going to Ponovezh. It's already been arranged."

Rav Chaim decided, and Meir went.

Reb Menachem ran into Meir's *maggid shiur* a few weeks later.

"How's my son doing?" he asked the man.

"I'm sorry to have to tell you that Meir doesn't seem to be fitting in at the yeshivah. I don't see him getting along with the other *bachurim* and he's become very quiet and withdrawn."

This wasn't good at all. Meir had been the life of his class in *yeshivah ketanah* and his father was very concerned.

"Meir," he told his son, "I met one of the *maggidei shiur* from the yeshivah and he told me that you haven't been yourself since the beginning of the *zeman*. He said that you don't participate and that you haven't been learning well. What's the matter?"

"I don't feel connected to the other *bachurim*," Meir replied. "I don't feel comfortable here."

"Why don't you discuss your feelings with Rav Chaim?"

Meir did just that. That Friday, he told Rav Chaim how he felt about the yeshivah and how Ponovezh wasn't working out for him.

Rav Chaim's answer was decisive and unorthodox.

"From now on, I do not want you going to *shiur*."

"What should I do instead?"

"I want you to learn the entire *Masechta Megillah* this week. The entire *masechta*. *Daf* after *daf*. On Friday I will test you on everything you learned this week."

And so it was. Meir opened a *Megillah* on Sunday morning and started to learn. He had a goal. He needed to finish the entire *masechta*. He sat in the *beis midrash* and learned from morning till night, finishing the *masechta* by Friday. In the afternoon, he made his way to Rashbam Street where his rebbi was waiting to test him. Rav Chaim tested him on the entire *masechta* and was satisfied that he knew it well.

"Next week you will learn *Taanis*," he said. "On Friday I will test you on the entire *masechta*."

The next few years were an incredible period in the life of Meir Arava. Every Friday he'd present himself at the Kanievsky home, where Rav Chaim tested him on the material he'd learned that week. He would then be given his marching orders for the upcoming week.

At some point, Rav Chaim added *Tosafos* to the material that Meir would be tested on.

Week in, week out, Meir learned and was tested. It wasn't long before he finished *Shas*.

"Now you will begin learning sections of the *Mishnah Berurah*," Rav Chaim told him. Meir's extensive learning regimen meant that by the time he was ready to marry, he had learned vast amounts of both Gemara and halachah.

"What should I be focusing on after my marriage?" Meir asked his rebbi.

"I want you to begin writing a *sefer*."

"A *sefer* on what topic?"

"On *Mishnah Berurah*. I want you to explore the Chofetz Chaim's reasoning and the depth behind his *piskei halachah*. When he rules one way, I want you to delve into that ruling and explain why. I want you to write a *sefer* that can be used to illustrate the reasoning behind what is written in the *Mishnah Berurah*."

But Meir didn't feel suited for such a task. He felt it was too massive an undertaking for him.

Rav Chaim didn't force the issue.

Meir and his wife had been married for a year and still hadn't been blessed with a child. So Meir asked his rebbi what he should do.

"I told you what to do," Rav Chaim said.

"What?"

"Write a *sefer* on *Mishnah Berurah*."

So Meir wrote a *sefer* on *Mishnah Berurah*, calling it *Meir Oz*. The *mem* stood for Meir. The *vav*, for the family name back in Poland, and the *zayin* for Zohar, the name he'd gone by before Rav Chaim told him to change it.

As Rav Chaim had foreseen, Meir and his wife were blessed with their first child. And, as I said earlier, every time he published another installment of *Meir Oz*, they were blessed with another child.

This, my friends, is the story of my cousin's husband, Rav Meir

Arava — the fourteen-year-old boy who had trouble learning. The boy who became Rav Chaim's *chavrusa*. The boy who would end up writing deep and learned *sefarim* on complicated issues of halachah. Imagine for a second what would have happened had Meir presented himself to a different *talmid chacham* who didn't see what Rav Chaim did, and wasn't willing to do what Rav Chaim did? Might he not have sent Meir away? And then what would have happened to all those pages of Gemara, and finishing *Shas* with tests, halachos learned and *sefarim* written…

How many *bachurim* have been lost because nobody recognized their potential and took the time to help them realize what they could become?

Rav Chaim, who was busier than probably anyone alive, somehow managed to find the time to learn with that boy and to help him develop into a *talmid chacham* of note.

Let this story serve as a lesson to every one of us about the potential that lies inherent in every single Jewish soul.

And let us act on that knowledge — and change lives. Just as Rav Chaim did.

Part Two:

The Beis Yaakov Treasury

The Stature and Role of the Jewish Woman
Collected From *Zera Shimshon*
and *Toldos Shimshon*

My Tent or Your Tent?

וַיַּעְתֵּק מִשָּׁם הָהָרָה מִקֶּדֶם לְבֵית אֵל וַיֵּט אָהֳלֹה בֵּית אֵל מִיָּם וְהָעַי מִקֶּדֶם וַיִּבֶן שָׁם מִזְבֵּחַ לַה' וַיִּקְרָא בְּשֵׁם ה' (בראשית יב:ח).

From there [Avraham] relocated to the mountain east of Beis-El and pitched his tent, with Beis-El on the west and Ai on the east; and there he built an altar to Hashem and invoked Hashem by Name (Bereishis 12:8).

Hers or His?

*R*ashi explains that Avraham Avinu first pitched Sarah's tent, and only when hers was up did he pitch his own.

In the Torah there is a concept called מִקְרָא וּמָסֹרֶת. What does this mean?

מִקְרָא (*mikra*) is the way we read a word in the Torah.

מָסֹרֶת (*masores*) is the way we write the word in the Torah — even though at times it is not pronounced the way it is written.

This *pasuk* is discussing the period when Avraham Avinu arrived in Eretz Canaan, and he pitched his tent. When we read the Torah, we pronounce the word אָהֳלֹה as if it were written with a *vav* at the end of the word, אָהֳלוֹ, which means "*his* tent." However, the word is actually written אָהֳלֹה, with the letter *hei* at the end, which can mean "*her* tent." *Rashi* explains that the fact that the Torah wrote the word in such a way that one would think it is referring to Sarah's tent teaches us that Avraham Avinu erected his wife's tent before putting up his own.

The *Re'eim* (Rav Eliyahu Mizrachi) has a problem with this reasoning. He writes: Elsewhere in the Torah, we do not derive the order of events from a discrepancy between the way the Torah is written and read, between *masores* and *mikra*. So, he declares, it cannot be done here either. Yet if that is the case, on what basis does *Rashi* learn that Avraham pitched Sarah's tent first?

Now even if you say that *Rashi* knows this because it seems to him that such an idea makes sense — since, as we know, a person is obligated to honor his wife more than himself — we are still left with a question. Why did *Rashi* say that the word is written אָהֳלֹה — her tent? Wouldn't we have assumed that Avraham would put up his wife's tent first? And why are we praising Avraham Avinu for erecting his wife's tent before his own? Isn't that what every person is supposed to do?

Why Two Tents?

Furthermore, why did Avraham Avinu erect two tents in the first place? Wasn't one tent enough? Wouldn't he want to live in the same tent as his wife?

Rashi explains (*Bereishis* 31:33) that Yaakov slept in Rachel's tent, though he had three other wives. He did not have a tent of his own. Avraham Avinu had only had one wife, Sarah Imeinu. It would seem that he should have slept in her tent. So why did he pitch his own?

Zera Shimshon provides several answers:

In order for us to understand what was going on here, we first need to know that the reason Avraham was building the tents was to host guests and convert them to believing in Hashem. Avraham operated a "hotel," where he would feed travelers and wayfarers. By providing them with food, he had the opportunity to teach and convert them. As a good host, Avraham would give his guests a private and modest place to enjoy their meal — a tent! And while they were eating, Avraham would speak with them and tell them all about Hashem.

We learn this from the words, "and he invoked the Name of Hashem," which the Sages tell us means that Avraham taught the travelers about Hashem's Name.

So we know that the tents were being built for *kiruv* purposes, to bring as many people as possible to a belief in the One G-d. Because of this, they needed two tents: one for Sarah Imeinu for teaching the women, and one for Avraham, who was converting the men.

The *pasuk* therefore writes the word אָהֱלֹה (her tent) and it is read אָהֳלוֹ (his tent), and both of these things are true, since there were two tents, which were equally necessary. With two tents, Avraham could work with the men and Sarah with the women at the same time — but in separate places.

Since Avraham Avinu put up two tents, the Torah informs us that he put his wife's tent up first.

Ladies First!

Before *Mattan Torah*, too, Hashem had Moshe speak to the women of Klal Yisrael first, as it says, "So you shall say to Beis Yaakov, and relate to Bnei Yisrael" (*Shemos* 19:3). The members of "Beis Yaakov" — that is, the women — were called before "Bnei Yisrael," the men.

The Midrash relates (*Bereishis* 17:7):

> A pious man, and his equally pious wife, got divorced. The pious man remarried a woman who was not on a high spiritual level. He ended up becoming like her. The pious woman married a wicked man, and she turned him into a pious man.

From this story, we can see that a wife has a powerful influence on her husband, and she can help him become a much better person. And this is why the Torah was given to the women first, because if the women of Klal Yisrael wanted the Torah, they would cause their husbands to want the Torah too.

Zera Shimshon continues:

And because women influence the men, Sarah was more successful at converting the women than Avraham was with the men. Why?

Because a woman who converted would not waver in her commitment, even if she married someone who was not as committed. But a man might falter if he married someone who did not recognize Hashem.

When the *pasuk* tells us that Avraham erected two tents — learned from the usage of the אֲהֳלֹה, which is read אָהֳלוֹ — we can say that the reason the *pasuk* went out of its way to stress the point of the two tents was because the Torah wants us to know that he erected Sarah's tent first and then his own.

Now if the *pasuk's* point was for us to know that Sarah also converted women, and thus needed her own tent, we already learned that fact from the words (*Bereishis* 12:5), "the souls they made in Charan," which *Chazal* explain refers to the men and the women that Avraham and Sarah converted. Since this is the case, the fact that the word is written אֲהֳלָה, even though it's pronounced אָהֳלוֹ, is coming to teach us something else.

What the Pasuk Teaches Us

What is it teaching us?

That there were two tents, and that Avraham pitched his wife's tent first because it was more important to convert the women than the men, since they are the ones who motivate, inspire, and cause their husbands to become great.

With this we can also answer the *Re'eim's* question as well. He pointed out that we do not figure out what happened earlier or later in the Torah from the *mikra* (the way something is read in the Torah) or from the *masores* (the way it is written) — so why are we saying that it's clear from the way the Torah wrote the word that Avraham put hers up first?

Zera Shimshon explains that the Torah is alerting us to the fact that Avraham made sure that Sarah had her own tent. She was also heavily involved in their joint "outreach" operations — with the women and not with the men — and therefore she needed her own tent. And not only did she need her own tent, but the Torah wants us to know that it had to go up first because converting the women was more important than converting the men!

We can also answer our second question — why do we even need a *pasuk* to teach us that Avraham put up his wife's tent first? Isn't it obvious that Avraham would do that?

We need the *pasuk* to tell us that he put up two tents — and Sarah's first — so that we will understand that it was more important to convert the women first. It is also making sure we comprehend that since Sarah was working with the women, she needed a separate tent since it wouldn't have been modest for the men and women to have been taught together.

Loyalty Above All

אִמְרִי נָא אֲחֹתִי אָתְּ לְמַעַן יִיטַב לִי בַעֲבוּרֵךְ וְחָיְתָה נַפְשִׁי בִּגְלָלֵךְ
(בראשית יב:יג).

Please say that you are my sister, so that it will go well with me because of you, and that I will live on account of you (Bereishis 12:13).

Zera Shimshon asks: Why did Avraham say, "…so that it will go well with me…"?

Another question:

The obvious meaning of the statement "so that it will go well with me" is that Avraham would receive gifts from the king in exchange for the woman they assumed was his sister. But did Avraham Avinu think for a second that Sarah would want to be put into such a situation — even if they would be given presents and even if Hashem would no doubt come to her rescue?

And if you say that the main point of those words is that Avraham's life would be saved if the Egyptians believed that Sarah was his sister rather than his wife — we already know that information from the previous *pasuk,* which says that "[if the Egyptians find out that] you are my wife, they will kill me and let you live."

So what could Avraham have meant when he said "so that it will go well with me"?

Zera Shimshon answers:

Avraham Avinu was telling Sarah two separate things.

"First, I want you to tell the Egyptians that you are my sister so that I will be saved from death, since the moment they realize we are married they are going to kill me so that you will no longer be a married woman and they can abduct you.

"Second, I am sure that nothing will happen to you and that you will remain loyal to me. I am also sure that Hashem will save me and give me *berachos* in the merit of your loyalty."

Proof of this is found in the Gemara (*Bava Metzia* 59a) that says, "A person should always be careful to treat his wife with honor, since the blessing in a home comes only on account of his wife."

So here is still another question: Why does the blessing in a home come only on account of the wife?

The answer is that this is referring to a woman who is loyal to her husband — and whose loyalty brings blessing to the house. The Midrash (*Shemos Rabbah* 51:1) states, "Hashem brings blessing through people who are loyal." Therefore when a woman is loyal to her husband, Hashem sends His blessings.

This, then, was what Avraham Avinu was telling Sarah when he said, "...so that it will go well with me." Not that he was counting on receiving presents because the Egyptians would abduct her. Rather, since he knows that she is completely loyal to him and would never agree to do anything that would compromise their marriage, he is one hundred percent sure that blessings will come his way and everything will work out for them in the best possible way.

The *Zera Shimshon's* commentary on these *pesukim* makes clear the importance of the *eishes chayil*'s contribution to the well-being of the home — either because she is the one who keeps her husband strong in his convictions, or because it is through her loyalty that blessing comes to their house.

In the following story, you will read about an *eishes chayil* who characterized the traits of *chesed* and *emunah* — and the incredible blessing that came to many houses in the wake of her actions.

The first email was sent out to the members of the local N'shei by one of their own.

Sunday, August 23, 2020 at 7:48 PM
Subject: You can make a difference to someone I know…
Hi ladies,

There is a very special girl from my seminary who is getting married next week and who does not even have the cash to buy herself socks! Her chassan is from a broken and complicated background. I was wondering if any of you have any towels, linen, or anything nice or new that you can give her for her new home. I am turning to all of you because I really hope that her home will not be completely empty when she moves into it.

If anyone has anything for the cause, I will be happy to pick it up and have it taken to her.

I feel very uncomfortable writing this email, but because I got to know our group, I felt able to do this. I know you will want to help and will try to do what you can.

Thanks for being such an amazing group! I hope that we never need to post such emails again.

Waiting to hear from you ASAP,
*Chavi Meller

Chavi sent out the email to the members of the N'shei and sat back in her chair. Knowing the kind of women she had met at the last event, she was pretty sure they would be receptive to her appeal. She had never done anything like this before and it felt a little strange. Still if it helped, it would have been worth it.

"I guess now I just wait and see what happens," she said to herself. "At this point, it's out of my hands."

Then she went to do something else because, as they say, "A watched computer never pings…"

The second email was sent out the next day.
Monday, August 24, 2020 — 10:19 AM
Subject: Wow!!! I can't believe what I am seeing!!!

Ladies! Dear, dear ladies!

I want us all to know what kind of a community we are part of!

I am typing these words with my fingers running across the keyboard and tears streaming down my cheeks.

You women are unbelievably amazing!!!

I want to update you all on the incredible events that occurred after I sent you (uncomfortably) the email about my friend, the kallah.

Within less than an hour, I received emails asking where I live, since women wanted to come over to drop off the brand-new things that they wanted to donate. One super-special woman went tremendously out of her way to buy stuff for the kallah, also arranging for her to be able to shop and buy dresses at a store for free and doing her best to help with many more things.

So many of you have been in touch, donating money and reaching out with different ideas for how to help.

Sisters — בזכות נשים צדקניות נגאלו ישראל

Yes, seeing each of you give of your utmost and do your best for our kallah, I truly feel as if we are all sisters, all of us in this together!

Even though you do not know my friend and I don't really know most of you, you all pitched in and showed Hashem what a beautiful circle of sisters we have in this neighborhood. People who are here for one another. People who care!

Can you hear my heartbeat? I am overwhelmed by your open hearts and hands, by your generosity and by your kind-ness.

May we all always be here for one another!

May we all be on the giving end, with Hashem showering us with His eternal good. And may it be a year filled with health, happiness and besuros tovos for gantz Klal Yisrael.

With deep admiration for you all,
Chavi Meller

In all honesty, Chavi had not known what would happen when she sent out that first email about her friend. Her fingers had trembled a little when she wrote it, and trembled some more when she pressed the send button. She knew that it was the right thing to do, and she also knew that her friend really, really needed a miracle, so there wasn't much choice. But she'd had no idea how her appeal would be received. People are bombarded with so many emails asking them for *tzedakah*. Who was to say that hers would touch a chord in their hearts?

And yet –

The email touched their hearts and the response had been off the charts. Every time she looked at her computer, she still couldn't get over what had happened and the amount of help that had come in for her friend. The whole story was overwhelmingly beautiful.

And, as she had written to all her new friends, she really was proud of being part of such a wonderful community. She hoped that everyone who read the email understood just how grateful she was.

The third email was sent out almost a year later.

Thursday, June 10, 2021 — 3:28 PM

Subject: Your part in my personal story....

Hi ladies.

I've thought about this a lot and I have decided to share something personal with you, even though it is very unlike me to do so.

Allow me to remind you about an awesome chesed that you all did about ten months ago. That week, when all of you were calling and sending in new and beautiful stuff for a kallah who was about to begin her life with two small pots and four hand towels, was a life-changing experience for me.

At that time, I witnessed the depth of your giving hearts, your warm generosity and your true desire to help as much as possible, even though you didn't even know who the kallah was.

I remember how I received over forty emails from women wanting to help in a million ways — when I had sent out the email only an hour before! I remember how, by the end of the week, I had received almost a hundred emails from people wanting to help...

I will never forget how I went onto the balcony of my home with tears in my eyes and a heart filled with amazement. I looked up at the stars and said to Hashem,

בזכות נשים צדקניות נגאלו ישראל

ובזכות נשים צדקניות עתידין להיגאל

At that moment, I felt truly uplifted. Taking advantage of what I instinctively comprehended was a special moment, and still overwhelmed by the chesed I had just witnessed from all of you, I davened to Hashem from the depths of my heart to send me more children...

At the same time, I also used the opportunity to daven for my sister-in-law, who had been married for close to six years and was still waiting to be a mother — and for my sister as well, who had been waiting for four years...

"Hashem," I said, "please look at the special women in my neighborhood and accept my tears in their zechus!"

Ladies, I am overwhelmed, overjoyed and so, so thankful to Hashem for His endless kindness. And so, I am taking this opportunity to inform you all — every one of you — that my Rina Malka is now five weeks old!

I also want to tell you that my sister-in-law became a mother for the first time last Wednesday, to a precious baby girl.

And that my sister just had a baby boy two hours ago!

My dear sisters, did you ever in your wildest dreams imagine, when you came over to bring your new towel/knife/peeler/linen, that three babies — three beautiful Yiddishe kinder — would be born in the merit of your awesome chesed?!

Look how powerful one deed can be!!

Thank you for being a part of bringing these children into the world!

May Hashem shower each and every one of you with

endless joy and nachas, and may you be happy and healthy,
along with every member of your families!!

I am proud to be part of such a special community,
Good Shabbos,
Chavi Meller

The Eishes Chayil
and the Three Types of Reward

וְהָאֱלֹקִים נִסָּה אֶת אַבְרָהָם... וַיֹּאמֶר קַח נָא אֶת בִּנְךָ אֶת יְחִידְךָ
(בראשית כב:א-ב).

G-d tested Avraham... and He said, "Please take your son, your only one..." (Bereishis 22:1-2).

---

*A*keidas Yitzchak was a *nisayon,* a test that would bring Avraham Avinu reward even in this world.

Discussing this *pasuk,* the *Yalkut Shimoni* quotes (*Tehillim* 60:6): "To those who fear You, You gave a banner to be raised high..."

Says the *Yalkut Shimoni* (95):

> Challenge after challenge and test after test come to people in order to make them great. It is like the sail of a ship that is buffeted by the wind.
>
> Why so many challenges for Avraham? So that if a person comes along and says to you, "Hashem can make any person wealthy or poor or even turn him into a king, and in fact He actually did this to Avraham Avinu, making him rich and turning him into a king"; you can reply, "Yes. And you can have the same type of life. Just remember that Avraham was one hundred years old when his son Yitzchak was born, and even after all that pain, he was then told to take his son, his only one — and he did not refrain from doing so."

The Midrash is telling us that Avraham was tested so that Hashem would make his life better — even his life in this world, and even though in general, the Gemara (*Kiddushin* 39b) says, there is no reward for mitzvos in this world.

Zera Shimshon tells us that Avraham Avinu asked Hashem to test him and he was rewarded in this world, even though that is not usually the case. Since Avraham Avinu went above and beyond what was expected of him, Hashem did the same for Avraham. More: Hashem's reward to Avraham was given so that everyone could see that Hashem can reward in this world as well as in the next.

Women's Rewards

We will now use this as a means to evaluate the reward that an *eishes chayil* receives from her husband's learning — and how, when she goes above and beyond for him, the Torah that he studies and the Torah that his *talmidim* study is all connected to her.

The Gemara (*Berachos* 17a) relates that the promise that Hashem made to women is greater than the promise He made to men.

What promise is that?

Hashem promised the women of Klal Yisrael that they will be granted *Olam Haba*, the World to Come, as it says (*Yeshayahu* 32:9), "*Nashim shaananos*, rise up and hear my voice; confident daughters, listen to my speech."

What is the meaning of the word "*shaananos*"? It means filled with serenity and sure of themselves, since they know that they will merit a portion in the World to Come.

Rav said to Rabbi Chiya, "What is the *zechus* that helps women merit the World to Come?"

The answer?

They take their sons to the *beis knesses* to learn *Chumash* and Mishnah (in those times children studied in the shuls), they give their husbands permission to go study Torah in other cities, and they wait for their husbands to return home from learning (whether late at night or after a long period of being away from home).

Partners

The *Zera Shimshon* now raises a question:

The Gemara (*Kiddushin* 31a) states that someone who performs a mitzvah because he was commanded to do so receives more reward than someone who does a mitzvah without being commanded to do so. Men are commanded to study Torah, and women are not. So why is the Gemara telling me that women are assured a place in the World to Come as a reward for their enabling Torah study when they are not even commanded to study Torah in the first place? It would seem that a woman's reward would be less than that of a man — and definitely not more than her husband's!

The Gemara (*Sotah* 21a) says that while it is true that women are not obligated in the mitzvah of learning Torah and therefore you might think that she doesn't warrant reward, however, "She will be rewarded for helping her sons learn *Chumash* and Mishnah and for waiting for her husband to return from the *beis midrash*." And since she does this and gives her family members support, she is considered a full partner in the learning — and doesn't a partner deserve half of the profits?

Of course she does.

This Gemara isn't saying that women receive more reward than men — only that they are full partners in every sense of the word. But the Gemara in *Sotah* is still difficult to understand. Why should women — who, after all, are not commanded in the mitzvah of Torah learning — receive as much reward as their husbands? Yes, they should receive a certain amount of reward — but why fifty-fifty?

The Gemara (*Nedarim* 50a) tells us that when Rabbi Akiva returned home after twenty-four years of learning, he brought 24,000 *talmidim* with him, and when his wife, Rachel, came to greet her husband, the students didn't know who she was and didn't want to let her come before their rebbi. That was when Rabbi Akiva uttered the legendary line, "Leave her, for my [Torah] and your [Torah] are hers."

A line that implies that she was the recipient of all of the merit of their Torah study.

But how could that be? How could she have all the merit? After all, the Gemara told us that a woman gets half the reward — yet Rabbi Akiva seems to be saying that she gets all the merit of their learning!

To sum up:

The Gemara in *Berachos* taught that women receive lots of reward.

The Gemara in *Sotah* taught that they receive half the reward of their husbands.

And the Gemara in Nedarim quoted Rabbi Akiva, who seems to be saying that all the Torah learned and all the reward belongs to the wife!

What exactly is the meaning of all this?

On the *pasuk* (*Shemos* 19:3), "So shall you say to Beis Yaakov, and relate to Bnei Yisrael," the *Midrash Rabbah* (*Shemos* 28:2) says "Beis Yaakov are the women, Bnei Yisrael are the men."

Why is Hashem telling Moshe Rabbeinu to speak to the women about the Torah first, when men have more mitzvos? The answer, says the *Zera Shimshon*, is that Hashem told Moshe to let the women know about a command that He was directing straight to them — שֶׁתִּהְיֶינָה מְזָרְזוֹת אֶת בַּעֲלֵיהֶן לְלִמּוּד תּוֹרָה — "They should encourage their husbands to learn Torah." For that reason, the women were told first — because through their alacrity, they would cause their husbands to learn.

So while they do not have an obligation to actually learn Torah, they do have an obligation to encourage their husbands to learn — and for that they are rewarded, even though this is not included in the mitzvah of *talmud Torah*.

Reward 1: The Husbands Who Need Encouragement

From all this we can see that it is the wife's role to encourage her husband to learn when he needs her to give encouragement.

The Gemara (*Chagigah* 15a) states that when people are lazy about doing their mitzvos, the *tzaddik* in their midst who is not lazy and does the mitzvos will receive the lazy people's share as well.

Because this is the case, *Chazal* (*Berachos* 17a) tell us that the promise made to women is greater than the promise made to men. This is referring to a situation where the husband has a difficult time motivating himself to go learn, and his wife is the one who encourages him. When that is the case, her reward is greater than his. He will have his reward for going to learn, but she will receive half of his *schar* for learning, plus additional reward for encouraging him to fulfill his mitzvah of *talmud Torah*.

Reward 2: The Husbands Who Don't Need Encouragement

Of course there are many husbands who are excited about their learning and do not necessarily need much encouragement from their wives. Here it is less about her encouragement and more about her obvious pride and support in what he is accomplishing — and the fact that she is waiting for him when he comes home; all significant acts on her part and that will all make a difference to him.

There is a concept of giving encouragement to someone who, by his nature, is eager to do something. This is discussed in the Gemara (*Makkos* 23a) that states that encouragement should be given to someone even if he is naturally spirited and gets things done.

When this is the case, the Gemara (*Sotah* 21a) says that the wives divide the reward with their husbands, since both of them did what they were obligated to do: the husband through his learning and the wife through her encouragement.

So even though the *eishes chayil* doesn't have a mitzvah of *talmud Torah*, her mitzvah is to encourage her husband. She receives the same reward that he gets for his Torah study, since she has done her part and given him support, which is what Hashem commanded her to do at the time of *Mattan Torah*.

Reward 3: The Wife Who Sacrifices for Her Husband's Learning

We now come to the story of Rabbi Akiva, who famously said

that all of his Torah and all of his students' Torah belonged to his wife. This is a very different type of situation from the first two and means a very high-level reward for the wife.

Why?

In the case of Rabbi Akiva, who was away for twenty-four years, there was no way that he could have been away from his wife for that long had she not insisted that he do so. More: He left her in a penniless state — to the extent that the Gemara (*Nedarim* 50a) writes that she didn't even have proper clothing to wear (which is one of the reasons the students didn't want to allow her to approach their rebbi).

According to halachah, Rabbi Akiva was obligated to take care of her and to provide for her material needs. But that was not what she wanted. She preferred to suffer extreme poverty so that her husband would have the opportunity to become great in Torah. Rabbi Akiva owed Rachel a great debt, because there was no other way he would have been able to develop into the *tzaddik, talmid chacham* and *gadol* that he became. And since that was the case, it made sense for him to say, "What's mine and what's yours are hers."

To sum up:

We clarified the three types of situations where the *eishes chayil* receives reward for her involvement in her husband's learning.

The Gemara in *Berachos* is discussing a case where the husband needs encouragement and that is why, when the *eishes chayil* provides that push, her reward is very great.

The Gemara in *Sotah* is referring to a case where the husband doesn't actually need encouragement, yet the wife finds ways to support him and to make him feel good — especially when he returns home from a long day of learning. In this case she receives half of his reward.

The Gemara in *Nedarim* is a situation where she makes the choice to work incredibly hard and to give up many things that other women take for granted — for the sake of her husband's Torah learning. And when the *eishes chayil* does that, then all of her husband's Torah and all the reward of his Torah are hers.

Offering someone encouragement is the gift that never stops giving. You never know when the words you say to someone else will penetrate their mind and heart and be there for them when they most need to be strengthened. In particular, we are focused on the *eishes chayil* and her unique brand of encouragement to her husband.

But there are many people who give one another *chizuk*. Sometimes even to an individual who barely knows them.

Even so, their words can literally mean the difference between life and death. This story, which happened to my friend Rabbi Yaakov Morgan, is a classic example.

Rabbi Morgan's story:

Each year, I sell *lulavim* and *esrogim* from my home in Yerushalayim. On Motzaei Yom Kippur 2020, a yeshivah *bachur* came to work for me. The next day he learned that many of his fellow *talmidim* had come down with Covid-19, and as anticipated he, too, become a card-carrying member of the Coronavirus team.

Since I had been near him for quite a few hours, I wasn't surprised when I started to cough the next day. However, despite my cough, I wasn't sure if I had the virus, since I generally become ill every year during my *arba minim* sale. It might have been due to the amount of work I do during the season, or the change of weather at that time of year. Whatever the reason, I wasn't surprised that I had suddenly started to cough, and I was not convinced that it was Covid.

"I think I should get it checked out, just to make sure," I told my wife.

"We'll need to take a Corona test," she said.

And so the entire family went off on the first day of Chol HaMoed to be tested for Corona. It was a whole different kind of Chol HaMoed trip from the kind we usually did. On Monday, I got the results. I was positive for COVID-19.

My doctor, Dr. Munter, happens to be in charge of one of the Corona wards at Shaarei Tzedek, and we were in close contact in the days following the big news.

"I want you to start taking blood thinners and steroids," the doctor told me.

I started following his instructions, but my mother was unhappy that I wasn't being monitored in the hospital.

"I don't want to go to the hospital," I told my mother. "I've heard too many stories of people who went to the hospital and were cut off from their families, with detrimental results."

My mother, however, wouldn't give in. I called the doctor, who promised to prepare a bed for me in his ward and to personally oversee my case. I called Magen David Adom at eleven o'clock that night and they came down to take me to the hospital. I was coughing, running a fever and feeling very weak.

There were three people in my hospital room. The first bed held an 80-year-old man. The second patient was an Arab. I was in the last bed, closest to the wall. The old man in the first bed made a habit of calling for the nurses at least once an hour — at the top of his lungs. This meant that the Arab patient and I were never able to get any sleep. Whenever the old man raised his voice, the Arab would raise his, complaining at being disturbed. And because the other two patients in my room were so demanding, the nurses never really ended up coming to see me.

Since it was a Corona ward, I was not allowed to leave it. I was therefore visited by a medical team who came to my bed with an X-ray machine. Dr. Munter called me a little later.

"Yaakov, we're not so happy with how the X-ray looks."

"What does that mean for me?"

"It means that we are going to have to keep you here for a few days."

That was Thursday.

A doctor came to see me on Friday morning.

"Can I ask you a question?"

"Yes."

"How come they aren't giving me any antibiotics?"

"We only dispense medication that has been proven to work for Corona."

My breathing became a little worse as the day progressed and the staff switched me onto a machine called an Optiflow, which was stronger than a regular oxygen tank. Feeling that I could just as easily take oxygen and look after myself at home, I called the doctor and asked him if there was any way I could be released.

"Definitely not until after Shabbos."

It was Erev Simchas Torah, and I was stuck in the hospital.

Many people sent me packages all Friday. Unfortunately, I had no appetite and no energy. I told the nurses to leave the food at the side of my bed.

Another Corona patient came into my room to make *Kiddush* for me on Simchas Torah night. I tried singing a few Simchas Torah songs to myself to get into the mood. The night was more or less uneventful, but on the morning of Simchas Torah I was feeling pretty horrible. I had no interest in eating, but I knew that I had to force something down if I wanted to stay alive.

"Why aren't you eating?" the nurse asked, when she noticed that I hadn't touched anything.

"I have no energy."

"But look, there's some really nice stuffed chicken."

"I told you, I don't even have the energy to cut it up."

The nurse cut the stuffed chicken into pieces for me.

I picked up a piece of chicken. Held it in the air.

"Hashem," I said, "I'm eating this because it's Yom Tov."

I took a bite. Then a few more. I also tried to sing a little. It was Yom Tov, after all.

On Motzaei Simchas Torah, I felt truly terrible. By this point, my Optiflow machine was up to fifty percent. I was breathing half on my own, and half with the help of the machine. The problem was that I didn't even have the energy to pull the oxygen into my lungs. Which meant that the oxygen wasn't really doing much for me. Suddenly, a doctor walked into the room. He was wearing a Hazmat suit like the rest of the medical staff, so that only his eyes were visible.

"What's the problem?" he asked.

"I feel really bad. Please do something for me!"

He looked at my numbers and he looked at the machine. Then he turned up the oxygen level from fifty to ninety percent.

"You should know that the step after this is a respirator. I know many people who were put on a respirator and never got off. You need to get strong."

So saying, he gave me a pat on the shoulder and walked out of the room. I never saw him again. At the same time, I knew that I would never forget those intense eyes, and the way he warned me against getting too comfortable with the machine. He had been very serious, and the way he spoke frightened me badly.

After he left the room, I began reciting *Vidui*, sure that this was the end. I wasn't going to make it. Thoughts of the *chevrah kaddisha* began swirling through my mind as I drifted up and out of the hospital ward. I saw my father, who had passed away from Corona several months earlier. Part of me felt that I was heading in the same direction unless something drastic happened...

And then I recalled the encouragement that a visitor had given me. He was a chassidishe Yid who'd already had Corona and was given permission to come and go. He was the one who brought me a *lulav* and *esrog* and spent time with me when I was all alone.

"Reb Yaakov," he said, "I was in your situation. I already had Corona. But you have to know something. The only way you are going to get out of this is if you fight!"

As I recalled those words, I said to myself, "You are going to walk out of this hospital alive!! You are not going to end up on a respirator! You are going to fight!"

I began taking tiny breaths, and after every third or fourth breath, I said, *"Ein od milvado!* Hakadosh Baruch Hu, I will only be able to get out of here if you give me the strength to do so!"

I did a little more breathing.

Then I undertook a few *kabbalos*.

A few more breaths. Another *"Ein od milvado."*

"Hashem," I whispered, "if I get out of this hospital, I will do my best to spread my story, so I can show the world how much Hashem loves His people."

I felt extremely close to Hashem at that moment. The words, *"U'mal'ah ha'aretz de'ah es Hashem,"* entered my mind, as if to back up my earlier thought, and I knew that I was on the right path. I also knew that Hashem was taking care of me. Each time I was successful at taking a breath, it was another gift from the One Above.

One of the doctors entered my room the next morning. I especially liked this doctor, who had learned in the Mir as a *bachur*. I knew who he was since the doctors had started putting pictures of themselves on their Hazmat suits, so that the patients would know what they looked like.

"I've just learned about some new research," he said. "There's a certain medication that seems to have proven itself beneficial for Corona patients, and because the research has been done by a really professional group of people, we want to give our patients this medicine. It's expensive, but we are going to make sure that we get it covered by the Kupat Cholim for you."

"Great," I said.

The medication which the doctor was referring to needed to be administered over a five-day period. This meant I was now going to be in the hospital at least until the end of the week.

On Monday, they took another X-ray. Dr. Munter called me a little while later, letting me know that he was very unhappy with my X-ray.

"We want you to be closer to the heavier machines."

From his words, I understood that he wanted me moved closer to the respirators.

"I told the nurses that I want you moved to the ward that is next to the ICU."

"Do whatever you feel is right," I said.

The next thing I knew, a big, burly security guard entered my room with a wheelchair. He was accompanied by two nurses, one of whom had a huge oxygen tank for when they removed me from the breathing machine and transferred me to the next room. The second nurse had come to move my stuff to my new room. There was a lot of stuff.

"Get into the wheelchair," the guy said.

I got into the wheelchair.

He then wheeled me into the same back elevator that they used when I came into the hospital. When we emerged onto the new floor, I couldn't get over what I was seeing. Men with guns stood at every intersecting hallway, making sure that nobody got close to me. As I was wheeled down the hall, they yelled at anyone who came too close, "Go back! Corona!"

When they brought me into my new ward, I knew that they would bring me an Optiflow machine. Until they did, I had an oxygen tank. I was fairly comfortable and not in too much pain. The linen on the bed was pink, and upon closer inspection I saw that it had been brought from the maternity ward. I found that cute and even a little uplifting.

"I feel reborn again," I said to myself. I would have liked to have been able to use the line, since it was a good one, but there was never anyone around when you needed them.

Everyone else in the ward was heavily sedated and on a respirator. I was the only one there who was still awake. It was a surreal feeling, to put it mildly.

They gave me some medicine to help me fall asleep that night, and I slept very well from about twelve till four. Suddenly, I noticed that I was feeling markedly better. There was a noticeable difference. I looked at my phone. The entire time I had been in the hospital, it had been ringing off the hook. I hadn't been up to talking to anyone other than my wife. Now I called my mother. Then I called my brother.

By the middle of the week, I was really feeling better. They informed me that I was going to be moved yet again.

"I like it here."

"Don't worry, we're moving you to an even better place."

This time, a nurse moved me instead of the big, burly security guy. It wasn't easy for her, since I'm not the smallest person in the world. Somehow, she managed to move me into my new room, which, for whatever reason, contained only one bed. This was a nice surprise. I finished my medicine that Thursday, and by Friday I was back on a regular oxygen tank, whose level they were slowly lowering as I became able to breathe better and better on my own.

I called the doctor.

"Can I please go home for Shabbos?"

"Sorry. You have to stay at least until Sunday."

I was ready for Shabbos and sitting in the chair in my room, when a brand-new melody suddenly popped into my head to the words of *"U'mal'ah ha'aretz de'ah es Hashem k'mayim lamayim mechasim."*

I sang the song to myself over and over, knowing that I was going to want to remember it. I am not in the habit of composing songs, and this was a big deal for me. That was the way I went into Shabbos.

An Arab orderly brought me a bottle of grape juice from another ward. I made *Kiddush* and had my *seudah*. I took my time that night, singing every one of the *zemiros* in the book. Meanwhile, they had set the oxygen machine to its lowest setting, since my breathing was almost back to normal. When a nurse came in to see me, I told him, "There's no reason for me to be here anymore. Please let me go home."

"We have no interest in keeping you here for no reason," he replied. "Here's an idea for you. If you don't feel like you need the oxygen machine anymore, then take it off and see what happens."

I took it off, and my numbers were okay.

That was a pretty great moment.

I ended up going home on Sunday afternoon. The first thing we did after I entered my own house, after so many days of lying stranded in the hospital, was to say *Mizmor L'sodah* together as a family.

Today I am back to myself, after coming very close to never returning home. Very often I find myself thinking of my experiences in the hospital, and how that chassidishe *yungerman* told me that I had to fight, and how the doctor told me that the last thing I wanted was to be put on a respirator.

I will never forget the moment when I composed my song of thanks, while sitting up and feeling good for the first time in so long. As I said, it was a time when I felt extremely close to the Ribbono shel Olam. While I would never want to go through something like that again, I have tremendous *hakaras hatov* for the incredible kindness from Above of which I was, and continue to be, a grateful recipient. I have also done my best to publicize my story, as I promised I would.

The Segulah of the Zera Shimshon

"My father-in-law is a very respected Yid from Yerushalayim," said *Reb Avigdor Lehrfeld. "Though no longer young, he is an agile person who gets things done and is very active in the area of *gemilus chasadim*. He also possesses a sharp sense of humor and an instinctive understanding of people, and always knows which people need help.

"When Shabbos comes, he doesn't let up on himself despite the fact that it's much more difficult to get around. Instead, he actually works harder. He likes to say, "The people who normally help aren't around, so my help is needed even more…"

Because this is his philosophy, he is constantly busy throughout Shabbos with a wide range of mitzvos. He gives *shiurei Torah*, visits sick people who are stuck at home, and goes out of his way to bring cheer and joy to the homes of widows and orphans.

Two years ago, my father-in-law was diagnosed with diabetes. It became harder and harder for him to get around, until it reached the point where he needed to be wheeled from place to place in a wheelchair. This meant that he was no longer able to do the acts of *chesed* that had once been such a natural part of his life, and to which he had shown such endless *mesiras nefesh*. It goes without saying that the new developments in his life pained him very much.

My wife and I visited many doctors and consulted with numerous specialists in our quest to help him recover, but nothing came of our efforts. Instead, his pains grew worse and he became less and less mobile. In addition to all of his health issues, my father-in-law was suffering from something else that bothered him no less: the fact that his youngest son, my brother-in-law, was already thirty years old and still unmarried. My father-in-law had both of these hardships sitting squarely on his mind at all times.

It was not in my father-in-law's nature to pick up his hands and admit defeat. He was a person who had always been optimistic by nature and was never willing to give up hope. In his mind, the answer was simple. It was merely a question of davening for Hashem to light up his eyes and give him direction.

My father-in-law had been suffering for a while when he first heard about the *segulah* of the *Zera Shimshon*. From that day on, everyone around him was treated to a wide array of beautiful ideas from the Torah of the *Zera Shimshon*. Shabbos and Yom Tov meals began turning into *shiurim* in Rav Shimshon Chaim's Torah. My *shver* had become a chassid.

Every time he had the opportunity to introduce someone new to the *Zera Shimshon's* Torah, he would read to them from Rav Shimshon Chaim's *berachah*, written in the *sefer's* introduction. He would follow that by repeating a piece or two from the *sefer*. At the end of every *seudah*, he would conclude with the words, "I want you to know that the *berachah* of such a holy *tzaddik* will come true without a doubt!"

Some members of the family expressed their reservations, worried that he was placing so much hope in the *sefer*. After all, what if his hopes and dreams didn't come true and everything remained the same?

Some people even tried to cool him off a little, hoping to help him avoid the "inevitable disappointment." But he shrugged them off and continued learning the *sefer* with even more passion, always saying, "I believe in the *koach* of the *tzaddikim*."

And you know what? The *Zera Shimshon* didn't disappoint.

A few months later, and against all the odds, my father-in-law's condition began to improve. In a year, he was walking around on his own two feet, as if nothing had ever happened! And to top it all off, my brother-in-law got engaged a short while later as well.

It goes without saying that after my *shver* experienced such wonderful miracles, he never stopped learning *Zera Shimshon*. When he spent the following Succos at my home, he brought the *Zera Shimshon* along, explaining, "There was no way I could leave my *sefer* at home. With such an important thing, one doesn't take chances of going without it..."

The Enigma of Devorah

וַתָּמָת דְּבֹרָה מֵינֶקֶת רִבְקָה (בראשית לה:ח).

Devorah, Rivkah's wet nurse, died (Bereishis 35:8).

Shlomo HaMelech wrote (*Mishlei* 10:1), "A wise son gladdens his father, while a foolish son is his mother's sorrow."

Zera Shimshon raises a question. Why does the wise son bring happiness to his father, while the mother suffers because of her foolish son? You would think that if a son is intelligent the joy would belong equally to both parents, and if the son is a fool, both parents would be sad.

Why is the father mentioned in reference to wisdom and the mother in reference to foolishness?

Zera Shimshon answers that a wise son brings praise to his father, since the father provided guidance to his son and led him on the right path.

What about the foolish son? Here, his foolishness is attributed specifically to his mother.

Why?

Mothers and Sons

Zera Shimshon begins to answer by giving a few other examples where the mother seems to be "blamed" for her foolish or wicked son.

Rashi asks why the *Chumash* tells us that Devorah, Rivkah's wet nurse, died. He explains that the mourning was not only for Devorah's passing, but also for Rivkah's death, because this was when Yaakov learned of his mother's passing. Why didn't the Torah discuss Rivkah's death openly, rather than just hinting at it?

The Torah did not want people to curse Rivkah for having given birth to a son like Esav. Therefore the Torah only alludes to her passing by telling us that Devorah died — and through this we understand that Rivkah passed away as well.

When Yitzchak Avinu passed away, the Torah recorded the event and was not concerned about what people would say. Yet when it came to Rivkah, the Torah went out of its way to protect her because of people's tendency to blame the mother of a problem child.

Zera Shimshon now reminds us: Just as people look askance at a mother who raises an evil child, so too do they praise a mother when her children turn out well, as the *pasuk* says, "Blessings of the bosom and the womb" (*Bereishis* 49:25), meaning, "Blessed is the breast that nursed such [a son], and the womb that brought forth such [a son]" (*Bereishis Rabbah* 98:20).

Batsheva and Shlomo

Zera Shimshon cites another example of a foolish child being blamed on the mother and not the father. The Gemara (*Sanhedrin* 70b) quotes the *pasuk* (*Mishlei* 31:1), "The words of Lemuel the king [i.e., Shlomo HaMelech], the prophecy with which his mother disciplined him," informing us that Batsheva — David HaMelech's wife and Shlomo's mother — reprimanded him.

This, says the Gemara, is what Batsheva said to her son Shlomo:

> "How could it be that you, my son, are choosing to take a wrong path? Everyone knows that your father David is God-fearing. Yet you made a party to celebrate your marriage to the daughter of Pharaoh, and now you have risen late in the day. People are going to say that it was I, your mother, who caused this type of behavior. They will blame me and not your father."

From here we see once again that when a son acts foolishly, his behavior is attributed to the mother and not the father — which is why the *pasuk* in *Mishlei* says "his mother's sorrow."

Why do people have the tendency to blame the mother and not the father? And why does the *pasuk* speak about "blessings of the bosom and womb"?

A Nursing Mother's Influence

Zera Shimshon explains:

The Gemara (*Sotah* 12b) discusses the portion in *Chumash* where Miriam tells Pharaoh's daughter that she will go and call a Jewish woman to nurse the baby that Bisya found floating in the water. The Gemara states that Bisya first tried to have Moshe nurse from the Egyptian women in the vicinity, but he refused to nurse from them.

Said Hashem, "Can a mouth that will speak with me in the future eat something impure?"

A *pasuk* (*Yeshayah* 28:9) says: "To whom shall one teach knowledge? To whom shall one explain a message? To those weaned from mother's milk." This is referring to Moshe Rabbeinu, who nursed only from his mother, who made sure that she didn't consume anything impure.

From this and other examples, we learn that the nourishment a child receives from his mother has an influence on whether the child grows up to be righteous or evil.

For that reason, Shlomo HaMelech's mother said, "People are going to say that you acted improperly and are following your heart's impulses because I ate impure food and you nursed from me."

The implication? Mother's milk has an effect upon the child, whether he will become a *tzaddik* or a *rasha*.

Of course, a wise child is a product of both his father and his mother — who went out of her way to eat only kosher food. The Mishnah (*Avos* 2:8) praises the one who gave birth to Rabbi Yehoshua ben Chananiah, attributing his greatness to his mother. Yet at the same time we find the *pasuk* we cited earlier that states, "A wise son gladdens his father," without including the mother.

The *Zohar* writes (*Parashas Chukas* 183b) that when a man's name is mentioned, even if there are one hundred women and only one man, the people are referred to in the masculine; that is, they are included in his name. For this reason the *pasuk* says, "Let the father rejoice," without mentioning the mother — since the mother is included in the father. So when it says in *Mishlei*, "A wise son gladdens his father," and the mother isn't mentioned, it's because she doesn't have to be, since she is included with the father. More: She had a very important job.

What job?

The job of being careful not to consume anything impure, which would have caused him damage when he nursed from her.

And what about the second half of the *pasuk,* that connects the foolish son to his mother?

This is attributed to the mother, and has nothing to do with the father, because it was the mother who ate the impure foods and caused her son to become a fool and to go on the wrong path, by nursing him with milk that was impure.

Who Comes First?

Zera Shimshon suggests another approach to the *pasuk*, "A wise son gladdens his father, while a foolish son is his mother's sorrow." This explanation is based on a Gemara (*Kiddushin* 29b) that details what should be done if both a father and his son want to learn Torah, but there are not enough resources to allow both of them to study instead of work. The Gemara says that if both are capable of learning, the father takes precedence. However, if the son is particularly quick and gifted, and he retains what he has learned, the son takes precedence and is the one who is allowed to sit and learn.

So when a father has a wise son, he will send his son to learn before going himself. Since the son possesses a sharp mind and knows how to ask questions and supply answers and retains his learning, it makes sense that he should be the one to learn.

In such a case, the father rejoices because he has such a wise son, even if this means that he himself cannot go learn.

But when the son is a fool, the father won't be as sad as the mother, because at least he can comfort himself with the fact that now he can go and learn himself, since he is more deserving than his son.

The mother, on the other hand, is filled with sorrow, since her husband is going away to learn, leaving her at home with their foolish son. And that is why the *pasuk* writes about "his mother's sorrow." ˙

Zera Shimshon stresses an important point — in a very real way it is the mother who causes her son to have the propensity to develop into something great or, Heaven forbid, the opposite, depending on the choices she makes in her life.

And yet, even if a mother does take her children down winding and torturous paths, there is always hope that she will find a way to bring them back one day. It may take years, but there is always the chance that in the end, the natural goodness in her heart will prevail and her children will return.

Consider the following example:

I had the privilege of spending a couple of years doing *kiruv* work in the English city of Nottingham. There was not much going on for Jewish people in Nottingham, and I ended up becoming the sole connection to *Yiddishkeit* for quite a few people there — especially the college students who were living in the nearby dorms. I met a lot of interesting people during my years in the city. I'd like to focus on two of them.

The first one went by the name of Johnny Cohen. Johnny had been raised as a non-Jew, but at some point decided to move to Israel and join the IDF. There he acquired some sort of Jewish identity. He wasn't religious at all, but he did appreciate the fact that he was a Jew. Johnny was a well-built individual and when he returned from Israel, he found a job working as a bouncer at the largest bar in town.

After the two of us met, I made a point of spending time with him and we became very close.

"Johnny," I said to him one day, "you know that I would do anything for you, right?"

"Yes, Rabbi," he replied, his eyes serious.

"Good, because that's the truth. But I also want something from you."

He looked at me curiously, wondering what I could possibly want from him.

"Johnny, I want you to promise that if a Jew should ever happen to get in trouble in your bar, you will be there for him. Can you promise me that?"

Johnny considered my words and eventually made the promise. At the time, I had no idea how important a promise it was going to be...

One evening, a Jewish boy from the university named Alex was hanging out at the bar when he made a potentially fatal mistake. In England, one of the popular sports is rugby. In general, rugby players tend to be on the larger side and are no strangers to violence, as rugby tends to get extremely rough. The mistake the Jewish student made that night was when he somehow managed to pick a fight with the captain of the university rugby team. Since the rest of the team were all sitting and drinking with the captain, the response was quick and brutal.

Alex was lifted up and off his feet and carried by the team out the back door of the bar and into the alley just beyond. There the team began pounding him enthusiastically. If not for the fact that Alex managed to get out a few screams before the beating commenced, there is every chance that he would have been pounded to death that night.

However, in those final moments before he was lifted off his feet and bodily thrown through the door into the alley, Alex remembered me — his rabbi — telling him that if he was ever in trouble at the bar he should seek out Johnny Cohen. In the split seconds that he had before he couldn't speak anymore, Alex managed to call out Johnny's name a couple of times. Then he was on the ground, being pummeled by the entire rugby team.

"I heard Alex calling out for my help," Johnny told me later.

"I knew that he'd been pulled outside and was in danger of being beaten to within an inch of his life, or even losing it entirely. However, I had a problem. If the fight had taken place inside the bar, it would have been okay for me to break up the fight since I was the bar's bouncer and my job was to deal with violence. But once they had grabbed him and moved him outside the bar and into the alley, the fighting was no longer taking place under my jurisdiction and I really had no business getting involved.

"Except —

"Except that I had promised you, Rabbi, that I would help any Jew who was in trouble in the bar, and I wanted to keep my promise. Even if that meant putting myself in danger.

"How could I ignore the fact that a fellow Jew might be killed just outside the bar where I worked?

"The answer was: I couldn't ignore it. I had to get involved.

"The next thing I knew, I was running outside, throwing myself into the center of the melee as I separated the wild rugby players who were punching and kicking Alex on the ground. Seeing me leaving the bar, some of the other security fellows came along and helped me pull everyone apart. Yet even with all the help, one of the rugby players hit me hard enough that I suffered a concussion and ended up in the hospital."

Of course I told Johnny how impressed I was with him for being willing to put his own life in danger for a fellow Jew. He just looked back at me, meeting my gaze, and said, "I had to help him. I couldn't let them kill another Jew."

While Johnny didn't become *frum* during our time together, I admired his willingness to be *moser nefesh* for another Yid — just because he was a Yid. To me, his behavior was a real lesson that every member of Klal Yisrael would do well to learn. Yet while Johnny's story was fascinating, something else occurred while I was in Nottingham that showed me that, no matter where a person comes from or what he has done in life, there is always a chance that things will change and that they will become an authentic Jew. Maybe even a *ben Torah*.

It all began on Chanukah. It was a big night for us because I was throwing a Chanukah party for all the Jewish students at a local venue, complete with music, plenty of food, and entertainment. People were turning up at a rapid rate and I was busy greeting everyone who walked through the door, making them feel welcome and looked after. Suddenly, one of the security guards we had hired for the evening approached me.

"Excuse me, Rabbi?"

"Yes?"

"There's a man outside who wants to see you."

"Why don't you show him in then?"

"Because he looks like a Nazi."

"What do you mean?"

"Exactly what I said. He has the look, the coloring, the manner and the haircut of a neo-Nazi."

"What did he say when he tried coming in?"

"He said that he wanted to attend the party. But I took one look at him and wanted to make sure that you were okay with such a person coming inside when there's a real possibility that he is up to no good and might even be dangerous."

"I guess I might as well go and meet this man."

I went to the front of the building, where I found a man waiting in the cold. It was just as the security man had said. He really did have the stereotypical look of a neo-Nazi. At the same time, he was here because he wanted to attend a Chanukah party. The question was — where did the truth lie?

"The life of a rabbi," I mused to myself...

"How can I help you?" I asked the man.

"Are you the rabbi here?"

I nodded.

"Can I please speak with you?"

"What's your name?"

"Johann."

"Where are you from?"

"Austria."

So the guard was on the right track. Maybe he really *was* a Nazi. On the other hand, I wasn't getting that kind of vibe from him. Besides, I had hired security at the party for a reason. If there were any problems, I was pretty sure they would be able to handle it.

"Okay, come on in."

Five minutes later, we were seated at a table.

"So, what's the story?" I asked.

"I was born in Austria," he began. "Growing up, I always knew that my grandfather had been a member of the Nazi party. I didn't put much thought into it. It was just a part of my life and had always been.

"However, not long ago my grandmother, my mother's mother, became very sick and grew progressively weaker and weaker. Near the end, she asked me to come and see her. When I was sitting at her bedside, she said, 'Johann, there is something that I need to share with you. You know that your grandfather was a Nazi. But there is something else that you need to know. I was born into a Jewish family, and grew up that way from the beginning of my life.'

"I was completely shocked, and looked it.

"'I know that I am shocking you,' she said. 'It really is a crazy story. I was sent to a labor camp along with the rest of my family. It was there that I met your grandfather, who was a guard at the camp. I don't know why he was willing to do what he did next, as it put his life in danger, but your grandfather made the decision to save my life. He obtained false papers for me and used those papers to clear my name from the records of Jewish prisoners. Because of his actions, I was able to survive the war.

"'When the war was over and I realized that my entire family had probably been killed by the Nazis, I didn't know what to do. That was when your grandfather told me that he wanted to marry me.

"'As a Jewish girl, I should have never agreed to do such a thing. But I was all alone in the world— and he had put his own life in danger to save mine. In the end, I agreed to marry him.

"'Although I agreed to marry your grandfather, I never forgot that I am really a Jewish woman. I knew that the day would come when I would tell someone the truth. I know that I will soon be leaving this world, and I made the decision to tell you the truth so that you could go and find out what it means to be a Jew. You will be able to see what I gave up.

"'No doubt the Jewish people you will meet will want proof that you are in fact of Jewish descent. I prepared for that as well, since I saved the papers that I had at the beginning of the war. There you will see my real Jewish name and the names of my parents and siblings. I want you to take the papers and use them to prove that you are telling the truth.'

"My grandmother passed away a few weeks after our fateful meeting," Johann said.

"Of course," Johann continued, "it was hard to believe the story I had just been told. But my grandmother had never lied to me before, and her story had the ring of truth. Besides, she had real proof to back herself up, proof that I have with me.

"I took her story seriously, and I told myself that since she was a Jew, I should probably try and find out what the Jewish religion is all about. I did a lot of research and spoke to many people. I even left Austria and traveled to England in search of the truth. When I found out about your Chanukah party tonight, I knew that I had to come here, tell you my story and ask you what I should do next."

Johann's story was one of the most far-out tales I had ever heard in my life. But I knew it was true, and so did the *beis din*. In the end, he underwent *giyur l'chumrah*, but everyone knew that he was a genuine Jewish boy, born of a Jewish woman who had been the daughter of a Jewish woman.

Once he figured out what life was all about, you couldn't slow him down. Johann jumped into the ocean of Torah as if he had been swimming there his entire life. Eventually he left England and moved to Eretz Yisrael, where he continued learning. Today he is married and learning in kollel — yes, the grandson of an

Austrian Nazi — *shteiging* away, still blond and blue-eyed, still tall and muscular, still good-looking in that Aryan way.

But at the same time, a *ben Torah*, through and through. And I couldn't be prouder of him if I tried.

A Paid Vacation

תְּנוּ לָהּ מִפְּרִי יָדֶיהָ וִיהַלְלוּהָ בַשְּׁעָרִים מַעֲשֶׂיהָ (משלי לא, לא).
*Give her from the fruits of her hands, and they will
praise her actions at the gates* (Mishlei 31:31).

he *Shulchan Aruch* (*Orach Chaim* 670:1) discusses the custom
some women have to refrain from working during specific
times on Chanukah.

As he examines this issue, *Zera Shimshon* quotes the *pasuk* from
Eishes Chayil: "Give her from the fruits of her hands, and they will
praise her actions at the gates."

He then raises several questions:

First, the words "from the fruits of her hands" imply that she
already has the fruit in her hands. If so, why does the *pasuk* begin
by saying "give her," which implies that the fruits will be given to
her? Also, "from the fruits of her hands" seems to imply that she
will be given some of the fruits, but not all of them. Why?

And one final question: Why is the *eishes chayil* specifically
praised "at the gates" and not elsewhere?

There are some women who do not work on Chanukah during
the entire night. There are also some women who add to that custom,
and do not work on the first and eighth days, daytime as well. Others take this even further and do not perform any labor throughout
the entire Chanukah. (Nowadays, many women have the custom not
to do work during the first half-hour that the candles are burning.)

The Acharonim debate whether the custom of women refraining

from working on Chanukah is an authentic *minhag*, or something that does not have to be adhered to closely.

There is a school of thought that posits that the husband should be able to insist that his wife do work on Chanukah. Why? Since he provides for his wife's needs, the halachah says that the work of her hands belongs to him, and one can argue that she is therefore not allowed to be *machmir* on her husband's account, since by not working she is causing him a loss.

Another opinion suggests that if the wife insists on not working on Chanukah, then the husband is not obligated to provide her with her needs during those days, as it says in the *Shulchan Aruch* (*Even HaEzer* 85:15) that any woman who refrains from doing the work that she is obligated to do does not have to be provided for until she takes responsibility for her obligations.

Along Comes the Taz

The *Taz* (*Turei Zahav, Orach Chaim* 670:2) compares this case to the case of women not working on Rosh Chodesh. He cites a halachah (*Bach, Orach Chaim* 410) that says that though some women have a *minhag* not to work on Rosh Chodesh, husbands cannot compel them to work.

That being the case, says the *Taz*, the same halachah should apply to Chanukah, and the husband should not be permitted to insist that his wife work.

In addition, the *Taz* adds, even if halachically a woman may work on Chanukah, since the women of Klal Yisrael have taken upon themselves not to do so, we should not say it is permitted. If we do, there is the risk that they may permit themselves to do other things that are halachically forbidden.

Keeping all this in mind, we can now understand why the *pasuk* says "give her from the fruits of her hands." Even though she didn't do her regular work during the days of Chanukah, her husband should give her what he's obligated to give her. Working on Chanukah would have been considered "extra," and as such, would belong to her — the fruits of her labor.

And why didn't she do her work? Since a big part of the Chanukah miracle happened through the hands of a woman, therefore "they will praise her actions at the gates," i.e., while lighting the menorah. Why "gates"? Because the mitzvah of lighting the menorah is done close to the doorpost of the gateway of the house.

The verse in *Mishlei* makes a point of stressing to the husband that he must continue to take care of all his wife's needs even though she isn't working on Chanukah — and this makes sense, since he is really giving her "from the fruits of her hands."

The Fruits of Her Labors

Why does the *pasuk* say מִפְּרִי יָדֶיהָ — "from the fruits," and not מִמַּעֲשֵׂה יָדֶיהָ — "from her labors"?

Zera Shimshon quotes a Gemara (*Kesubos* 64b) that discusses a dispute between Rabbi Akiva and the *Chachamim* on the question of what happens when a woman pushes herself to do more work than is expected of her; for example, she rose in the middle of the night to work at a time when everyone else is sleeping.[1]

Now the question becomes, who receives the extra money, the woman or her husband?

The *Shulchan Aruch* (*Beis Shmuel, Even HaEzer* 80:2) says that the custom is not to take the money away from her. Instead, the money is used to purchase a piece of real estate that belongs to her, while the husband benefits from the profits made off the land.

The money that she has made from doing the extra work is not called "her labors" because that term is used in reference to the usual kinds of work that all women do. But work that she does because she pushed herself beyond normal limits has a different name. That kind of work is called "the fruits of her hands."

Why?

Again, because this kind of work is like "the fruits of her labor" — extra work, whose fruits belong to her. The *pasuk* tells the husband, "give her from the fruits of her hands," meaning, provide for

---

1. This concept is discussed earlier, in the section on "She arises while it is still nighttime," page 85.

your wife even if she isn't working on Chanukah — because of the work that she does when she goes above and beyond, from which you, the husband, profit.

And because she works so hard at those times, she deserves to have a "paid" vacation during Chanukah!

And she is right for not wanting to work then, because "they will praise her actions at the gates," as they remember that the main Chanukah miracle came about through a woman.

Questions: Answered!

To summarize, *Zera Shimshon* has answered all the questions he's raised:

1. The husband should be considerate about his wife's Chanukah "vacation." He should "give her" — that is, continue to provide for her — even if she is not working, because she is an *eishes chayil* who works extra all year round to bring him "from the fruits of her hands," when she works extra and he retains the profits from the fruits of that extra work.

2. He profits only partially from those extra earnings, because the capital remains with her.

3. They praise her "at the gates" because of candles lit by the gates. The women are an essential part of the Chanukah miracle.

At the end of the day a person's *parnassah* comes through his wife. And he has to remember that and to appreciate everything that she does for him — whether she has an official job or not. Because she brings the *mazel* into the house.

Let me give you an example of what I mean. It happened that an *eishes chayil* decided that her family needed to go away. Even if they didn't have the money to do so. And Hashem took her wishes into consideration.

The whole story was something I never would have imagined. I wasn't planning to take a trip at the time — things were crazy enough as it was. But when I arrived home from shul one morning and went to make myself a cup of coffee, *Shevi sat down across from me and gave me the news.

"We need to go away."

"What are you talking about?"

"We need to take the family on a trip."

"But we're in the middle of a Corona pandemic," I protested. "What kind of trip can we take?"

"We'll figure out an itinerary and decide where to go," she said. "The main thing is that we need to take the kids and go away."

"What's the emergency?"

"The emergency is that the kids have been cooped up in the house for months on end, and they are going out of their collective minds. Shaya, especially, needs to get out before he loses it completely. You know what I'm talking about."

I did know what she was talking about, and it was true — Shaya did need to get out of the house. But going away for a trip meant renting a car, and renting a car for a family our size is no simple thing. It would be quite expensive, even for just one day.

"Shevi," I said, "I am not arguing with you. But the fact is, renting a car for the Neuman family is going to cost *harbei kesef* (plenty of money), and we don't exactly have *harbei kesef* right now."

"I know that," she replied. "But we still need to rent the car and go on a trip."

I looked at her, she looked at me. I nodded in resignation.

"I will rent the car," said I.

"When?"

"I guess we can take the trip tomorrow. So I will rent the car after Shacharis."

By then my coffee was cold, and I decided to prepare another one. As the water boiled and I spooned some coffee and sugar into the waiting cup, I reflected that even though the money wasn't there and I didn't know how I was going to pay for it, my rebbeim had educated me that it is always a good idea to listen to your wife. Having been married for quite some time, I knew this to be true. Which is why I left shul early the next morning, after davening, and headed over to the local rent-a-car.

I'm sure you won't be surprised to learn that there were not a lot of people waiting in line ahead of me. Very few people were renting cars those days, because there are very few places to visit. Minutes later, I found myself behind the wheel of a nice-looking vehicle for which I was being charged the grand sum of 1,700 shekel for one day.

I had no idea where I was going to find the 1,700 shekel to pay for the car, but I was listening to my *eishes chayil* and I had a feeling that it was all going to work out just fine.

I parked the car outside my building, slipped the keys into my pocket, and entered the apartment, stowing my *tallis* bag in the hallway closet on my way in. As I was making my way toward the kitchen, which was filled with the happy sounds of an excited family getting ready to leave for a trip, my phone rang.

I glanced down at the screen. It was an American number.

"Hello?"

"Hi, Reb Uri. How's it going?"

"*Baruch Hashem.* Who is this?"

"Moshe Mermelstein. Do you remember me?"

The name was vaguely familiar.

"Remind me, please."

"You learned with my son Nosson ten years ago in yeshivah. You were his morning *seder chavrusa.*"

I remembered Nosson Mermelstein. We had been *chavrusos* for about a year. I recalled our time together, and how the learning had been very good. Of course, even good *chavrusos* don't last forever. There comes a time when they pack their bags and return home to the United States.

At least I had been left with nice memories.

All this flashed through my mind in the second after he'd introduced himself.

"What can I do for you, Reb Moshe? Do you have another son coming to learn in Eretz Yisrael?"

"No, that's not why I'm calling."

Now I was getting curious.

"Okay. What is it, then?"

"This is going to sound a little funny, but I recently made a nice business deal and I wanted to send some money to some *yungeleit* in Eretz Yisrael."

"Wow! That's really nice of you, Reb Moshe," I said. "But I don't need money."

You may be wondering why I said such a thing, when you know that I did in fact need money. The answer is that long ago I made the decision to try my hardest not to become a person who makes a practice of accepting money from others. I cannot tell you how many times people have looked at me strangely due to this resolve of mine. In fact, I recall one particular occasion when the father of one of my *talmidim* came to visit his son at the yeshivah. He had already paid me for that month, but after we finished talking and I'd given him a report on his son's progress, he thanked me profusely for everything I was doing and handed me an envelope.

"What's this?"

"Just a little token of my appreciation."

"You mean, like a tip?"

"Exactly."

I handed it back to him.

"Thank you, but I'm really okay."

What can I say? I just don't like taking money from people.

So there I was, standing in the hallway and talking to Mermelstein.

"Look," he said. "Just give me your bank account information so I can send you the money."

"That's really not necessary."

"Reb Elimelech," Mermelstein said, "I am sending you the money. So stop arguing with me and tell me what I need to know."

I kept my voice steady.

"Reb Moshe, I don't need the money. Let me give you an example of how much I don't need the money. I just came from the rental place, where I rented a car for a nice sum. If I am willing to spend that kind of money just to rent a car, you will admit that I am not the right candidate for a bank transfer. Do me a favor and give the money to someone who really needs it."

"No, I want to give it to you. And if you don't cooperate, I will call your home number and ask your wife for the bank details. Stop fighting me and just give in. It's not that much money and I am going to do it, come what may!"

In the end, I gave in and provided the account information. Sometimes it's just not worth the fight. If he was so intent on giving me money, then clearly Hashem wanted this to happen.

But I did have one question.

"Reb Moshe?"

"Yes?"

"I have to ask you something."

"Please."

"Why now?"

"What do you mean?"

"Well, think about it. I learned with Nosson ten years ago and haven't heard from you since. What made you decide, after all this time, to pick up the phone and call me specifically today?"

"I'll tell you what happened. A few hours ago, I happened to pick up a *sefer* off my bookshelf. I don't know why. It just caught my eye. As I opened the cover, I realized that someone had written something on the flyleaf. Obviously, I was curious to see who the writer was and what he had written. Anyway, it didn't take me long to realize that you were the one who wrote the inscription. You wrote it to my son. The *sefer* was a present from you to him, celebrating your time and what you accomplished together.

"When I saw your warm and meaningful words, I suddenly recalled how much you cared for Nosson and how you helped him that year, and I wanted to show you a small token of my appreciation. I know that you were *chavrusos* a long time ago, but I thought to myself, "better late than never..."

We got off the phone a short while later. I stood in the hallway thinking about the conversation, and how the things you do for a person can sometimes come back to benefit you even a decade later.

Then I went to eat breakfast before starting to load up the car.

I checked my bank account that night.
Mermelstein had made a transfer of 1,700 shekel.
Just saying.

The Segulah of the Zera Shimshon

Since this *parashah* discusses matters pertaining to Chanukah, I want to share the following story involving the *Zera Shimshon*. There was some confusion in this story as to the role played by the *Zera Shimshon*. *Baruch Hashem*, it was all cleared up on Chanukah.

Rabbi Shimon Prague is a rebbi in the Mir and a true advocate and enthusiast of the *Zera Shimshon*. He related the following story:

I was introduced to the incredible Torah of Rabbeinu Shimshon Chaim Nachmani, *zt"l*, through his *sefarim Zera Shimshon* and *Toldos Shimshon*. At some point, I began giving *shiurim* in his Torah in many locations. And because I am so involved, I have heard many stories of *yeshuos* from trustworthy people, some of whom come to the *shiurim*. I've heard about how they personally experienced wonderful things, and how they have seen firsthand that the *Zera Shimshon's* promises, which he wrote in his *sefarim*, are still working for Klal Yisrael so many years later.

Now, to the story at hand.

One of the *bachurim* from the yeshivah was walking near Kikar Shabbos one day, when a piece of a crane fell on his head! He collapsed on the spot, terribly injured, and was in danger of losing his life. Everyone who knew him was extremely worried that he would not recover from the trauma.

I discussed the story with my friend, Rabbi Yaakov Chaim Sofer — Rosh Yeshivas Kaf Hachaim — and he advised me to visit the *bachur* and arrange davening and learning sessions next

to the hospital bed, where he lay unconscious and unrespon-
sive. Following my friend's advice, I began giving *shiurim* at the
bedside of the comatose *talmid*, one of which was a *shiur* in
Toldos Shimshon, the author's first *sefer*. I knew that Rav Shimshon Chaim had written in the introduction that anyone who
learned his *sefer* would merit לְמֵיטַב חַיֵּי אֲרִיכֵי — to enjoy a long,
good life. We davened that in the merit of the public learning
of the *tzaddik's* Torah, we should see real change in the *talmid's*
physical condition.

Despite the doctors' depressing prognosis, and even though
it had seemed as though there was no chance for recovery, we
didn't give up hoping that our *tefillos* would help him experience
a true recovery. And our hope proved well-founded. We began
to see a steady improvement, which continued on a daily basis. It
wasn't long before the *talmid*, who had been hovering between
life and death, had made a full recovery and had come back to
himself, to the shock of the doctors and the overwhelming happiness of his family and friends.

This is far from the only story I have heard about people
who have seen *yeshuos* through learning the *sefarim* of the *Zera
Shimshon*. I therefore advise everyone that it is a very good idea
to learn his Torah and to bring his *neshamah* happiness. This is
a good thing, because the Torah ideas are sweet and *geshmak*,
and because you will be fulfilling the desire and request of a
tzaddik. And hopefully, by doing so, you too will merit to receive
the Heavenly bounty enjoyed by so many.

Three months after this story was made public, Reb *Nesanel
Rubin called the *Zera Shimshon* office to share a continuation
of the story.

"Around Chanukah time," he said, "I had a conversation with
the *bachur* who was hit in the head. We discussed the accident
and the great miracle that he had experienced. I couldn't help
asking him about a number of details I had heard people saying.
I wanted to learn if they were completely accurate, since people
have a way of embellishing the stories that they hear. One of the

things I asked him was whether there really was a *shiur* in the Torah of the *Zera Shimshon* around his hospital bed. The *bachur* looked at me.

"What does the *Zera Shimshon* have to do with my story?" he asked.

I was completely taken aback to hear him say that.

"Rav Shimon Prague did visit me in the hospital, and he did daven and give *shiurim* at my bedside. But they had nothing to do with the *Zera Shimshon.*"

I was shocked to hear the denial coming from the mouth of the "*baal ha'maaseh*" himself. I found myself thinking, "I guess people like attributing every miracle to the *Zera Shimshon...*"

The next day, I met the *bachur* again.

He ran over to me and said, "Guess what? You were right! Last night, just a short while after we spoke, and I told you that the *Zera Shimshon* had nothing to do with my coming back to life, I attended a Chanukah *mesibah*. There was a large group of *bachurim* at the party. In the middle of everything, one of the *bachurim* suddenly approached me, and said, "I'm very happy to have met you here."

I asked him why.

"I was one of the *bachurim* who visited you in the hospital while you were unconscious and fighting for your life. I wanted to tell you how we publicly learned the Torah of the *Zera Shimshon* to give you the *zechus* to have a *refuah sheleimah*. I am very happy to see you are whole and healthy again!"

"When I heard his words, I couldn't get over how, just a few hours earlier, I had told you that the *Zera Shimshon* had nothing to do with my *yeshuah* and how I had been completely and utterly incorrect. *Baruch Hashem*, a messenger was sent from *Shamayim* to give me the real information — so I should know to whom I owe a debt of gratitude, and for the honor of the *Zera Shimshon.*"

Beis Yaakov Comes First

כֹּה תֹאמַר לְבֵית יַעֲקֹב וְתַגֵּיד לִבְנֵי יִשְׂרָאֵל (שמות יט:ג).
*So shall you say to Beis Yaakov
and relate to Bnei Yisrael* (Shemos 19:3).

*T*he *Midrash Rabbah* (*Shemos* 28:2) writes about this *pasuk*:

To Beis Yaakov (the house of Yaakov): These are the women.

To Bnei Yisrael (the Children of Israel): These are the men.

The Midrash continues: Why are the women mentioned before the men? Because they are more eager to do the mitzvos.

Zera Shimshon asks: What does it mean when it says that women are more eager to do the mitzvos than men?

Furthermore, in another Midrash (*Bereishis Rabbah* 45:5) the Sages said that women have a tendency toward laziness.

And even if they are faster when it comes to doing mitzvos, why is that a reason to put them first? After all, women are not obligated to fulfill time-related mitzvos, nor are they obligated in the mitzvah of Talmud Torah. Shouldn't that mean that men should be put first?

Zera Shimshon strengthens the question even more. In a number of places we find that men are put before women. In fact, the Gemara (*Berachos* 61a) says, "The way of the world is for men to walk before women." If that is the case, why did Hashem give His commands to women first when it came to accepting His Torah?

And still another question:

The whole point of Hashem giving the Torah to Klal Yisrael was for them to learn it and then fulfill the commandments. If women are not obligated to learn Torah, shouldn't the men have been commanded first, since they are the ones who are going to have to keep *all* the mitzvos?!

Zera Shimshon explains:

The Gemara (*Kiddushin* 34a) writes that it makes sense that women should be obligated in the mitzvah of *mezuzah*. Since the mitzvah of putting up a *mezuzah* is a *segulah* for long life [as it says (*Devarim* 11:20-21), "And you shall write them on the doorposts... in order to prolong your days"], the Gemara asks rhetorically, "What? Only men need life, women don't need life?" Since both men and women need life, it must be that women are also obligated in the mitzvah of *mezuzah*.

Tosafos (ibid., s.v. *"gavra"*) asks: What about the fact that it says כִּי הוּא חַיֶּיךָ וְאֹרֶךְ יָמֶיךָ — "... for it [Torah] is your life and the length of your days" (*Devarim* 30:20), which means that the Torah is life? Since women need life as much as men do, one would think that women would also be obligated to study Torah.

Tosafos's answer? The words "your life and the length of your days" are not referring to Torah learning, but rather to fulfilling the mitzvos of the Torah, which will keep a person alive.

Another answer: The words "your life and the length of your days" are, indeed, talking about learning Torah, which would mean that women also have to learn, in order to obtain life. The reason they are not obligated to learn is because of a *pasuk* that specifically excludes them from having to do this mitzvah — "make them known to your sons, and your sons' sons" (*Devarim* 4:9). *Chazal* learn from these words that a person has to teach Torah to their sons — and not their daughters. The mitzvah of *mezuzah*, on the other hand, does not have such an exclusion, and women are therefore obligated in that mitzvah since they need life just as much as men.

Which Is Greater?

This discussion in *Tosafos* brings us to another intriguing question: Which is greater — learning Torah or actually fulfilling the mitzvos?

If we look back at the first answer that *Tosafos* gave — that the words "your life and the length of your days" are referring to mitzvah observance — then mitzvos are greater than Torah learning.

According to *Tosafos's* second answer — which says the words are referring to learning Torah — then *talmud Torah* would be greater.

Zera Shimshon asks another question: Why does *Tosafos* even feel the need to offer a second answer? Why couldn't *Tosafos* adhere to their first answer — that the words "your life and the length of your days" refer to mitzvah observance? Especially since the Gemara (*Bava Kamma* 17a) discusses this topic and concludes that the performance of mitzvos is greater than learning.

Zera Shimshon answers: We can say that these words apply equally to the study of Torah and to the fulfillment of mitzvos — because both of these things fall under the category of being "life-giving." And while it is true that performance of mitzvos is greater than Torah study, one does receive the reward of long life for learning as well. So while both learning and doing mitzvos share the same type of reward, women are exempt from learning since they are specifically excluded.

To sum up this discussion:

Doing mitzvos is greater than learning.

The *pasuk* כִּי הוּא חַיֶּיךָ וְאֹרֶךְ יָמֶיךָ — "For it is your life and the length of your days" can be referring to doing mitzvos.

However, it can also be referring to both mitzvah performance and learning Torah.

According to both views, women are obligated in the mitzvos, but they are exempt from Torah study since the *pasuk* (*Devarim* 4:9) does not refer to them.

Back to Our Original Questions

At the moment that Hashem gave us the Torah, He wanted Klal Yisrael to grasp the idea that doing mitzvos is the most important thing — which is why the *pasuk* begins with the words "Beis Yaakov" (the women), and only afterward "Bnei Yisrael" (the men).

So while women are exempt when it comes to learning Torah,

they were still called first by Hashem, because they do mitzvos eagerly.

From here we see that mitzvah performance is the primary focus for a Jew.

Eager to Do Mitzvos

We will now return to what the Midrash told us — that women do mitzvos with more eagerness than men.

Let's analyze this. Small children are not obligated in any mitzvos until they are at least five or six years old. While we begin teaching children the *aleph-beis* earlier than age five or six, we do that so that the child will recognize the letters and the *nekudos*. This obligation is incumbent on us and not on the child, as it says, "And you shall teach them to your sons" (*Devarim* 6:7).

Since the *pasuk* specifically wrote "your sons," we understand that the obligation of teaching Torah to children when they are small is an obligation to teach it to the boys, but not the girls. That changes when they grow older, because at that time parents are obligated to educate the girls in the mitzvos that apply to them.

To sum up:

We educate boys to study Torah (beginning with recognizing the *aleph-beis*) earlier than girls. We start when they are very young, and only when they grow older do we begin educating them in doing mitzvos as well.

When it comes to girls, on the other hand, we begin teaching them to read at a later age [keep in mind that the *Zera Shimshon* wrote this at a time when girls were educated at home] but we give them *chinuch* for mitzvos at an earlier stage. We do this because *Chazal* write, "[Women] are more eager to do mitzvos." Because the performance of mitzvos is so important to Hashem, in a sense there is more importance to what the young girls are doing than to what the boys are doing, because while the boys start with learning, the girls begin with actual mitzvos.

That is another reason why the Torah writes that the Torah was given to "Beis Yaakov" first — so that we should know that fulfilling the mitzvos, which girls start with, takes precedence over learning — which is where the boys begin their *chinuch*.

Hashem and the Name Chavah

In the next piece, *Zera Shimshon* begins by quoting a "*Midrash Peliah*," a Midrash that is difficult to understand. This Midrash comes from the *Yalkut Reuveini* (page 18).

מִדְרָשׁ פְּלִיאָה: כְּשֶׁעָלָה מֹשֶׁה לַמָּרוֹם, מָצְאוּ לְהַקָּבָּ״ה שֶׁהָיָה אוֹמֵר חַוָּה, אָמַר לוֹ, רִבּוֹנֵיה דְעָלְמָא מַאי חַוָּה, אָמַר לוֹ ״כִּי הִיא הָיְתָה אֵם כָּל חָי״. אָמַר לוֹ רִבּוֹנֵיה דְעָלְמָא, אִם כֵּן תִּקְרְאֶנָּה חַיָּה, אָמַר לוֹ חַוָּה בְּמִסְפָּר קָטָן אֵם כָּל חָי.

The Midrash tells us that when Moshe Rabbeinu went up to heaven to receive the Torah from Hashem, he found Hashem saying the name "Chavah."

"Ribbono shel Olam," Moshe said to Hashem, "Why is Hashem saying Chavah?"

"Because Chavah is the mother of all humankind," Hashem replied, as it says (*Bereishis* 3:20) "She was the mother of all the living."

"Ribbono Shel Olam," Moshe responded, "if so, why not call her Chayah?"

"The name Chavah," Hashem replied, "equals the words אֵם כָּל חָי (mother of all the living), if you use *mispar katan* (which is a form of *gematria*)."[2]

This is a puzzling Midrash, a real מִדְרָשׁ פְּלִיאָה. It is very difficult to understand why Hashem was uttering the name Chavah just when Moshe ascended to heaven to receive the Torah. More: Why did Moshe ask Hashem about Chavah's name? Didn't he know that she was called Chavah because she was the mother of all living beings?

Zera Shimshon answers:

Shemos Rabbah (28:2) quotes the *pasuk*, "So you shall say to

---

2. *Mispar katan* is a *gematria* in which the tens and hundreds are reduced to single units. Ten and one hundred (*yud* and *kuf*) are reckoned as one. Twenty and two hundred (*chaf* and *reish*) are equal to two. Thirty and three hundred (*lamed* and *shin*) are considered as three. Forty and four hundred (*mem* and *tav*) are equal to four. Fifty (*nun*) is five, etc. Using this method, אֵם כָּל חָי can be reduced to nineteen, which is the same *mispar katan* as Chavah.

Beis Yaakov," and explains that it is referring to the women of Klal Yisrael. And why was the Torah given to the women first? So they could raise their sons to learn Torah.

When Moshe went up to heaven and found Hashem saying "Chavah," he understood that Hashem was telling him through a *remez* (hint) that he should give the Torah first to the daughters of Chavah — the "Beis Yaakov."

At that point Moshe asked Hashem, "Why is Hashem saying 'Chavah'?" — meaning, "Why should we give the Torah to the women (the daughters of Chavah) before the men?"

Hashem replied, "Because Chavah is the mother of all human-kind, and since it is the women who will raise their sons to study Torah, I will give it to them first."

Her Quality of Life

The Gemara (*Kesubos* 61a) discusses a case where a man and his wife have a disagreement. For example, when they married, the woman was accustomed to eating meat a few times a week or wearing elegant clothing, and she wants to continue doing so, while the husband does not want to maintain this luxurious lifestyle. In such a case we side with the wife, since her marriage is intended to raise her quality of life and not the opposite.

On this the Gemara asks, "How do you know that a husband may not provide his wife with less than she was used to before their marriage?"

Rabbi Elazar explains that we learn this from the *pasuk* "because she was the mother of all the living" — which implies that the woman was given to her husband to have a good life, or at least as good as it was when she was living in her father's house. Her married life should definitely not be less than it was before.

The Maharsha

The *Maharsha* writes that before the sin, in Gan Eden, Chavah was known as *ishah* (woman), as the Torah writes (*Bereishis* 2:23), "This shall be called *ishah* (woman), for she was taken from man (*ish*)." However, after she sinned she stopped being identified as *ishah* and was known as Chavah. Why?

Hashem wanted people to understand that she hadn't lost her exalted status because of her sin. She was still considered the mother of all living beings — every human being descended from her.

Zera Shimshon now raises another question: Why does the *Maharsha* write that everyone in the world comes from Chavah? After all, didn't *Chazal* tell us (*Kiddushin* 30b) that there are three partners in a person's creation — a mother, a father and Hashem? That would mean that Chavah is only one-third of everyone! If that is the case, why do we go out of our way to stress that everyone in the world is descended from her? After all, there was a husband there as well!

The reason we say that everyone comes from Chavah is because even more than does her husband, the woman raises her sons to study Torah.

The Gemara (*Sanhedrin* 19b) speaks about five children to whom Meirav, Shaul's daughter, gave birth. These children were raised by Meirav's sister, Michal, after Meirav's death. The interesting thing is that those children are considered Michal's, as we see in the *pasuk* (*II Shmuel* 21:8) that calls them the children "to whom Michal gave birth." Michal is identified as their actual mother, though Meirav had actually given birth to them.

From here we see that one who raises a child is considered its parent. Because women are more involved in raising their children than men are, all living beings are therefore attributed to Chavah, the mother of all living beings.

This is the reason that Hashem said Chavah's name when Moshe Rabbeinu came to get the Torah. It was as if He gave the Torah first to Chavah — and by extension, to all women. Because it is they who raise children to learn Torah.

The Conversation Between Hashem and Moshe Rabbeinu, Continued

"Okay," Moshe Rabbeinu said. "I understand that Chavah is called the mother of all living things because she raises her children to Torah — and Torah brings life to the world. I also understand that based on this, it makes sense that women should receive the Torah before men.

"But now I have a question. Why is she called Chavah? She should be called Chayah! After all, Chayah comes from the word 'chaim,' life. Since the women are the ones who bring life to the world by teaching their children Torah, it would make sense for her name to include a reference to that. Why Chavah and not Chayah?"

"I specifically called her Chavah," Hashem told Moshe Rabbeinu. "Why? Because Chavah has the *mispar katan* (a type of *gematria*) of אֵם כָּל חָי — mother of all the living."

"I understand that women have an important job and are busy raising their children to learn Torah," Moshe told Hashem. "But if that is the case, she should have been called Chayah — from the *pasuk* (Devarim 30:20) that states, כִּי הִיא חַיֶּיךָ וְאֹרֶךְ יָמֶיךָ — "for it is your life and the length of your days." And she should have also been commanded to learn Torah, since Torah is life, and women need life as much as men. So why call her Chavah and not Chayah?"

Hashem's reply? The *pasuk* "It is your life and the length of your days" doesn't refer to Torah learning. It is speaking about mitzvos. And since doing mitzvos is the most important thing, as the Gemara writes (*Bava Kamma* 17a), her mitzvah of raising children is of the utmost importance.

At the end of the day, Chavah was not commanded to learn Torah, since she already possessed the merit of raising children for *talmud Torah*.

Someone to Talk To

The name Chavah is also important for another reason, and that's because it is defined by *Targum* as coming from the word "speech." What is the connection between Chavah and speech?

First: When Chavah was created, the world acquired speech.

How is that? Wasn't Adam able to speak before she came along?

Until Chavah came along, Adam didn't have anyone to speak with, since animals do not speak.

And if you ask — didn't Adam communicate with the angels? The answer is: that is not called speech, since it is spiritual.

When Chavah was created, Adam finally had someone to speak with.

The second connection is that women like to talk, as *Chazal* declared (*Berachos* 48b). So she was called Chavah, אֵם כָּל חָי — "mother of the entire world," because everyone in the world uses speech to communicate with one another.

The fact that she was called Chavah on account of her speech is appropriate, since speech is very important to a woman. Women use speech to teach and educate their children, as the Gemara (*Sotah* 11b) states, "Puah was another name for Miriam. The reason she was called Puah was because of the way she used to speak to and coo to the children in her care."

This, then, is another reason why Chavah was the mother of mankind — because it was she who educated people in the art of speech, an art that separates those who are alive and those who have since passed on and no longer possess the ability to use words.

The words "Because it is your life and the length of your days" are referring to the mitzvos that we do — and the more eager we are to do those mitzvos, the more Hashem appreciates it. Of course one would be hard-pressed to find someone who did the mitzvos with more eagerness than Rav Chaim Kanievsky *zt"l*, the Sar HaTorah. And there is no question that the Ribbono shel Olam looked at Rav Chaim's life with favor, because he was rewarded with incredible *kochos* and the ability to give *berachos* that were fulfilled.

"It was in the middle of Simchas Torah," related Rav Nosson Einfeld, "when the pain suddenly hit me. I was reciting *Hallel* at the time, and when I arrived at the words, *yasor yisrani Kah*, I suddenly felt an agonizing pain in my left foot.

I didn't pay attention to the pain at first, hoping it would go away of its own accord and that I would be able to continue enjoying my Simchas Torah with enthusiasm. But the pains grew worse and worse, and soon I realized that ignoring it was not an option.

There was no doubt that dancing was out of the question (I could barely move by that point). I asked the *gabbai* not to give me the Sefer Torah to dance with. As I sat there in the shul, the pain began to intensify until I was no longer able to move my foot. I was barely able to go up to the *bimah* when they called me for an *aliyah*, and it took tremendous effort for me to daven Mussaf, since the pain kept spreading from the sole of my foot and up my leg to my knee. When my foot was a throbbing mass of terrible pain, I asked a friend to please find me a wheelchair and take me home. When I arrived home, I collapsed onto my bed, hoping that the pain would begin to lessen. However, the opposite occurred, and I felt even worse.

By the time Yom Tov had come to an end, I was in the kind of pain that words cannot describe. I tried to locate a doctor who would examine me at home but was unsuccessful. In the end, I managed to find a doctor who agreed to see me at his house. Simply rising from my bed was excruciating, but I did it, knowing that I had no choice. I cannot describe how challenging it was for me to walk down the stairs, how the agony wouldn't end, how every nerve ending screamed to the heavens. Suffice it to say, getting in and out of the taxi was a nightmare, as was the seemingly endless journey to the doctor's home. But all of that was nothing compared to how I felt when the doctor began examining my foot. He laid me down on the couch in his room and began checking me. Every touch felt as if he were branding me with a burning-hot poker. When he tried turning my foot, I was unable to restrain myself and cried out from the pain.

The examination felt as if it went on forever. When the doctor finally finished his examination, he was at a loss. Not only couldn't he tell me which medicine to take, he wasn't even able to diagnose the problem. He gave me a shot for the pain, but it didn't help even a little bit. The pain remained with me all the way back home and kept me up through the night, as I twisted and turned in sheer agony. This was a truly untenable situation, the pain unprecedented and on a scale that boggled the imagination.

Many doctors were consulted, but none of them knew what to do. Finally, they took X-rays of my foot and then sat me down and informed me that the diagnosis was the worst one of all. The disease that nobody wants to hear about.

"What can I do for it?" I asked.

"At the moment, we haven't chosen a course of action."

"So what do I do about my situation?"

"Right now, you take painkillers."

You can imagine my feelings upon learning of the doctors' diagnosis. But instead of becoming depressed, I decided to be proactive and called Rabbi Elimelech Firer. He asked me all manner of questions, listened carefully to my answers, and recommended that I meet with a certain professor. I hastened to follow his advice.

The professor examined me, and within a short time let me know in no uncertain terms that he scornfully disagreed with the diagnosis made by his colleagues.

"So what is it then?" I asked him.

"The problem is located in your spine." He recommended that I go for an epidural for the pain.

Naturally, I was ecstatic at hearing that he disagreed with the previous diagnosis, but I still wanted to know how long I should expect to be in pain.

"In my opinion, the pain will last for at least another six weeks, after which you will need to go for physiotherapy for a full year at least."

"That's a long time to feel pain," I commented.

"There's no other option. That's the situation."

That night, I suffered terribly. While I was extremely happy to hear that I wasn't facing a life-and-death situation, it was still very difficult for me to deal with the jagged spasms of pain that I experienced in every part of my foot and that continued unabated throughout the night. The shots didn't help. The pills didn't help. Nothing helped. Simply speaking, I was on fire.

That Thursday morning was a week from when the pain began. I suddenly recalled what the Gemara in *Shabbos* (32a) states: "A person should daven for mercy before they become sick, because once a person is sick he is told to present his merits if he wants to get cured..."

"If I would have known what was coming my way this year," I reflected, "how different my Yom Kippur and Hoshana Rabbah would have been!"

When my wife left the house to go shopping for Shabbos, I told her to lock the front door from the outside and take the keys with her. I wasn't expecting any visitors, and even if someone did come to the house, I didn't have the strength to get up and go to the door. Feeling extremely overcome with emotion, I donned my *tallis* and *tefillin* and began to daven with a broken heart. As I finished davening, the bell rang downstairs. When I didn't answer, someone entered the building and began knocking on my front door. I couldn't get up to walk to the door, so I called out "Who's there?" from my seat at the table.

I heard the voice of Rav Epstein — one of the *gabbaim* of Rav Chaim Kanievsky — calling out, "Rav Chaim is downstairs in the car and wants to come up and visit you!"

I cannot describe how hearing those words made me feel. I rose from my place — somehow managing to ignore the raging pain — and began searching for the key to the front door. I hadn't carried a key with me for an entire week, and I began searching in all my pockets while trying to remember where we kept another key. But no matter how I wracked my brain, I couldn't think of another place where we kept a key. I resigned myself to the fact that I was unable to open the front door.

Rav Epstein heard my words and went to tell Rav Chaim that there was no reason to come up, since the house was locked and there was no key.

"How do you know all this?" Rav Chaim asked. "How did you talk to him?"

"Through the door."

"If you spoke to him through the door," Rav Chaim said, "I can do the same."

So Rav Chaim Kanievsky got out of the car and climbed the stairs to my floor, Rav Epstein walking behind him. Later, Rav Epstein told me that Rav Chaim said as he climbed, "הַמְבַקֵּר אֶת הַחוֹלָה נוֹטֵל חָלְיוֹ," and he also heard him say, "We need him."

When Rav Chaim was standing outside the door, Rav Epstein called out, "Reb Nosson, the Rav is right outside."

In my wildest dreams, I never imagined that Rav Chaim would go to so much trouble to visit me — especially knowing that the door was locked and that he wouldn't be able to come into the house. When I heard the words, "The Rav is right outside," I became very emotional and my entire body started to shake. I called out in a tear-filled voice, "Rabbeinu, I have terrible *yissurim*."

I made my way over to the door, ignoring the agony I felt with every step.

And then I heard his holy voice: "Reb Nosson, *refuah sheleimah, refuah sheleimah*!"

And then again, "Hakadosh Baruch Hu will send you a *refuah sheleimah b'meheirah*."

He called out, "Shalom," and then again, "*Refuah sheleimah b'meheirah*.

His voice is still ringing in my ears, every letter of every word of his *berachah* engraved on my brain for all time. I made my way as quickly as I could over to the window, and when I caught sight of Rav Chaim I screamed out, "Rebbi, I have such terrible pains!"

He lifted his holy eyes in my direction and repeated his earlier *berachah*: "*Refuah sheleimah b'meheirah*!"

I saw him approach his car. Just before he entered the vehicle, he looked up and saw me. He gave me a big smile and called out in a voice so loud it carried all the way up to my window, "*Refuah sheleimah*!"

I stood there watching until I couldn't see the car any longer. Only then did I return to my place. Suddenly I stopped in my tracks. Something was different. Something had changed. With wonder, I suddenly realized that as I walked from the window to the table in the middle of the room, I hadn't felt any pain at all! Not only that, but I had used both my feet — equally!

Could it be?

Was I imagining my suddenly pain-free existence?

I lifted my right foot and concentrated on leaning all my weight onto my left foot.

No pain.

I lifted my left foot and rested it on a chair. Then I touched it gingerly with my finger, recalling my screams when the doctor examined me the last time I had been in his office. Yet now I felt no pain. None at all. From one moment to the next it was all gone, as if it had never been there in the first place — and this without any shots or medicines! It was a miracle, an absolute miracle! I began to dance with joy, calling out, "Thank you Hashem, Master of the world!"

I danced and I sang, calling out the words of *pesukim* as I whirled around the room.

מָה אָשִׁיב לַה׳ כָּל תַּגְמוּלוֹהִי עָלָי

I danced some more.

הוֹדוּ לַה׳ כִּי טוֹב כִּי לְעוֹלָם חַסְדּוֹ

I continued dancing for the next ten minutes, my feet jumping through the air of their own accord. That's the way my wife found me when she returned from the store, hands full of bags. She had left behind a sick husband who was unable to touch his foot, and returned to find a different man, singing and dancing with elation. She was overcome at the sight and began to cry out of sheer emotion. I did, too.

"What's this?" she asked me.

"I'm making up for all the dancing I wasn't able to do on Simchas Torah."

"But what happened? How did the miracle occur?"

"While you were away, a professor came to visit me."

I then described how Rav Chaim, the Prince of Torah, came to visit me, bringing a complete *refuah sheleimah* with him and accomplishing his miracle from behind the door. I cannot tell you how disappointed she was at having missed that particular visit, especially since, had she been home, the door would not have been locked in the first place and we would have merited a visit by the *tzaddik* of our generation.

I immediately called Rav Epstein. He had heard me crying with agony just a short while before — and now I asked him to please run over to Rav Chaim's house to let him know that his visit had accomplished incredible results and that I had been cured shortly after his *berachah*.

"I am completely cured," I told him. "The pain is gone. And it happened right after Rav Chaim blessed me!"

Rav Epstein became very emotional, and he ran over to Rav Chaim to tell him what had occurred. When he heard the news, Rav Chaim said, "But of course. Doesn't it say in the Gemara (*Megillah* 15a), אַל תְּהִי בִּרְכַּת הֶדְיוֹט קַלָּה בְּעֵינֶיךָ — that the blessing of an ordinary man should be taken seriously..."

It was classic Rav Chaim: referring to his *berachah* as the blessing of an ordinary person instead of what it really was.

It goes without saying that my story made waves, shocking everyone who heard it. So many people had seen me during my time of suffering. They knew how terrible it had been, and how I hadn't been able to walk. Now they joined me in my happiness and were overcome by how the turnaround had come about. When I saw that the pains were really and truly gone, I made my way to the home of Rav Chaim, giving thanks to Hashem for every step I was able to take along the way.

When I arrived, I stood before Rav Chaim and burst into tears. I told him about the terrible pain I had suffered, how the doctors had diagnosed me incorrectly, how the professor had given me shots and medicine which hadn't helped. "But then Rabbeinu came, and the sickness fled from me."

Rav Chaim arose from his spot and, removing a *Maseches Avodah Zarah* from the shelf, turned to 55a and began to read with enthusiasm. When he finished, Rav Chaim turned loving eyes on me and said, "From this Gemara, we see that when a person has *yissurim*, they are decreed on him from Above. It is decreed which day they will begin and which second they will stop. I must have arrived at your home a second before the *yissurim* were supposed to leave you. I then performed the mitzvah of *bikur cholim,* and a second later the illness left you — just as it had been decreed Above. "

I also paid a visit to the professor who had examined me. I arrived at his office on time for my previously scheduled appointment, and I came without anyone assisting me, walking on my own two feet. What an incredible difference there was between this visit and my previous one, when I'd barely been capable of movement! I walked into his office and took a seat across from him. He stared at me, shocked by how light I was on my feet.

"Are you Rav Einfeld?" he asked.

I nodded, a smile on my lips.

"Please explain something to me," he said. "You came to my office a few days ago in a wheelchair and cried out in pain when I barely touched your feet. Is that not correct?"

"It's one hundred percent correct."

"So how is it that you are healed?"

"Someone came to my house and healed me."

"Who is the incredible doctor who succeeded in healing you?"

"The biggest *tzaddik* of the generation came to my house, blessed me, and the pain immediately disappeared."

The doctor thought about what I had told him. He said, "If someone else had told me this story, I would have had a very difficult time believing him. But in your case, I have no choice. I saw your situation, I saw how much pain you were in, and I know that there was no way for the pain to just disappear without a miracle."

He rose from his place.

"If you don't mind, I want to check your foot. Is that okay?"

He gave me a thorough examination.

"You are right — your foot is better than ever. There is no question in my mind that a miracle happened here. However, I still feel you should be careful for a while. Don't carry heavy objects or packages yet."

"I do travel extensively. Is that okay?"

"As long as you don't lift your suitcase by yourself."

"I'm marrying off my daughter in a few weeks. Can I dance at the wedding?"

He thought for a few seconds.

"Look," he said at last. "This is a serious situation, and you need to treat it as such. There was something terribly wrong with your foot, and even though it's better now, you have to be very careful so that it doesn't revert to the way it was before."

"So no dancing?"

"No dancing."

When I presented myself at Rav Chaim's house to invite him to the wedding, I told him how the doctor had forbidden me to dance since the pain was apt to return at any time. When Rav Chaim heard this, he waved his hand and said, "*Chas v'shalom*, the pains will not return. And I will be attending the wedding, where we will dance together."

And so it was. Rav Chaim came to the wedding and we danced together for about fifteen precious minutes.

We have come to the end of this miraculous tale. I was the recipient of Hashem's kindness through the merit of the *berachah* of the Sar HaTorah, and I thank Hashem for showing me His mercy.

The Segulah of the Zera Shimshon

Just as Rav Nosson was a recipient of a *berachah* that helped him, so was the hero of the following story a recipient of a *berachah* — the *berachah* of the Zera Shimshon.

We were busy dealing with our son's *shidduchim* for a very long time. There were many ideas, but none of them went anywhere. So it went for more than five years. While we had heard about the *sefer Zera Shimshon* and were familiar with the *segulah*, it was difficult for us to understand what Rav Shimshon Chaim was saying and we never ended up learning it on a regular basis.

And then we heard that an English edition of *Zera Shimshon* had been published. It included pieces from the *sefer*, written in a clear style by the famous author Rabbi Nachman Seltzer and published by ArtScroll, in conjunction with the *Zera Shimshon* team dedicated to spreading the Torah of Rav Shimshon Chaim Nachmani. I was, of course, excited to hear the news, and I purchased the *sefer* and began learning from it with my family at the table every Shabbos. We did this as a *zechus* for my son to find a *shidduch*. To my delight, I found the learning extremely enjoyable and it brought the entire family pleasure. We loved every *vort* and idea and felt that we were fulfilling the verse (*Tehillim* 199:9), פְּקוּדֵי ה' יְשָׁרִים מְשַׂמְּחֵי לֵב — "The orders of Hashem are upright, gladdening the heart." This continued, week after week.

Our son became engaged about nine months later. It took us some time, but we eventually grasped something very interesting. Everyone knows the idea of doing a *segulah* for forty days, be it going to the Kosel, reciting *Shir HaShirim*, or saying *Tehillim*. *Chazal* (*Midrash Rabbah, Devarim* 2:17) advised us to do so with the words: יֵשׁ תְּפִלָּה שֶׁנַּעֲנֵית לְאַרְבָּעִים יוֹם.

After we did an exact calculation from when we started learning *Zera Shimshon* at the Shabbos meals, we figured out that we, too, had managed to take advantage of the idea of forty days. Our son was engaged after exactly forty weeks of learning the *sefer* every Shabbos, week in and week out...

Conversion? Great! Marrying a Talmid Chacham? Even Better!

הֵיטַבְתְּ חַסְדֵּךְ הָאַחֲרוֹן מִן הָרִאשׁוֹן לְבִלְתִּי לֶכֶת אַחֲרֵי הַבַּחוּרִים אִם דַּל וְאִם עָשִׁיר (רות ג:י).

You have made your latest act of kindness greater than your first, in that you have not gone after younger men, whether poor or rich (Rus 3:10).

The *pasuk* in *Megillas Rus* seems to imply that Rus's marriage to Boaz was even more important than her conversion. Yet how can one possibly suggest that her conversion was less important than her marriage?

Zera Shimshon paraphrases a Gemara (*Berachos* 17a) to give us an explanation:

Women are more assured of attaining *Olam Haba* than their male counterparts. This is derived from a *pasuk* (*Yeshayah* 32:9) in which women are referred to as שַׁאֲנַנּוֹת — confident and secure — since they know that they can rely on a future portion in the World to Come.

Here Rav asked Rabbi Chiya a question: What special merit makes women so sure that they will merit a portion in *Olam Haba*?

The answer? Their special merit lies in the fact that they take their sons to learn *Chumash* and *Mikra*, and because they give their husbands permission to go and learn Torah at yeshivos that are far away from home. In addition, they also have the merit of waiting for their husbands to come home late at night from the *beis midrash*, or sometimes after being away for quite some time.

Zera Shimshon continues: When Rus converted to Judaism, she received the same type of reward that any Jewish woman can expect, but she didn't have a special promise that she would merit *Olam Haba*.

After she married Boaz, who was a *talmid chacham*, and she intended to wait for him to return from the *beis midrash*, her reward was increased, for now she received the promise given to Jewish women who allow their husbands to go learn.

This, then, is the meaning of the words "you have made your latest act of kindness greater" — because Rus married a Torah scholar and was ready to wait for him to return home from the study hall. Because Rus did this, her reward was greater than that of other women who were not in such relationships, and she was now promised a share in the World to Come.

This is the reason why her marriage to Boaz was even more important than "the first" — her conversion. Of course, the fact that she chose to become a convert was a powerful thing and came along with its own type of reward. But it didn't guarantee her a place in *Olam Haba*.

And this is what Boaz said to Rus: The reason that you are now going to merit this is because you chose not to marry for money or other mundane reasons, but rather you made the decision to marry a *talmid chacham*. And for that you have earned yourself a definite place in *Olam Haba*.

The "convert" has long held a place of prominence in Jewish thought and literature, with Rus even meriting to marry Boaz and have a *Megillah* named for her; indeed, she will be the ancestor of Mashiach! Yet while the fact that a person chooses to convert is something incredible and worthy of admiration, it is just the start of the process and needs to be followed by a long life or living the right way — with Torah, mitzvos and becoming the best Yid one can possibly be.

I met Reb Mordechai Yosef ben Avraham during Succos of 2021. Mordechai was raised in L.A. and had lived an exciting life before embarking on a fascinating journey which took him from his native city to Eretz Yisrael. An African American convert to Judaism, Mordechai is married and living in Yerushalayim, where he is involved in many interesting and inspirational projects, including a book he wrote called *Mind of the Black Jew*, which he plans to release later this year.

We shared some great conversation during the meal we had together, and I enjoyed meeting him very much. For most of the *seudah,* we focused on his life and journey. It was only near the end of the evening that Mordechai shared the following story with me.

"I was spending Pesach in a house in the German Colony in Jerusalem," Mordechai told me. "We had a nice group of people staying there together. One of them was my good friend Amare Yehoshafat Stoudemire, who played professional basketball for the NBA and was a star player on the Phoenix Suns, New York Knicks, Dallas Mavericks, and Miami Heat. Amare eventually ended up in Jerusalem, where he played for Hapoel Yerushalayim. Today he is back in the States, coaching for the Nets."

According to the way Mordechai explained it to me, he shares a close relationship with a large group of African American *geirim* and has become close friends with both Amare Yehoshafat Stoudemire and Nissim Black. And while those are two of his more famous friends, he is a person who connects to everyone he meets in a very short amount of time. He is open, honest, and extremely friendly. In addition to all of that, he is a truly bright individual and much in demand as a popular public speaker and personality.

It was Motzaei Yom Tov, Mordechai said, and our group of guys left the house where we were staying and went to daven Maariv. It was still during the pandemic, and all the *minyanim* were held outdoors.

On our way back to the house, we were having a nice time,

laughing and joking around. Nobody was in a rush to go anywhere. Pesach was coming to an end and we had enjoyed the Yom Tov immensely, Corona or no Corona.

Turning down one of the streets that would lead us to the house, we saw that an outdoor *minyan* was just finishing Maariv. As we approached, they finished davening and began disbanding, with every person heading to his own house.

Since we needed to hear *Havdalah*, we turned to one of the men who had just finished davening and asked if we could hear *Havdalah* at his home. He was very nice and welcoming and asked us to wait.

"I'm just going to call my family," he said. "Then we'll make *Havdalah* outside."

He went into his house. A few minutes later, the door opened and his family began pouring into the street. Everyone was very excited to welcome us, and it looked like we were going to experience a first-class *Havdalah* ceremony.

We figured that the whole thing was just going to take a few minutes, after which we would be on our way. But something huge and unexpected happened in those few minutes.

Before making *Havdalah*, our host turned to Amare and said, "Amare, I have to tell you something."

The fact that the entire family seemed to have recognized Amare was no surprise, considering the fact that he was a huge superstar with the NBA and was an internationally known sports icon. Amare waited to hear what the man had to say.

"I know that you don't know us," the father of that beautiful family said, "but I just want you to know that we know you."

Again, the fact that they knew Amare was not surprising, because everyone in the world knows Amare. But from the way the man was talking, it was clear that he wasn't referring to just recognizing a famous face. Without question, there was something much deeper happening. We waited to see where he was going with the story.

The father took a long pause before continuing, and it was clear to see that he wasn't having the easiest time getting it all out.

"The reason we know you, Amare," he finally said, "is because you used to come and visit our son when he was in the hospital."

His words hung in the pleasant air of Motzaei Pesach.

"You visited our son many times during his stay in the hospital, and the two of you became very close. I don't know if my son told you this, but he had a dream that he was hoping to pursue when he recovered."

Again a pause.

"My son dreamt of being able to invite you — the guy he loved so much — to spend a Shabbos at our home, here in the German Colony. You see, he felt that the two of you had really connected during your visits and he was looking forward to sharing the beauty of Shabbos with you at our home."

Everyone was silent now, listening to the father tell his story.

"Unfortunately, my son was never able to invite you for Shabbos," the father continued. "You see, he passed away a month later."

The story hit every one of us hard. Instinctively, we all grasped that something awesome was taking place right before our eyes.

"There's just one more thing I have to tell you," the father said. "My son passed away on the final day of Pesach — one year ago. Today we mark his first *yahrtzeit*. It is also the day that you, Amare Yehoshafat Stoudemire, walked down my block and asked if you could join me and my family for *Havdalah*. I cannot help but feel that my son sent you here to join us this evening. While he never was able to fulfill his dream of hosting you at our home for a Shabbos, he did his best to send you here on his *yahrtzeit* for *Havdalah*. He wanted you to join us right now, on this important day."

Reb Mordechai Hazan has heard *Havdalah* many times since he joined Klal Yisrael and became a *ger*. But there is no question that the *Havdalah* he heard that night on a Jerusalem street, outside the home of a boy who had come to meet and love Amare during his time in the hospital, was the most emotional *Havdalah* of all. It was certainly a *Havdalah* he knew he would never, ever forget.

A Son to Be Proud Of

רַבִּי יְהוֹשֻׁעַ בֶּן חֲנַנְיָה אַשְׁרֵי יוֹלַדְתּוֹ (אבות ב:ח).

[Rabban Yochanan ben Zakkai would say of his student,]
Rabbi Yehoshua ben Chananiah: "Praiseworthy is the
woman who gave birth to him" (Avos 2:8).

Zera Shimshon explains that the five *talmidim* of Rabban Yochanan ben Zakkai who are mentioned in the Mishnah were his greatest and most exceptional students. He also explains that, metaphorically, Rabban Yochanan ben Zakkai was the "arm" of Moshe Rabbeinu, and these five students were the "hand," with each one of them corresponding to one of Moshe's fingers.

Rabbi Yehoshua ben Chananiah represented the finger that is called קְמִיצָה — the fifth finger on the Kohen's hand. This finger was used in the *avodah* of "*kemitzah*" for the *korban minchah*.[3]

We know that it was common for poor people to donate the *korban minchah*, rather than an animal or bird *korban*, because that was what they were able to afford.

The fact that Rabbi Yehoshua ben Chananiah was chosen to represent that particular finger implies that he was a poor man.

This was in fact the case, as the Gemara (*Berachos* 28a) writes: "Rabbi Yehoshua ben Chananiah said to Rabban Gamliel, 'You don't

---

3. When a poor person brings a meal offering, the Kohen first takes a handful of the offering and then removes the excess of the handful with his pinky, and with his thumb he removes the excess on the other side of the hand. Thus, the *kemitzah* that remains is in his hand, under the three fingers. This *kemitzah* is then burnt on top of the *Mizbei'ach*.

know the pain of the *talmidei chachamim*, how they have such trouble trying to make a living.'"

Rabbi Yehoshua was singularly equipped to make such a statement because he was a poor man himself — and because that was the case, he was the student who represented the *kemitzah* finger that was used to do the *korban minchah*, brought by the poor.

Zera Shimshon continues:

We find in the Zohar (*Bamidbar* 125b) and in the *sifrei mussar* that a woman who isn't modest causes her husband and sons to become poor — and that her sons do not grow up to maximize their potential. If that is the case, when people saw Rabbi Yehoshua ben Chananiah and understood the extent of his poverty, they might have thought that this was his mother's fault, and his situation had come about because she wasn't a modest woman.

For that reason — so that people should understand that this was certainly not the reason — Rabban Yochanan ben Zakkai said "Praiseworthy is the woman who gave birth to such a man," who merited a son like Rabbi Yehoshua, a true *talmid chacham*.

The implication of those words was to stress the point that his mother was a modest woman — for had she not been modest, there is no way she could have possibly merited such a son. This is similar to what the Gemara (*Yoma* 47a) makes clear in the story of Kimchis and how she merited to see her seven sons all serve as Kohanim Gedolim because of her modesty.

And so it must have been here as well.

The fact is, there is no substitute for good behavior on the side of parents. If we want our children to live righteous and meaningful lives, we need to exemplify those types of behaviors ourselves. Remember — the payoff is worth the investment. After all, who doesn't dream of having children about whom one could say "praiseworthy is the woman who gave birth to him."

I'll never forget what I saw at the contest. It was the kind of memory that stays in your mind and finds a place to live, comfortable with the atmosphere and happy to be there. In fact, I wouldn't want it to leave. It was just that incredible. And although it happened a while back, when my brother was just a kid, it's still as clear in my memory as if the whole story took place just a couple of days ago.

Enough with the introduction. Here goes.

When my brother was a child, he was one of those kids who liked to participate in Mishnayos contests. He did this for years, memorizing as many Mishnayos as he could and presenting himself on the day of the contest, to join the throng of excited boys waiting to get up on stage and show the crowd how much they knew. My brother always did well. He was lucky to have been born with the kind of brain that lent itself to learning Mishnayos by heart — or to any kind of learning, really. Some people have that good fortune.

But there was another kid who also used to come to get tested, and this story is really about him. You see, although he showed up at the hall on the appointed day every single year, and although he took a seat onstage alongside the other kids, all clad in their white shirts and dark pants, this boy never did well. I happen to know that it wasn't due to lack of effort. I know this because the boy made a point of coming over to my house to study with my brother. But no matter how much he tried or how hard he worked, the boy never managed to accomplish what he so clearly hoped to achieve.

I remember how he used to arrive at the hall accompanied by his father, and how the father would take a seat in the audience while his son went to sit on the stage. I used to watch the father, and I used to think that he really looked like a nice person.

Then I'd glance up at the stage and watch his son get ready to be tested. And I'd cringe when his turn came and the questioner looked his way, because although you could see how hard he was trying, he just couldn't seem to get the answers right. It was almost heartbreaking to see it.

Now, some people would learn their lesson after a few years and decide that they would have to find their talent somewhere else. Learning reams of material by heart is not for everyone. Some people are better at learning when they can look at the words. I would have understood if the kid had given up and stopped participating in the contest. But that didn't happen. When the next year rolled around and it was time for the contest again, he would show up at my house to learn with my brother. He would arrive at the hall with his father. And he'd get up onstage and get all the answers wrong.

That's the way it went, year after year.

And then we heard that the father of the boy who always got it wrong had passed away.

Since this tragic event happened two weeks before the Mishnayos contest, I was sure that this year the boy who always tried and never succeeded would sit it out. He had only finished sitting *shivah* a week before the contest, giving him very little time for the final cramming sessions before the big event. Besides, his father had been the one to take him every year and to sit and sit in the audience. How would he be able to sit on that stage, knowing that this year he was there all by himself?

I spent the week watching my brother go about his usual pre-contest routine. As I watched, him walk the room from side to side, muttering to himself, I could almost see the Mishnayos adding up inside that brain of his. I had mixed feelings about this year's contest, because this was going to be the first time in my memory that the boy who never won wasn't going to be up on stage.

And then it was the day of the event, and my brother woke up early and nobody could talk to him since he was on edge, and eventually it was time to leave. We drove over to the hall and waited in line to get inside. When we were finally admitted, we found seats while my brother went up onstage. And even though I knew there was no chance that the other boy would be there that day, I couldn't help looking for him in his usual seat in the second row.

I looked once. Then I looked again. I found myself blinking in surprise.

To my utter shock and complete surprise, the boy was there in white shirt and dark pants, just like the rest of them.

Before I was able to recover, the contest began.

I watched as the questioner began asking the first round of

questions. They were not very difficult — yet. My brother was asked a question and he answered correctly. I cheered for him, but my mind was not very focused, because I was waiting to see what was going to happen with the other boy, who hadn't even come to study with my brother this year. How would he do? Would he know any answers, or would it be the same story as last year and the year before?

The questioner reached the boy whose father had always watched him from the audience, but was no longer there to watch.

The question was asked.

I held my breath. How would he do? Would he know the answer?

The boy answered.

"Correct!"

I burst into wild applause. I couldn't help myself.

The contest continued. Questions were asked. Most of the boys knew the answers. They were serious kids who had prepared well for the day. They knew their stuff.

Soon it was time for round two. Again the questioner reached the boy who was there all by himself. The question was asked.

Again I held my breath.

He answered.

"Correct!!"

I cheered out loud for him once more. It was so exciting. This was a kid who had never had two right answers before — but this year he was on fire! When it happened for the third time, I was bursting myself with sheer pride. I wanted to jump up and down and start to dance. But I couldn't. It's just not the kind of thing you do at a Mishnayos contest.

The whole scene was somewhat surreal. The kid who had never done well before was getting them right, one after the next. For the first time ever, it was as if he could do no wrong.

The next part of that Mishnayos contest was something straight out of the books — and I do not say this lightly, or with any form of exaggeration. What had begun as a happy surprise, where someone who had been in the constant position of underdog for many years, suddenly rebounded to head seamlessly for the top, didn't stop, but just kept on getting better and better. I tried to put myself in the boy's head, asking myself how he could deal with the incredible pressure when he had just risen from *shivah*, and I didn't have an answer. But the facts were the facts. It seemed clear that he was intent on going all the way.

Question after question came his way, and each received a clear and concise answer that was deemed correct by the contest administrator. The applause grew louder as the evening progressed and he nailed each additional question. And then we reached the point where there were just a few kids left on the stage — and he was one of them. It was unreal. A kid who had never gotten anything right in the past was a step away from being proclaimed the winner!

Question to one of the kids. He answered. He was wrong. He left the stage. Now there were only three kids left. My brother was not one of them. He had given a wrong answer in the previous round and left the stage.

The questions were asked, the answers were given. Round and round they went. And then the third kid got one wrong. It was now down to the two last contestants — the boy who never got anything right, and one other.

I would like to be able to make you happy and say that he won. But he didn't. He missed an answer and had to be content with the title *"Mishneh l'Chassan,"* instead of *"Chassan."*

I'm sure you can imagine how much noise the crowd made when he almost won, and the admiration that filled the room as we watched his incredible performance of the night.

When it was all over and the prizes had been awarded — his first time receiving a prize — I turned to my father and said, "Abba, how on earth did he do it? I don't understand! He never won before, and his father just passed away!"

"You know what?" my father replied. "Why don't we go over to him and ask how he did it?"

That's exactly what we did.

We approached the boy and waited until all the well-wishers had finished congratulating him. And then we moved in.

"*Mazel tov*," we said.

"Thank you," he replied shyly, still not used to being anywhere near the limelight.

"That was a magnificent performance," my father said. "We just had to ask you: How did you do it?!"

He was quiet for a few seconds.

Then he replied.

"You know that my father used to come with me to the contest every year," he began.

We nodded.

"He came with me every time, and I used to come and study with you (he said to my brother) because I wanted to make him proud and do well on stage. But somehow, no matter how hard I tried, I never succeeded.

"Two weeks ago, he passed away. And as I was sitting *shivah* for my father, I knew that this year I was not only going to get up on that stage and participate in the contest, but that I was going to go all the way — or at least come in a close second. In the last week before the contest, I studied harder than I have ever studied for anything in my life. I wanted to do well. More than that, I needed to do this. For my father."

He was silent for a few more seconds.

"I know that you were here every year," he continued, "and that you used to see my father coming in with me, taking a seat and watching me.

"But here's something you didn't know.

"My father was blind. He chose not to use a stick here inside the hall, and I used to help him find a seat. And then he would sit and listen to what was going on, but he could never see it for himself.

"But now he can.

"This was the first year that my father could finally see me up on stage. And because I knew that he was going to be able to see me for the first time, I worked as hard as I could. And it paid off — because I wanted to make him proud of me."

Author's note: If this story reminds you of a song, it should. It is very similar to the famous, "Deaf Man in the Shtiebel," by Country Yossi.

And I quote: "*Well you knew my dad was deaf,*" he said, "*last night he passed away, it's the first time that my father's heard me pray.*"

Unlike Country Yossi's song, however, which although a beautiful story is, to the best of my knowledge, fiction — the story you have just read is, to the best of my knowledge, true.

And that makes it absolutely phenomenal.

The Segulah of the Zera Shimshon

Yet another letter sent to the *Zera Shimshon* team:

I have been learning the *Zera Shimshon* newsletters for a long time, and I wanted to share a story that I personally witnessed. I take my daughter to *gan* every morning. Since I am there every day, I have become friends with the man who guards the entrance. We exchange hellos every morning, along with a smile and a wave.

One morning, I noticed that he wasn't his normal, cheery self. Sometimes people are sad, but they manage to keep it to themselves. He was unable to do so. The sadness was plastered all over his face.

I asked him what was wrong.

"It's my daughter."

"What about her?"

"She's been married for a while and still hasn't had any children."

"I have an idea for you."

"What is it?"

"Do you think your son-in-law would be willing to learn from a *sefer* every Shabbos? That might really help them." I explained about the power of the *sefer*, so that he would understand why there was a special reason behind my request.

"I need to ask him."

A few days later, he got back to me.

"My son-in-law said he would be willing to learn from it, even though he never heard of this *segulah*."

I purchased the *sefer* for him. Now it's a year later, and he has a baby girl.

Shortly after his daughter was born, I met him on the street. He told me all about his *simchah*, and that he knew I had a part in it. Then he grabbed me right there in the middle of the street and started to dance. It was a dance of genuine happiness and joy. A dance of *hakaras hatov* to me for being a faithful messenger. And that's the way it went for a while, with both of us just jumping and dancing in the street while passersby looked at us strangely, not understanding why two ordinary people were dancing away for no apparent reason.

How wonderful it is that the Master of the World gives the *tzaddik* the ability to work for Klal Yisrael!

With wishes of *shalom* and *hatzlachah* for those who are עוֹסְקִים בִּמְלֶאכֶת הַקּוֹדֶשׁ — who busy themselves with the work of Heaven.

Amus Porat, *gabbai* of the Beit El Shul in Raanana